Horizon

SUMMER, 1968 · VOLUME X, NUMBER 3

© 1968 by American Heritage Publishing Co., Inc. All rights reserved under Berne and Pan-American Copyright Conventions. Reproduction in whole or in part of any article without permission is prohibited. U.S. Copyright is not claimed for pages 97–104 or for the color plates on pages 4–5, 8, 15, 16, 24, 31, 32, 74–75, 79, 83, 86, 87, 89, 90. Printed in the United States of America.

Must Progress be Terminal?

The Environment. There must have been a time, so fondly sought after these days, when the word did not exist. Why should a man standing alone amid wooded hills, bright skies, clear streams, and an abundance of open space bother to consider it at all—a man who can joyously call down a valley and hear only the echo of his own voice in reply? That is the ideal, of course; and for most of us the ideal environment, with its intimations of a pioneer Arcadia, has vanished forever. The trees are cut down, and the hillsides are covered with monotonous frame houses, clapboard cheek by asbestos jowl; the skies are suffused with a sulfurous haze, and our lungs are choked with smog; the streams are dark and their surfaces irridescent with pollution; the open spaces are being divided, subdivided, and redivided—and the man who would shout down the valley, now thronged with smokestacks and motels and bowling alleys, is judged mad or arrested for disturbing the peace.

As if by some sullen chemical process, and not by the customary evolution of philology, the word "environment" has become synonymous with nightmare.

> "Thou canst not stir a flower
> Without troubling of a star..."

Francis Thompson wrote in lines that have become for us more than a poetic conceit. The environment, in all its interrelationships, can no longer be denied or romanticized.

For the moment we must content ourselves with stopgap remedies: devices to control exhaust fumes in cars, laws to forbid the dumping of refuse in our rivers, acts to save virgin stands of redwoods from the power saw, new and cheap diet supplements to feed the undernourished. The present symptoms of the environmental crisis can be cured—there is little, apparently, that technology is not capable of—but will they only be replaced by new ones? Nor should we congratulate ourselves too heartily for our ability to "manage" nature. We can save Lake Tahoe by ingeniously pumping our filth over the Sierras—but what happens to the other side? We can dam the Amazon to create a giant lake in the South American interior (a proposal of Herman Kahn's thinkers at the Hudson Institute), thus opening a new environment to that continent's impoverished millions—but what will be the effect on the ecology of the region, on the ecology of the whole Western Hemisphere, for that matter?

Beyond all this despair, beyond all this theorizing and improvising, lies the most urgent need of all: a total examination of the permanent relationship of man to his environment—or "ecosystemics," as scientists are beginning to call it. "Man at War with Nature," the cluster of articles starting on page 16, sets forth the ideas of four thinkers

---

Horizon is published every three months by American Heritage Publishing Co., Inc.

PRESIDENT
James Parton

EDITORIAL COMMITTEE
Joseph J. Thorndike, *Chairman*
Oliver Jensen
Richard M. Ketchum

SENIOR ART DIRECTOR
Irwin Glusker

SENIOR EDITOR, HORIZON
Marshall B. Davidson

PUBLISHER, HORIZON
Paul Gottlieb

Editorial and executive offices:
551 Fifth Avenue, New York, N.Y. 10017.

EDITOR
Joseph J. Thorndike
MANAGING EDITOR: Charles L. Mee, Jr.
ARTICLES EDITOR: Robert Cowley   ART EDITOR: Jane Wilson
ART DIRECTOR: Kenneth Munowitz
ASSOCIATE EDITORS: Shirley Tomkievicz, Barbara Klaw
CONTRIBUTING EDITOR: Walter Karp
ASSISTANT EDITOR: Charles Folds
COPY EDITOR: Mary Ann Pfeiffer   *Assistant:* Carol R. Angell

ADVISORY BOARD: Gilbert Highet, *Chairman*, Frederick Burkhardt,
William Harlan Hale, John Walker
EUROPEAN CONSULTING EDITOR: J. H. Plumb, *Christ's College, Cambridge*
EUROPEAN BUREAU: Gertrudis Feliu, *Chief, 11 rue du Bouloi, Paris 1er*

HORIZON
A Magazine of the Arts

SUMMER, 1968 · VOLUME X, NUMBER 3

who, in different ways and disciplines, have devoted their lives to such an examination.

George Perkins Marsh, the Vermont visionary whose *Man and Nature* predicted in 1864 our present global environmental crisis, would say that the examination is too long overdue—by three millenniums at least. "Thou canst not stir a flower . . ." In Marsh we have a prophetic appreciation of the world as a single complex unity. The same recognition—embodied in a call for a rational organization of our technological civilization—is at the heart of the thinking of Lewis Mumford and R. Buckminster Fuller. But it is a measure of the present crisis that the two differ so widely, not only in their prescriptions for a remedy but even in their diagnoses.

To a scientist like the oceanographer turned demographer Roger Revelle, one remedy is inescapable: stabilization of the world's population. The correction of so many of our environmental ills—as well as closely related social and political ones—depends on it.

Must Progress be terminal? Perhaps we have become too obsessed with the possibility of self-destruction by one rampant by-product of our technology or another. Eventually even councilmen in Jersey City will choose not to have their lungs rotted by air pollution. The real question, then, is not life but quality of life. It is likely that man will endure: but can he prevail? —R.C.

All correspondence about subscriptions should be addressed to: HORIZON Subscription Office, 379 West Center St., Marion, Ohio 43302.

    Single Copies: $ 5.00
    Subscriptions: $16.00 per year in the U.S. & Canada; elsewhere, $17.00

Annual indexes for Volumes I–IX are available at $1 each. A cumulative index for Volumes I–V is available at $3. HORIZON is also indexed in the *Readers Guide to Periodical Literature*.

The editors welcome contributions but can assume no responsibility for unsolicited material.

Title registered U.S. Patent Office

Second-class postage paid at New York, N.Y., and at additional mailing offices.

The Environment

MAN AT WAR WITH NATURE
  I. THE VERMONT PROPHET:
    GEORGE PERKINS MARSH   *Franklin Russell*   16
  II. WHICH GUIDE TO THE PROMISED LAND:
    FULLER OR MUMFORD?   *Allan Temko*   24
  III. TOO MANY BORN? TOO MANY DIE.
    SO SAYS ROGER REVELLE   *Milton Viorst*   32

Archaeology

THE SEARCH FOR KING ARTHUR   *Christopher Hibbert*   4

Ideas

ON THE RAISING OF ARMIES   *Correlli Barnett*   40

Art

GOYA AND HORROR   *John Canaday*   90
A MODERN BESTIARY   *Drawings by Domenico Gnoli*   48
  WHAT IS A MONSTER?   *Robert Graves*   50

Letters

JOHNSON (?) ON JOHNSON   *Anthony Burgess*   60

History

SCHOLARES MEDII AEVI   *Morris Bishop*   66
THE ROYAL PORCELAIN CRAZE   *J. H. Plumb*   80
HIGH-SEAS SOCIETY   *Timothy S. Green*   106

Biography

SEX AND THE KING OF FRANCE   *Joseph Barry*   114

Entertainments

A SHORT PRIMER OF STYLE   *E. M. Halliday*   120

COVER: The Duchess of Alba, society's leading lady in eighteenth-century Madrid, was particularly admired by the artist who painted this portrait of her in 1797—the great Francisco Goya. He was, in fact, her lover for about seven years. But the rest of Goya's long life was hardly so gay, and his paintings were never again so serene. His gradual darkening of mood—which culminated in nightmare visions of sheer horror—is discussed in an article beginning on page 90. The portrait is in the collection of The Hispanic Society of America, N.Y.

The Search for King Arthur

Who was he? Did he exist at all? Where does legend leave off and history take over? Through the findings of archaeology, answers are beginning to emerge from the mists of time and fantasy

By CHRISTOPHER HIBBERT

Weekend Telegraph, LONDON—PHOTO DONALD MC CULLIN

N.Y. PUB. LIB. PRINTS DIV.

Rising abruptly out of a waterlogged west-country plain is the hill called Glastonbury Tor—perhaps the legendary Isle of Avalon where Arthur came to die. The chapel on the summit dates from the fifteenth century, but the Tor itself may have been a stronghold in Arthur's time, nine hundred years before. He was probably not a king but a cavalry leader who led his troops through the wilderness of Dark Age Britain, as in Gustave Doré's engraving, left, for Tennyson's Idylls of the King.

"For there was no man knew from whence he came;
But after tempest, when the long wave broke
All down the thundering shores of Bude and Bos,
There came a day as still as heaven, and then
They found a naked child upon the sands
Of dark Tintagil by the Cornish sea,
And that was Arthur, and they foster'd him
Till he by miracle was approven King . . ."
—Alfred, Lord Tennyson
IDYLLS OF THE KING

Are the crumbling walls of Tintagel Castle (opposite), clinging to a bleak Cornish headland, those of Camelot? Was the baby Arthur found here, in the manner of the Doré engraving above? The tradition is persistent. True, the remains of a sixth-century Celtic monastery uncovered on these cliffs do belong to the Arthurian period, but the "castle" is a Norman chapel, built centuries later.

For more than a thousand years the legend of King Arthur, Christian hero and paragon of chivalry, has inspired the human spirit. His exploits and adventures, his companions and his queen, have been the subject of countless books and poems, parables and paintings. Seventeenth-century operas, Victorian epics, and modern best-sellers, musicals, and films have been based upon the fantastic story of his life. Artists as diverse as Burne-Jones and Aubrey Beardsley, Gustave Doré and William Morris, have endeavored to interpret his person and his world; poets from Dryden to Swinburne have been moved by his virtues and the sad drama of his fate. Tennyson's *Idylls of the King*, Purcell's *King Arthur*, T. H. White's *The Once and Future King*, are but three works of art that owe their inspiration to the romance of his legend.

The sources of this legend have roots that stretch back far beyond the birth of printing to those Dark Ages of Britain's history when barbarian invaders were driving the people of the island to seek safety in the Welsh hills and across the channel in that part of France that became known as Brittany. These British refugees told tales of a great leader who had fought to save them from the heathen hordes; and their stories, repeated and embellished, became entangled in later generations with the fables of the people in whose lands they had settled. Centuries later, when the Normans conquered large tracts of Brittany and invaded England, the tales of King Arthur came to the ears of French poets, who set them down in epic verse.

In these poems—the written versions of the romances and folktales told by Welsh bards, French troubadours, and English west-country minstrels—King Arthur appears as an ideal of medieval chivalry, a kind of magical personage whose marvelous exploits were more daring and strange even than those of Charlemagne, whose brave knights shared attributes with Oberon's fairies; a romantic, courtly Christian warrior who could slay dragons and monsters, overpower the Giant of Mont St. Michel and the Demon Cat of Losanne; a hero who would one day rise again to destroy his followers' enemies; the immortal "King that was, and King that shall be." It is this view of King Arthur that we find in the pages of the book that ensured the perpetuation of the hero's legend —the *Morte d'Arthur*.

Sir Thomas Malory, the country gentleman who wrote it, paid tribute to one particular "Frensshe boke," but his sources in fact were numerous and varied. He collected them while the nobility of England were flying at each other's throats in the Wars of the Roses; and although the book was finished by 1470, it was not until the wars came to an end at Bosworth Field in 1485 that William Caxton, the first English printer, brought it out.

In the *Morte d'Arthur* Malory surrounds the legend with the atmosphere of the pre-Renaissance court, with knights in shining armor riding out to fight the wicked, contesting with one another in jousts and tournaments, competing for the smiles of the fair ladies whose favors they covet. Arthur is introduced to us as the ill-begotten son of King Uther Pendragon and Igraine, Duchess of Cornwall, a boy who proves his right to become king by drawing the sword from the stone, a feat beyond the power of other men. His reign begins in hope but is overcast by the fate that is doomed to overtake him—his betrayal by Guinevere, his beautiful fair-haired queen, who will, so Merlin the wizard warns him, be unfaithful to him with Sir Lancelot and so destroy the fellowship of the Knights of the Round Table; and his death in the battle of Camlan at the hands of the vengeful Modred, the son he has had by his sister, not knowing who she was.

The dreamlike quality of Malory's

The ruins of Glastonbury Abbey, supposed last resting place of Arthur and Guinevere, remain; but their bones have long since vanished

disjointed story, exemplified by Excalibur, the sword that rises from the magic waters at the behest of the Damosel of the Lake and by the search for the Holy Grail, is at one with the strange, ethereal atmosphere of King Arthur's unreal world, the fairy-tale jousts at the castle of Camelot, the enchantments that lie upon the Isle of Avalon, "hidden in the mist and the mysterious waters," whither Arthur was borne away wounded to die.

The harsh realities of Arthur's times were far removed from all this. And before considering how much truth lies concealed beneath the fabulous embellishments of the legends, we should look at the threatened land that gave them birth.

At the beginning of the fifth century the Roman Empire was crumbling and Roman Britain was crumbling with it. The legions were withdrawn to face threats closer to the heart of the empire; and as the military organization of the British province broke down, its governmental system began to distintegrate too. For generations now the Romanized island had been under recurrent attack—from Pictish tribes swarming south from the mountains and forests of Caledonia and across the ruins of the wall that the emperor Hadrian had built from Solway to the mouth of the Tyne; from the savage Irish tribesmen, then known as Scots, who sailed across the gray seas and drove inland from the ravaged western coasts; worst of all, from the Nordic pirates and raiders who stormed onto the eastern shores from the Continent, looting and pillaging, murdering and raping, burning the wooden farmhouses and the gracious stone villas of the cultured and the rich.

In 429 when Germanus, bishop of Auxerre, in Gaul, arrived in Britain to combat Pelagianism, a new heresy that was endangering the authority of the church, he found a people so accustomed to sheltering behind the power of Rome, so used to submitting to the authority of power, that they were incapable of withstanding the attacks of the heathen invaders. Germanus had been a soldier in his youth, and he undertook to save the Britons' bodies as well as their souls. He reorganized the bands of local militia and, placing himself at their head, taught them how to defend themselves; so that when next the barbarians came, instead of rushing inland with their victims flying in panic before them, they fell into the trap that Germanus had laid for them. They marched through the valley toward his camp, confident and unsuspecting, and when they had advanced too far for easy retreat, the bishop and his chaplains raised the shout of "Alleluia!" and sent the British army racing down to the destruction of their enemies. So Britain was not yet lost. Germanus had shown that with leaders to inspire them, its people were prepared to fight and to die for their homes, and for the kind of civilization that centuries of Roman rule had taught them to respect.

For Britain, although Rome had abandoned it, was still essentially a Roman province with Roman ideals and Roman aspirations, still willing to defend those ideals as no other Roman province ever had been. Long ago, even before the Claudian invasion of A.D. 43, Cymbeline, king of the Catuvellauni, the greatest of the tribes of southern Britain, was on the best of terms with the emperors Augustus and Tiberius; and on the silver coins that issued from his mint he described himself in the Latin style as *Rex Brittonum*. And after the invasion, when the Iceni and Trinovantes came pouring down from the northeast under the passionate Queen Boudicca to sack London and massacre its Romanized inhabitants, it was not so much the idea of Roman occupation that had enraged the tribesmen, but the brutal manner in which the Icenian royal house had been treated by the insufferably arrogant and far from characteristic local officials of the empire.

After the storm raised by Boudicca's revolt had died away, the Romanization of the island was completed. Towns were designed and built in the rectilinear Roman manner; a network of roads spanned the province from fortress to fortress, town to town, and coast to frontier; Londinium, its name eventually changed to Augusta in token of its grandeur, became one of the most important commercial centers north of the Alps; beautiful villas with painted walls and vine-clad courtyards with hypocaust beneath their mosaic floors dotted the lowlands of the south. Generation after generation, Roman influence spread and deepened, while Roman culture, Roman customs, and Roman manners became absorbed into British life. In the towns even the workmen spoke Latin, and many of them could read and write it.

Now, in the fifth century, this Romano-British way of life—civilized, orderly, prosperous, and by then widely Christian—lay open to attack and destruction. An outline for the means of its defense had, however, been bequeathed to the abandoned islanders by the former Roman command and by the organization of the Roman army. This organization had recently been overhauled. In the second century the legions in Britain had each contained fifty-six hundred men, of whom only one hundred and twenty were cavalrymen. But in 378, at the battle of Adrianople, huge columns of Roman infantrymen had been overwhelmed by charges of Goths on horseback; and since then the Roman army had come more and more to rely on the shock and weight of well-trained and heavily armored mounted troops to disperse and overrun the barbarian hordes. Squadrons of these cavalrymen were formed in Britain and placed at the disposal of one or another of the three commanders of the British troops—the *Dux Britanniarum*, Duke of the Britains, who from his headquarters at York defended the northern frontier; the *Comes Litoris Saxonici*, Count of the Saxon Shore, who was responsible for a series of forts on the southeastern coast from the Wash to the Solent; and the *Comes Britanniarum*, Count of the Britains, the officer entrusted with the direction of the island's mobile field army.

As the barbarian raids increased in numbers and intensity, it was upon the skills of this last commander, the Count of the Britains, and upon the heavy but fast-moving cavalry at his command that the hopes for Britain's survival were centered. And after the Roman legions had left, it was upon his example that any new British commander who assumed the authority to replace him would have to model his conduct of the continuing war.

Although no such commander had appeared by the time of Germanus' visit to Britain in 429, there was still time left for one to come forward. Germanus found Britain a "most wealthy island," with thriving communities governed by local kings whose families had been used to kingship even before the Romans came. Despite the constant inroads of the invaders, town life went on much as it had done before the legions left; for although the marauding barbarians could trample crops and orchards, destroy iso-

"But now farewell. I am going a long way . . .
To the island-valley of Avilion;
Where falls not hail, or rain, or any snow,
Nor ever wind blows loudly; but it lies
Deep-meadow'd, happy, fair with orchard lawns
And bowery hollows crown'd with summer sea,
Where I will heal me of my grievous wound."
—IDYLLS OF THE KING

Prostrating herself, Queen Guinevere confesses her infidelity to Arthur, above: she would go to a nunnery and he to battle and his mythical appointment in Avalon. In 1191 monks at Glastonbury dug up what they claimed were the bones of the unfortunate pair, and in 1278 monks removed them to the abbey.

lated villas, and burn down the wattle and daub huts of peasants and the timber hovels of fishermen, they were soon dispersed beneath the castellated walls and high stone towers of Roman forts and cities.

But as the years went by, the swirling tides of heathen Saxon invaders swelled ever deeper across the shores of Britain. Advancing down the now neglected roads, rowing their shallow-draught galleys far upstream on the wide rivers, they threatened with total extinction a culture they despised.

Leaving their galleys concealed in a tree-lined island inlet or protected by a palisade of timber torn from the walls of a riverside church, they sprawled inland. They were ill-trained for conventional warfare and ill-armed; few of them had swords, most carried a rough iron-spiked spear in one hand and a thick round wooden shield in the other; only the leaders had helmets, and of the leaders scarcely a handful could boast of a "hard war-net" of ring mail or even a jerkin of boiled leather. But they were strong and violent and ruthless, exulting in their animal energy, their hard bellies full of meat and spruce beer.

With experience allied to a native cunning they learned how to besiege and storm a stone-walled and defended city, how to discover its weakest point or batter down its gate; in massacring its inhabitants, in raping struggling girls, in selecting those upon whom to fix the collars of thralldom, they needed no instruction. They settled down in increasing numbers on the land they had at first come merely to plunder, scorning the towns—for towns were fearsome places where evil spirits clustered—and building instead rough shacks around the wooden hall of their leader, farming the rich land, taking fish from the clear waters and wild pigs from the oak forests.

Romanized Britain, or those parts of it still able to act collectively, made a final appeal for help from Rome against the Saxon incursions in 446. But there was nothing that Rome could do any more, and the emperor rejected their appeal. Then in desperation a call was made to a nearer, stronger ally, Vortigern. Vortigern was a rough and powerful king, with some respect for Roman ways, who ruled over a wild, expansive district in Wales, on Roman Britain's troubled borders, and who had much influence over the whole of the south of the island. He advised coming to terms with the Saxons, granting them an area of British land in exchange for their help against the Picts and Scots and any other invaders who might, thereafter, be presumed to be mutual enemies. There were precedents enough for this arrangement: the Roman Empire itself had not only taken men into its army from all the world's races but had recruited whole tribes, equipped their chiefs with Roman uniforms, and given them land as well as pay in return for military service. So it was agreed that a party of Saxons, under their chieftains Hengist and Horsa, should be admitted into the Isle of Thanet, an area of rich farmland separated from Kent (the land of the Cantii tribe) by a narrow channel at each end of which was one of the old Roman forts of the Count of the Saxon Shore.

t first the arrangement worked well enough; the Saxons proved successful mercenaries in their fights with Britain's enemies, and their settlement prospered. But gradually they spread themselves beyond their original limits and called in reinforcements from other tribes in their Continental homeland along the eastern shores of the North Sea: Angles (from whom the English were to take their name) and Jutes, as well as other Saxons. Sometime in 455 the quarrels between them and their British neighbors erupted into a long and bitter war in the course of which Vortigern's army was eventually overwhelmed and his dangerous policy thrown into ruins.

At this time there was, however, another powerful king in Britain, who had advised Vortigern against the arrangement with the Saxons and had stood aloof from its consequences. This was Ambrosius, a young man of Roman descent who ruled over a kingdom in the far west of Britain, the kingdom of Dumnonia, which lay on the far borders of the Roman island but which had jealously preserved the traditions of Roman culture. Its army seems to have been Roman in organization and training, its government Roman in outlook and construction. It was on the frontiers of Dumnonia that the final stand against the pagan host was ultimately to be made.

To this Romanized kingdom in the west country flocked all those who had need of its protection or who were prepared to fight for the ideals it celebrated. They came, said Gildas, the monk who chronicled the history of these times, with the urgency of bees seeking the hive when a storm is imminent. They were given shelter or arms, and under the leadership of Ambrosius, their accepted king, they suffered defeats but won victories, too; and they kept their enemies at bay. Toward the end of the fifth century Ambrosius died, and a new leader had to be found. It was then, say the chroniclers, that Arthur appeared like a *deus ex machina*, fully armed and mounted, on the center of the stage.

No one knows his parentage or provenance; some still doubt, despite the histories that mention him, his very existence. And the multiplicity of legends that have clustered round his name have hidden his achievements behind a miasma of fable and magic. Geoffrey of Monmouth, whose *Historia Regum Brittanniae* was written at the beginning of the twelfth century, confused the problem still further by mingling fact with myth and presenting Arthur, in the company of real figures like Ambrosius and invented ones such as King Lear, as one of the founders of the British kingdom, a powerful monarch feared all over

Europe, a hero to rival Charlemagne.

Geoffrey of Monmouth was not, however, the first historian to mention Arthur by name. Three hundred years before, the Welsh chronicler Nennius, whose *Historia Britonum* was completed within less than two centuries of the events it describes, had mentioned Arthur in a more succinct and less exotic way, describing him as a general rather than a king, but a general entrusted by the British kings with overall command of their forces: a kind of polemarch.

His name, Artorius, suggests that he came from a good family in one of the Romanized parts of the island—he may, perhaps, have been a kinsman of Ambrosius as some accounts indicate: Geoffrey of Monmouth says that his father, Uther Pendragon, was Ambrosius' brother. But it seems from Nennius's description that Arthur fought his battles in all parts of the island, acting as Count of the Britains, with a force of cavalry that he took wherever danger threatened and that gave power and inspiration to the levies called out by the local kings.

Nennius lists twelve battles, in all of which Arthur was victorious; but the names given to these battles are the old British names that have long since disappeared, and it is impossible now to discover exactly where they were fought. There can be little doubt, however, that Arthur's cavalry ranged far and wide, from the mouths of the rivers along the eastern coast to the frontiers of Wales, and from beyond the remains of Hadrian's Wall to the forests of Caledonia, which Nennius calls "the Wood of Celidon." Most of the battles seem to have taken place along the frontiers of the west country from the mouth of the Severn to the Solent; they were defensive battles, fought to keep the marauding Saxons, now established in all the rest of southern Britain, out of the last stronghold of Christian civilization.

The final battle, according to Nennius, "was on Mount Badon, where in one day nine hundred and sixty men fell in one charge of Arthur's."

Gildas, the earliest of British historians, also stresses the importance of this last victory on Mount Badon, an overwhelming success achieved by cavalry alone. Gildas, although a contemporary of Arthur's, does not mention the hero by name, perhaps because he fell short of the monk's strict ideals both in religion and morals: there are hints of this elsewhere. Gildas referred instead to a British leader whom he called The Bear. The Celtic for bear is *Artos*.

The Bear's great victory on Mount Badon appears to have been fought about 515 to break a siege by the Saxons of some British fortified position such as the immense earthwork known as the Wansdyke, which had been thrown up between the Bristol Channel and the Marlborough Downs. The victory was so utterly decisive that it assured an almost uninterrupted peace with the Saxons for nearly forty years.

The peace did not last so long, however, within the British kingdom. Some twenty years after Badon—the *Annales Cambriae* gives the date as 539 —Arthur was mortally wounded in a civil war between his followers and those whom one of his rivals, possibly the bastard son and nephew of Malory's story, had turned against him.

It is not surprising that the references to Arthur in the chronicles that have come down to us, fleeting, contradictory, and ambiguous as they are, prompted many nineteenth-century authorities to suggest that the whole Arthurian story was a fabrication, a characteristic result of wishful thinking at a time when a national hero was desperately needed, or at least an attribution to one man of the virtues and achievements of a score of lesser men who were fighting against the powers of darkness.

In more recent years this skeptical view of the Once and Future King has been strongly questioned. Within the past decade serious writers have painstakingly investigated the whole of the Arthurian Cycle and have concluded that its central figure *did* exist. Geoffrey Ashe, for example, has emphasized in two books and several articles such significant facts as the sudden fashion for Arthur as a Christian name in the sixth century, when it had been very rare before, and the ubiquity of Arthur in local legend and nomenclature: "Nobody else except the Devil is so renowned throughout so much of Britain."

The skeptical view is also now being questioned by archaeologists who have worked—and still are working—on sites in the western counties of England where the Arthurian legend is so particularly treasured. One of these sites is at Glastonbury in Somerset, long known in local lore as the magical Isle of Avalon.

nce Glastonbury was indeed an island, a fortified lake village whose inhabitants lived in huts supported on massive logs driven into the waterlogged peat of the lagoon, shot waterfowl—including pelicans—with terra-cotta pellets hurled from slings, and fished with nets and lines weighted by lead smelted from Mendip ore. It was here, men said, that Joseph, the rich man of Arimathea who had laid Christ's body to rest in the sepulcher, founded a church dedicated to the Blessed Virgin after his flight from the authorities in Palestine. It was here that Joseph conveyed the Holy Grail, the bowl that Jesus had used at the Last Supper and the source of those mystical ecstasies, supernatural visions, and mysterious graces to which Arthur's knights aspired. And it was here that Arthur was buried, in darkness and secrecy lest the fact of his death should overcast the spirit of his people.

Glastonbury was first connected with Arthur by Giraldus Cambrensis, a Welsh ecclesiastical writer of the twelfth century. In a far earlier time there was certainly a wattle church on the island, a church that developed into an important monastery with

Testimony of the Dot

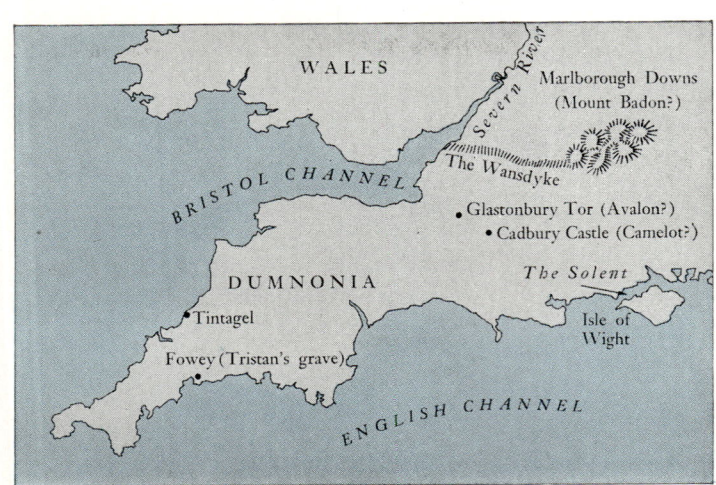

The search for Arthur is now centered at the hill called Cadbury Castle. Before digging began at the summit, geophysical instruments plotted the dot-density survey at right, different underground features giving different magnetic readings. The diagram next to it shows what was found: a ring-ditch from the Iron Age (gray), Iron Age pits (green), a medieval field boundary (oblique brown line), and the foundations of a church (blue), which could belong to the Arthurian era. (The other colors indicate various gullies and pits.) The cross section of one slope, below, reveals a stony bank on which ramparts were erected in the sixth century.

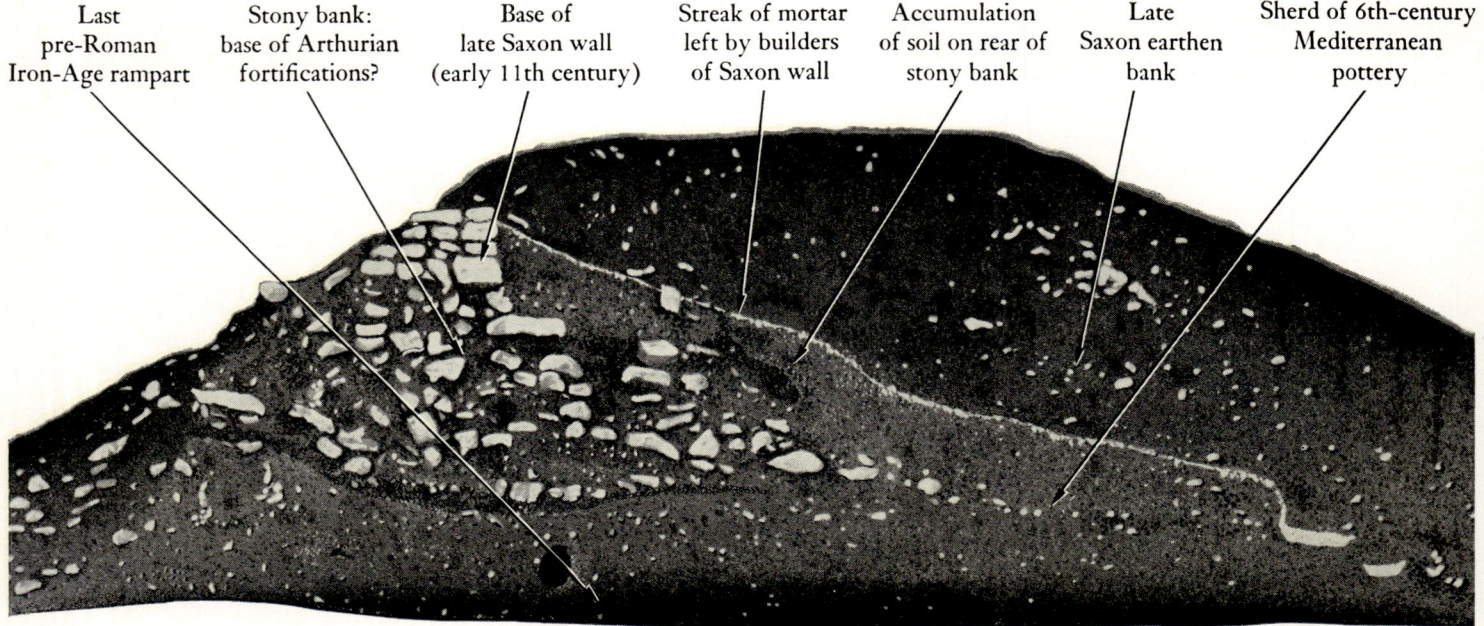

| Last pre-Roman Iron-Age rampart | Stony bank: base of Arthurian fortifications? | Base of late Saxon wall (early 11th century) | Streak of mortar left by builders of Saxon wall | Accumulation of soil on rear of stony bank | Late Saxon earthen bank | Sherd of 6th-century Mediterranean pottery |

DRAWINGS BY CAL SACKS, ADAPTED FROM *The Observer*, LONDON (CAMERA PRESS)—PIX which a number of the greatest saints of the Celtic world, including Saint Patrick the apostle of Ireland, were connected. According to Giraldus, the fine stone abbey was burned to the ground in the spring of 1184, and some years afterward its monks claimed to have discovered King Arthur's grave in an old cemetery where the bones of many saints lay buried. While digging a grave for a fellow monk, they came upon a stone cross inscribed with a Latin legend: "Here lies buried the renowned King Arthur in the Isle of Avalon." Excavating further in growing excitement, they hit upon a length of hard wood. They pushed the soil away to reveal a vast coffin fashioned from a hollow oak trunk. Inside were the bones of an enormously strong man—the shinbone was three fingers longer than the shin of the tallest monk present—and a skull that had been smashed by a blow above the left ear. Beside them were the bones of a far smaller body, its skull still encircled by traces of fair hair. A monk bent down to lift the hairs, but they crumbled at the touch of his fingers.

When a new and even more magnificent abbey rose above the ashes of the old—the abbey whose sprawling medieval ruins may still be seen at Glastonbury—later monks, in the presence of King Edward I and Queen Eleanor, moved the bones into a black marble tomb in a shrine in the center of the choir. After the dissolution of the monastery on the orders of Henry VIII, both the shrine and the original site of Arthur's grave were lost and the fanciful story of the monks derided.

In the mid-1930's, however, the base of the shrine was uncovered. And within the past few years Dr. Ralegh Radford, doyen of west-country archaeologists, has identified while excavating in the abbey grounds the site of a grave that he has convincingly demonstrated must be the one the monks dug up. More recently archaeologists digging in the summer of 1966 on Glastonbury Tor, which rises above the abbey to the east, discovered fragments of sixth-century Mediterranean pottery and so satisfied themselves of the occupation of the area in the Dark Ages by an elite such as a war leader of Arthur's fame would have collected around him.

Twelve miles farther to the southeast is the freestanding yellow sandstone hill known as South Cadbury Castle, and here the most exciting finds of all have come to light. For Cadbury, so local legend has romantically insisted for countless generations, is Arthur's Camelot, his camp and court. And now at last the persistent claims can no longer be ignored. A geophysical survey of the area carried out in the spring of 1967 has furnished hints and clues described by Leslie Alcock of the University College of South Wales, the archaeologist in charge of the excavations at Cadbury, as "the most exciting thing I've seen in all my archaeological experience."

ven to the untrained eye the hill that rises so sharply above the quiet little village of South Cadbury presents an intriguing appearance. The eighteen acres on its flat, grassed summit are surrounded by an artificial mound from which the ground falls away vertiginously in a series of ridges and ramparts. From the air it seems almost as though the hill has been dropped on the green Somerset plain in a series of gigantic lumps, each one of which has settled down into an area slightly less extensive than the one beneath it.

It has long been known that this hill was occupied by Neolithic man more than two thousand years before the birth of Christ; that it was occupied still at the time of the Roman invasion, when its stubborn British defenders were attacked and massacred by the empire's legions. What has usually been doubted, however, is that there was any extensive reoccupation of the fort in Arthur's time.

Still, the legends persisted. King Henry VIII's antiquary, John Leland, found that local people knew the place as Camelot and that they had heard it said that King Arthur often frequented Camelot, which was "sumtyme a famose town or castelle": two nearby villages are still known as West Camel and Queen Camel. These same local people spoke of the noise of ghostly horses clattering down into the village at night, of hunting horns sounding, and they pointed out Arthur's Well and Arthur's Hunting Causeway, which ran across the marsh beneath the ramparts of the camp and can still, indeed, be traced in parts along the now well-drained fields of the surrounding farms. As late as the nineteenth century an old man accosted a party of strangers who were prodding about for bits of pottery and coin and asked them nervously if they had come to take away the sleeping king from the hollow hill.

But it was not until the 1950's, when numerous sherds of imported pottery similar to those discovered at Glastonbury and a fragment from a Merovingian glass bowl were brought to the surface by plowing, that archaeological support was given to the tradition that South Cadbury Castle was in fact Camelot. And it was not until 1965 that large-scale excavations became possible through funds collected by the Camelot Research Committee.

The original organizers of the committee, Geoffrey Ashe and Dr. Radford, have now been joined by Sir Mortimer Wheeler, the energetic and versatile excavator of Mohenjo-Daro and the Indus civilizations in India, who has said that "it now begins to appear that South Cadbury Castle may under the impact of careful excavation produce yet another convergence of fact and tradition."

The first exploratory dig sponsored by the committee was undertaken by a team of young volunteers in July and August of 1966. The exploration was highly encouraging. Enough sherds of Mediterranean amphorae were discovered to confirm an occu-

"... Such a sleep
They sleep—the men I loved. I think that we
Shall never more, at any future time,
Delight our souls with talk of knightly deeds,
Walking about the gardens and the halls
Of Camelot, as in the days that were."
—IDYLLS OF THE KING

N.Y. PUB. LIB. PRINTS DIV.

Doré provided the romantic conception of Camelot above, but it is a castle of the imagination only—or, like the splendid citadels filmed in the movie Camelot, *a castle in Spain. The actual place—if it existed—would have been far more modest, and archaeologists now think they have found it beneath the grassy summit of Cadbury Castle (opposite), a hill no longer just a haunted pasture.*

pation by a rich settlement in the early sixth century; and the presence of numerous holes, some of them evidently dug at the same time for the support of thick building posts, shows that there were large buildings on the plateau during the Dark Ages.

A recent geophysical survey indicates how immense and extensive these buildings may have been, and a dig last summer revealed ruins of battlements that may well prove to have been the defenses of King Arthur's court and stronghold. Also discovered—in addition to medieval field boundaries, the longest stretch of Saxon wall now to be seen in England, and hints of a fourth-century pagan temple—was the plan of an early Christian church that the archaeologists working at the site had never expected to find. Further exploration this summer and in 1969 will answer many, if not all, of the problems waiting to be explained. Certainly none of the young students who will soon be helping to dig up the area again can fail to hope that buried beneath the turf is the vital proof—a medallion, perhaps, bearing the legend ARTORIUS. After all, in Cornwall in the ancient domain of King Mark—uncle to Tristan, who according to legend was one of Arthur's knights and the ill-starred lover of Isolde—there has been found a vast stone, seven feet tall, on which this Latin inscription of the sixth century can still be read: HERE LIES TRISTAN.

Certainly the discovery of a truth buried deep in a legend is nothing new. Had not the impulsive German archaeologist Heinrich Schliemann nourished a passion in his youth for the epic stories in Homer's *Odyssey* and *Iliad,* the reality of Troy and Mycenae might have lain forever concealed. So, too, the continuing excavations at Cadbury may one day help us to imagine Arthur as he really was and to believe that beneath each ornamentation of the legend lies a kernel of truth—that, as Beram Saklatvala has suggested, the Knights of the Round Table were Arthur's cavalry commanders and staff, the grand council of the last Count of the Britains in conference; that Arthur's enemy Carados was the warrior Cerdic, king of the West Saxons, from whom Queen Elizabeth II of England is directly descended; that the Latin phrase *Artorius gladium EX SAXO eripuit* may have been wrongly copied from an original that read *Artorius gladium EX SAXONO eripuit*—since medieval clerks often omitted the letter N—and thus that Arthur in reality took the sword from the Saxon and not from the stone; that Excalibur, the sword from the lake, was *ex cale burno*, from beside the river Cale, where the best swords were forged; that the Holy Grail was indeed some priceless holy relic preserved at Glastonbury as a symbol of Arthur's authority over Christian Britain; that Guinevere (or Winifrith), Lancelot (or Wlenca), and Galahad (or *Galerius Hadrianus*) existed in real life just as Arthur did.

And standing on the hill at Cadbury, shutting your eyes to the neat English fields below, imagining instead the haunted, misty swamps that Arthur would have known, it is possible to see him and his companions riding out to battle along the rough and narrow causeway. They ride down, not in the glittering panoply of medieval warfare, but with embossed cuirass and close-fitting helmet, carrying whitewashed shields, long spears, and heavy iron swords, wearing gold collars and strings of beads; men rough and hard and violent but fighting in a noble cause, stemming the tide of Saxon paganism, so that when at last they were defeated, they left behind them a legend that was one of the lasting inspirations of the English Christian kingdom.

Christopher Hibbert has written about characters as diverse as Lord Raglan, Garibaldi, and Dickens (see "The Early, Miserable Life of Charles Dickens," Autumn, 1967, HORIZON). He lives in Henley on Thames, England.

14

PORTRAITS PAINTED FOR HORIZON BY PAUL DAVIS

George Perkins Marsh

MAN AT WAR WITH NATURE

Three Articles on the Crisis in our Environment

I·The Vermont Prophet: George Perkins Marsh

He foresaw our problems a hundred years ago and invented a scientific study to deal with them. The study is called ecology, and we are only now beginning to learn how to apply it

When urban Americans feel nostalgic for the simple life, they invoke Henry David Thoreau. There was, however, another American, born sixteen years before Thoreau, whose union with nature was equally mystic and whose impact on this century is likely to be more important. George Perkins Marsh, a Vermont lawyer, created the concept of modern ecology, or the study of the interrelationships between organisms and environment. He cut through the Victorian complacency of his own age to prove that men were no asset to the earth; they were wrecking it. Indeed, Marsh anticipated many of the crises in resources, pollution, and overpopulation that plague our century.

Marsh once described himself as "forest-born," explaining that "the bubbling brook, the trees, the flowers, the wild animals were to me persons, not things." The intensity of his feeling for nature expanded, finally, to include *all* life; he became the complete watcher and the tireless collector of facts. (He calculated, for instance, that if all the domesticated four-footed animals of the United States were killed and piled together, they would, in one hundred years, form fifteen pyramids the size of Cheops's pyramid in Egypt.) He observed hummingbirds sipping nectar with the same attentiveness and appreciation he gave old John Quincy Adams dozing away during boring speeches in the House of Representatives.

It is fashionable today to sneer at the dilettante, yet each of Marsh's interests was strengthened by the variety of his life. He was a superb scholar who spoke twenty languages, an expert on architecture and an art collector, a congressman and a conservationist, a geographer and a historian, a lawyer, an ambassador, and a camel enthusiast. He was also one of the founders, and a director, of the Smithsonian Institution.

Marsh, like Darwin, had an immense breadth of vision, but, unlike Darwin, he was so far ahead of his time that even the most recent edition of the *Encyclopaedia Britannica* dismisses him in a paragraph as a "philologist" and a "diplomatist."

Yet soon after the American Civil War, Marsh expressed a devastating thesis: man, he said, was trapped in a crisis of environment. It involved him at every level of his existence, from his belly to his psyche. Moreover, the crisis was global and worsening rapidly. It could, and probably would, destroy civilization. This Marshian hypothesis was presented in 1864 in his chilling work *Man and Nature*, which was subtitled *Physical Geography as Modified by Human Action*. The destruction would involve forests, mammals, fish, and insects—life at all levels; and he foresaw the reduction of great areas of the earth to permanent deserts. Tied to this depreciation of environment was, he warned, the decay of man's moral being and the fall of empires. In an age of supreme optimism about the seemingly limitless possibilities of science Marsh wrote: "... we are, even now, breaking up the floor and wainscoting and doors and window frames of our dwelling, for fuel to warm our bodies and seethe our pottage, and the world cannot afford to wait till the slow and sure progress of exact science has taught it a better economy."

Marsh's genius, and his relevance to the present, were that he saw the earth as a single unit, a giant orchestra being conducted by Homo sapiens—and making agonizingly bad music. He was obsessed by the intricate chain of cause and effect. (The invention of the silk hat by a Parisian, he observed, caused the formation of many small lakes and bogs in the United States because it almost obliterated the demand for beaver fur, thus allowing the beavers to make their comeback.)

By FRANKLIN RUSSELL

He saw the earth as a series of environmental systems, which in *Man and Nature* he broke down arbitrarily into "The Woods," "The Waters," and "The Sands." All were governed by geographical rules that, Marsh noted acidly, man did not understand. Today these environmental systems have a name—*ecosystems,* or a series of "living and nonliving units interacting in nature," as one definition puts it. An ecosystem can be almost anything —an ant colony, Chicago, Africa, or two people in love. It is the interaction and interdependence of the parts of the system that are important.

The concept of the ecosystem has demanded the creation of a new science—the study of ecosystems. The science exists only as an idea. Nobody is quite sure where it should begin. It has no accepted name ("ecosystem ecology" is a possibility, or "ecosystemics"), but it is attracting the attention of many top scientists. They are, like Marsh, *macrocosmic* thinkers. They are concerned with wholes first, parts second, and so reverse the order of conventional scientific study.

Dr. S. Dillon Ripley, Secretary of the Smithsonian Institution, recently indicated the significance of the new approach: "The creation of this new science of ecosystem ecology is, without doubt, the most important single event that has occurred in the twentieth century. It may be the most important event in all history. It is our attempt to avoid the fate of the other great civilizations."

The genesis of Marsh's philosophy occurred, perhaps, in a Vermont forest fire. He was born in 1801 in Woodstock, then a village of some fifty frame houses. A year before his birth, fire burned off Mount Tom, a five-hundred-foot mountain that overlooks Woodstock. Until Marsh was three, the mountain remained bare of trees, and much of its soil probably eroded into the river at this time. Then new trees began springing up to cover it, as he, a precocious reader, was educating himself in his father's library. He saw the successive changes that followed the burn and noted them so carefully that years later he was able to write: "the depth of the mould and earth is too small to allow the trees to reach maturity. When they attain to the diameter of about six inches, they uniformly die, and this they will no doubt continue to do until the decay of leaves and wood on the surface, and the decomposition of the subjacent rock, shall have formed, perhaps hundreds of years hence, a stratum of soil thick enough to support a full-grown forest."

The Marshes of Vermont and their friends were gentlemen landowners. Ethan Allen once described them as "A Petulant, Pettefoging, Scribling sort of Gentry, that will keep any Government in hot water till they are Thoroughly brought under by the Exertions of Authority."

Despite Allen's sour estimate, George Marsh was proud of his family heritage. In later years he would make a giant leap to link them to the Goths, whom he vastly admired: "The intellectual character of our Puritan forefathers is that derived by inheritance from our remote Gothic ancestry, restored by its own inherent elasticity to its primitive proportions, upon the removal of the shackles and burdens, which the spiritual and intellectual tyranny of Rome had for centuries imposed upon it.... The Goths... are the noblest branch of the Caucasian race. We are their children. It was the spirit of the Goth, that guided the May Flower across the trackless ocean; the blood of the Goth that flowed at Bunker's Hill."

The Goth whose name was George Perkins Marsh was an odd child with an oversized head, who liked to play with girls. His father, Charles, tyrannized the children, and George sweated over his studies to win paternal approval. As a country child, he began his thinking at the soil and worked upward. He wanted to know everything, in more than the usual

Fire, savage agent of ecological change, destroys a woodland in 1959. A burned forest will be replaced by shrubs and grasses, a fact well known to ancient farmers, who helped to create the world's great prairies by purposely setting fires.

childish sense, and he went about it through years of systematic study of an encyclopedia. In his usual fashion he overdid it; by the time he was eight, he was almost blind and for four years could read nothing. But his passion for knowledge was undiminished.

He went out into the fields and woods to study the natural world. His father often walked with him, identifying trees and explaining the workings of watersheds. Young George himself was at the center of the grand, interacting system of life that he observed. The fast-flowing river Quechee, which runs past Woodstock and which at that time was studded with mills, shrank to a trickle during the summer, and the mills shut down. George noticed that as the hills were cleared of spruce and white pine, the spring floods of the Quechee became higher. When he was ten, a July flood smashed his father's stone retaining-wall on the river and swamped his sawmill. The system in which he lived was close to nature, yes; but its philosophy was destructive, and he witnessed the despoliation of his environment. His childhood was spent within the span of pioneer days in Vermont, when entire forests were felled for fuel and lumber. The roar of the floodwaters and the crash of falling trees were somber lessons for an observant boy. Marsh never forgot that as he watched, primeval Vermont was destroyed.

Erosion in New England may have carved the outlines of his philosophy, but to reach conclusions involving the world Marsh was forced to make a lifelong journey through time and space. His boyhood experiences were forgotten while he followed in his father's footsteps and became a lawyer.

"Work is life," he once said, and he used work to get him through a life of sustained personal disaster. Calamities hit him about as frequently as the floods hit Vermont. His first wife, Harriet, whom he had married in 1828, died in 1833, and his four-year-old son, Charles, died of scarlet fever eleven days later. In 1843 he was elected to Congress as a Whig representative, but during his campaign his second wife, Caroline, suffered a stroke, and his surviving son, George, got typhoid.

Politics, he found, dulled and degraded the mind. Besides, Marsh the politician needed a sinecure to support Marsh the scholar. In 1849 he wangled an appointment as U.S. Minister to Turkey. This, too, was a disaster. He had to spend thousands to supplement his meager government allowance.

On his return to the United States in 1854, pressed for money as usual, he tried the lecture circuit, but his fact-filled speeches stupefied his audiences. Marsh's biographer, David Lowenthal, explains that Marsh "never quite got rid of the notion that facts are virtues in themselves . . ." He had invested heavily in textiles a few years before the market collapsed, and now bought into a marble quarry that produced a type of marble nobody wanted. Eventually he went bankrupt from earlier investments in a railroad, losing valuable real estate in the process. "There have been Marshes," he wrote sadly to a friend, "who not only *had* money, but actually *kept* it till they died."

But none of this seemed to slow him down. He designed measuring and surveying instruments, wrote an Icelandic grammar, and launched a one-man lobby that was responsible for the Washington Monument's obelisk form.

In 1861 Abraham Lincoln came to Marsh's rescue, appointing him the first American minister to Italy. It was an odd choice, since Marsh was violently anti-Catholic; in the year of his appointment he expressed the hope that he would live to see Pope Pius IX hanged. Marsh set sail for Italy with his usual *mal de mer*. "I hate the sea," he once said, "and would be well content to pay my share of the cost of filling it up altogether."

When he finally sat down in a Genoa hotel room to work on *Man and Nature*, he was sixty-one. In addi-

The voracious goat, devourer of tender tree shoots, prevents reforestation wherever men do not stop it from overgrazing. By the beginning of the fifth century B.C. the goat's destructive nibble had already laid bare the hills of Greece.

A plow, abandoned in Oklahoma in 1936, lies in the dusty wasteland it helped to make—an area that farmers still call "the land that blows." The plowman, and his goats, can destroy the vegetation that protects the soil from wind and water.

tion to the Icelandic grammar and a work called *The Goths in New-England*, he had published *Lectures on the English Language* and a definitive book called *The Camel; His Organization, Habits and Uses, Considered with Reference to His Introduction into the United States*. No one could deny the dazzling variety of his work, but his life, though brilliant in parts, did not seem to add up to a significant whole.

However, Marsh's journey to Genoa and the beginning of the big book actually had nothing to do with his external life. This was the culmination of an *internal* journey—the summation of more than fifty years of watching and thinking. Added to Marsh's lifelong passion for collecting facts was an unmatched acuity of insight and an extraordinary capacity to observe, relate, interpret, and synthesize. He saw, for instance, that the great door of the cathedral at Ravenna was built of vine-wood planks, and calculated that the planks were thirteen feet long and fifteen inches wide. It was traditionally thought that the planks had been brought from the Black Sea, via Constantinople, in the eleventh or twelfth century. During his years in Europe he made a most careful search in Syria and Turkey, but he found no vine stocks more than six inches in diameter. From this he devised a commentary on what the state of Middle Eastern wine making had been a thousand years before his time.

It was, however, the ruins of civilization that really caught his attention. He analyzed ruins in North Africa, over much of the Arabian peninsula, and in Syria, Mesopotamia, Armenia, and other Roman provinces in Asia Minor, Greece, Sicily, Italy, and Spain. Dense populations of people had once occupied these areas, which in his time were little more than deserts. He recalled how the Persians, the crusaders, and the Tartars had moved great armies, supporting themselves solely off the land, across areas that in the nineteenth century could scarcely support a few nomadic shepherds. What had happened?

The answer was clear to Marsh. A steady depreciation of environment had occurred, ending in the almost total exhaustion of its original fertility. On this exhaustion hinged not only the fall of civilizations but the corruption of the moral state of man.

The fall of the Roman Empire fascinated Marsh. He compared ancient descriptions of the empire with his personal experiences in the region. "Vast forests have disappeared from mountain spurs and ridges," he wrote in *Man and Nature*. Alpine soils were gone, cisterns and reservoirs dried up, and famous historical rivers were shrunk to "humble brooklets." He denounced the tyrannical, despotic, brutal Romans of the empire who had left a "dying curse to all her wide dominion, and which, in some form of violence or of fraud, still brood over almost every soil subdued by the Roman legions."

Marsh was intemperate about Latins, but he was right about the scope of environmental damage. Adria, situated between the Po and the Adige, was a famous Adriatic seaport in Augustus's time, but when Marsh got there, it was fourteen miles inland. Marsh calculated that the combined outflow of silt from the Italian Alps and Apennines amounted to 220,000,000 cubic yards annually, enough to cover 360 square miles with seven inches of silt. Marsh became so concerned about the silt outflow—most of it, he noted, being carried toward the equator—that eventually he came to believe the equatorial diameter of the globe would be increased, its center of gravity displaced, and its rotation affected.

Man and Nature is full of such cosmic concepts. Locked in his hotel room, Marsh roared on around the earth, discussing the destruction of animal life, the transfer of plants, the damage done by fires, the effects of dams and dikes and floods, the shifting of sand dunes. He rounded out *Man and Nature* by speculating on the effects of the Suez Canal, then under construction, and by worrying about the proposed Panama Canal. There was a chance, he felt, that the Gulf Stream might plunge through such a canal into the Pacific and so cause an ice age in Europe.

Diverting the Nile into the Red Sea, turning the Rhine from its course, and draining the Great Lakes into the Gulf of Mexico were only a few of the many projects he played with as logical extensions of all his speculation about how physical geography was modified by human action.

Marsh's shotgun blast at the world is entertaining, though the reader may bog down in its chaotic organization and often prolix language, but even at its funniest it remains fascinating for the manner in which it presages later scientific evaluation of geographical modifications by man. With civilized man present, Marsh seems to say, the depreciation of environment—though it may be rapid or slow—is constant and inexorable. Vermont was hit suddenly, but in many regions of the world the process was so slow as to be immeasurable in one man's lifetime.

Apulia, in southern Italy, illustrates Marsh's theory. According to historical records, it was once fertile and well populated with Bronze and Iron Age farmers who subsequently gave way to thirteen centuries of the Roman principate, which left extensive remains of ditches, walls, and dwellings. Finally, the intensive grazing of sheep flocks after A.D. 1300 extracted the last of the wealth of the soil, and the region today is notable for its desolate landscape.

On a vaster scale the clearing of forests was carried out during the Shang dynasty in China, which began about 1600 B.C. The Chinese philosopher Mencius saw this forest destruction going on unabated thirteen hundred years later, with hordes of cattle and goats—which China cannot support today—gnawing away at the remains of the forests. ("To these things is owing the bare and stripped appearance of the mountain," he wrote, "and when people now see it, they think it was never finely wooded. But is this the nature of the mountain?") Modern China suffers the consequences of this early clearing; in the intervening thirty-five hundred years, the silt-laden Yellow River has dumped billions of tons of China into the Pacific. Such a loss is the sort of geographical change that would have fascinated Marsh.

The steady depreciation of the earth caused by man covers such a vast period that it is difficult to grasp its scope. Two thousand years before the founding of Rome, Sumerian temple records indicated a steady decline in the yields of crops and in the variety of game and fish available. There have been many major regional changes of environment throughout history. When Alexander invaded India, he found that beyond the Jhelum River in the northwest there was a great and stately forest. Today the region is desolate, holding only scattered acacia and Dalbergia trees. Five million square miles of Central Africa have been permanently transformed from forest land to savanna by fires, grazing, and primitive agriculture. Some modern scholars believe that all prairie lands—the American Middle West and the Russian steppes in particular—are the result of early man's use of fire for hunting.

In many ancient histories there are tantalizing clues to the range and period of man-made geographical change. Plato wandered in the Attic hills, chatting with his countrymen, and noted that the hills that in his time supported only thin grass and spring flowers had been covered just a few generations earlier with dense forests. Plato understood as well as Marsh that forested hills caused rain to be "received by the country...into her bosom" and prevented floods. Greek culture certainly did not flourish long after the loss of the upland soils.

The lunar desolation of Italy's Apennine mountains, grim handiwork of classical civilization, is the direct result of man's misuse of the land. Rain water, running unabsorbed down denuded hills, washed away the soil that nourished Rome.

Marsh witnessed the disastrous ecological consequences of the French Revolution. He climbed the Alps, wandered through the tributary valleys of the Rhone and other rivers, and saw flood destruction on a scale that made Vermont (which he thought the worst-eroded region in America) look like a well-managed garden. The French catastrophe was caused by the elimination of the prerevolutionary forest-protection laws. The resentment of the masses for aristocratic landowners was enormous; chopping down the forests of the privileged became at once a social virtue and an ecological tragedy.

Although Marsh viewed coldly man's interference with the earth, he was a positivist. "The multiplying population, the impoverished resources of the globe," he wrote, "demand new triumphs of mind over matter." But he knew, too, that he was ahead of his time and admitted there were not enough facts available for him to make really profound observations. "... all I can hope is to excite an interest in a topic of much economical importance," he said, "by pointing out the directions and illustrating the modes in which human action has been or may be most injurious or most beneficial in its influence upon the physical conditions of the earth we inhabit."

In the eighty-six years since Marsh died man's relations with his world have excited more than "interest." Something nearing a hysteria of concern has infected almost everybody who has looked at the world through ecologic, or Marshian, eyes. A minor flood of books and articles written by scientists and laymen predict catastrophe for the earth, citing its lack of food, its loss of soil, the pollution of its manifold parts. The writers do not need to dress up their figures; the facts are dramatic enough. About one-third of all American topsoil has been blown or washed away, and the soil is still disappearing at a grand rate. Lake Mead, formed by the Hoover Dam, which was completed in 1936 to irrigate five hundred thousand acres in southern Nevada, Arizona, and California, may be filled with silt by the year 2000. Thousands of tons of topsoil are rapidly filling up other reservoirs throughout the United States.

Recently a new depreciatory influence has been added to the environment—poisoning—and the long-term effects cannot be estimated. Like most technological modifications, it is global. Ducks in the Arctic, and penguins and seals in the Antarctic, carry DDT in their bodies. Much of the world's drinking water contains nitrates created by pollution filtering into reservoirs and wells—which in large doses cause cyanosis in children and kill domestic animals.

Such facts—and many more—have been cranked out so relentlessly by scientists that their shock value is pretty well gone. The most positive validation of Marsh's theories, however, is that the exhaust of man's engines is changing world climate. In the hundred years since 1860, combustion of man-made fuels into the atmosphere has added nearly 14 per cent to the carbon dioxide content of the air. Carbon dioxide tends to pass ordinary light and to absorb infrared. It lets sunlight into the earth but prevents, or slows, the redistribution of heat back into space. Eventually this could melt the Antarctic ice cap, perhaps within four hundred years. By that time the rising oceans will have drowned most of the major cities of the world, unless Marsh's demand for "new triumphs of mind over matter" prevails.

Marsh worshiped technology, which he saw as the answer to man's perennial problems of hunger and deprivation. He believed technology would free men. But he saw it in idealistic terms. It was, of course, technology—in the shape of axes, shovels, and plows —that had modified the geography he was discussing. However, in Marsh's view, that was merely the technology

The flood that devastated Florence in November, 1966, constitutes the last link in a causal chain instigated by man's ecological disbalancing act. Heavy rains ran off the barren hills and gorged a river constricted by factories and farms.

of ignorance. The technology of the future, he believed, would be in the hands of intelligent, informed, concerned men.

Unhappily, technology went right on being administered by the ignorant, the stupid, and the unconcerned. American farmers, equipped with the first steam plows, were breaking up the prairies in the west even as Marsh inveighed against erosion in the east. Ultimately, according to Dr. Hugh H. Bennett, former chief of the Soil Conservation Service of the U.S. Department of Agriculture, 280 million acres (or twice the area of France) of crop and range land were destroyed, and 100 million additional acres were so badly damaged that they cannot be restored.

Former Premier Khrushchev, beset by food shortages, put plows into the Russian steppes and upset thousands of years of fragile ecological balance. Some scientists believe the land will never recover.

If Marsh's theories on man-made geography are to be meaningful to us, we must find ways to avoid the climax that his work so clearly implies. There *are* ways, or rather, there *is a* way, born out of the kind of holistic thinking that Marsh used and that ecosystemic thinkers today are trying to use. In order to get the sort of knowledge that is necessary for such broad-gauge thinking—or, at least to start to get it —the five-year-long International Biological Program, which was begun in 1967 and unites fifty countries, will make a cell-by-cell analysis of international environments.

Marsh long ago foresaw the need for such a program. "In order to arrive at safe conclusions," he said, "we must first obtain a more exact knowledge of the topography, and of the present superficial and climatic condition of countries where the natural surface is as yet more or less unbroken."

"Ecosystemic thinking," says Dr. Frank Egler, an American ecologist, "co-ordinates the entire world—its plants, animals, soils, climate, man and other elements—as a single integrated whole which, though it must be 'managed' must also remain in relative balance if the human race is to persist in a healthy and culturally rich existence. It is a spider web where each strand is intimately connected with and dependent upon every other strand."

It is clear that a new type of man is needed in a future world where every man is dependent on every other man. Marsh, of course, would say that the new man should be a Goth, and because he understood the need so clearly, we can smile tolerantly at this small naïveté.

But was not Marsh himself the new man, or at least the *timeless* man who appears when he is needed? He was a combination of two Greek concepts: the Dionysian, or dynamic, ecstatic, and creative man, and the Apollonian, or reasonable, disciplined, and orderly man. Greek art synthesized these two concepts, and so did Marsh. He reconciled literature and science, reason and feeling, and this may well be the real reason why he tugs so hard on the scientific conscience today.

When Marsh died, in Italy in 1882, he was far from the "bubbling brooks" of his childhood, and he had become depressed because his optimistic hopes for man had coincided with the rise of the robber barons in America, the devastation and exploitation of the American South, and the "unification" of Italy—into apathy, poverty, and despair. Men learned nothing, he felt. They were stupid, dishonest, hopeless.

But if Marsh could hear the discussions about him today, he would not be so sure that man was hopeless. Men now listen to Marsh, and they understand him very well.

Franklin Russell, like Mr. Marsh, is a tireless collector of facts about our ecology. He has translated many of the facts into books and essays, including "Life and Death on the Funks" for the Summer, 1965, issue of HORIZON.

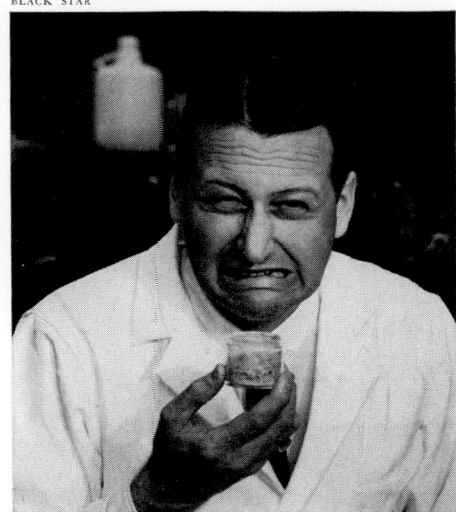

The noxious odor of "gunk," contaminants taken from the Mississippi River, contorts the face of Dr. D. W. Ryckman, director of Washington University's environmental laboratory. Despite such lessons as this, man *is not yet "housebroken."*

R. Buckminster Fuller appears in a moonscape with one of his tetrahedral cities floating in the sky and another nestling on the surface

MAN AT WAR WITH NATURE

II · Which Guide to the Promised Land: Fuller or Mumford?

They both understand the crisis; they both know all the facts; they are both brilliant and thoughtful men. It is a measure of our ecological crisis today that they disagree utterly on where to go from here

No matter how remotely separated Lewis Mumford and Richard Buckminster Fuller may be in temperament and thought—which is as far apart as ultraviolet and infrared in the diffused spectrum of modern environmental theory—they stand very close on several counts. Both believe that man's potentialities are virtually limitless, but that he has failed to make the most of them, or else has grievously misused them, so that technological civilization—which if rationally organized could transform the world into a heaven on earth—is in fact in a parlous way and needs a thorough overhaul on a global basis. Therefore they recommend, each from a radically different point of view but with equal fervor, that the chief components of the world environment, such as large cities, be renewed—not to say totally rebuilt—according to "comprehensive" and "integrated" design. Whatever else they may be, Mumford and Fuller are *integrators* who seek wholeness in a new order of man in an age of widespread cultural and physical disintegration.

Both of these "one-world" men believe, moreover, that before a valid global order can be established, man's spiritual and intellectual relationships with his physical environment, including of course machine-made environment as well as natural surroundings, must be profoundly redefined and revised. To Mumford the humanist, as to Fuller the technologist, man's relation to the machine itself is of supreme importance. Indeed, in an age of intercontinental missiles that has already witnessed genocidal exterminations, that is afflicted by hunger, ill-health, drudgery, ignorance, and squalor for hundreds of millions of people, not only the welfare but the very survival of civilization hinges on the humane use of depersonalized technology. Consequently Mumford and Fuller insist that the machine must be put more fully at the service of man, although their diagnoses of man's technological dilemma, together with their prescriptions for sweeping remedial action, differ so markedly that it would seem they are grappling with utterly separate problems.

Yet both Mumford, the spokesman for man in all his human complexity, and Fuller, who enthrones technics as the single solution to the difficulties of mankind, are nothing if not "generalists." Each, with some pride, describes himself as such and disdains slavish specialization as a bane of the present age. Even when they address themselves to comparatively narrow subjects—Mumford to the neolithic village, perhaps, or to the psychology of Jung, or to gardening at his home in Dutchess County; and Fuller to the etymology of the word "dome," to sailing off the Maine coast, or the design of drainage systems—each of them thinks within the frame of a much larger conceptual scheme. The hyphen is a formidable device in their intellectual arsenals, enabling them to interconnect a bewildering range of disciplines within their broad, unifying philosophies.

Such catholicity scarcely endears them to conventional pedants; and for their part Mumford and Fuller, who are otherwise kindly men, have little patience with conventional wisdom, whether exhibited by professors, politicians, or plumbers. Neither of them, it goes without saying, is an academician, although both have held famous professorships and have spent much time in universities. (Fuller, who never got past a tumultuous freshman year at Harvard, is actually a research professor at Southern Illinois University at Carbondale, but he is seldom there; whereas Mumford, whose studies at City College, Columbia, the New School for Social Research, and the museums and libraries of New York were so free that his only academic degrees are honorary, was installed last year as scholar in residence at Leverett House at Harvard.)

On the campus, understandably enough, their all-encompassing doctrines often evoke the private gibes of pedagogues who resent their brilliant forays into carefully fenced scholarly terrain, but such professorial skepti-

By ALLAN TEMKO

cism does not dampen the unreserved enthusiasm of students who are "turned on" by these vigorous and fearless septuagenarians. For even though their styles could not be more different—Mumford's measured eloquence and smiling dignity contrasting sharply with Fuller's bombastic and garrulous monologues—they are both inspiring and very great teachers who, like Henry Adams and H. G. Wells before them, fear that time is running out and that the fate of civilization may soon be decided, in Wells's phrase, by "a race between education and catastrophe."

Finally, and not least important, Mumford and Fuller are unmistakably Americans. Both were born in 1895, Fuller in Massachusetts, and Mumford in New York. The differences in their backgrounds are significant. Fuller, the descendant of generations of Harvard men, whose forbears came to this country in 1630, attended a Milton Academy that was far removed from the Stuyvesant High where Mumford, whose old New York family had come to know "genteel poverty," learned at firsthand the inexhaustible variety and vitality—and the crushing realities—of the melting pot of the modern industrial metropolis. Fuller was exposed to comparable experience later, at the nadir of his career in the 1920's, when he lived for a time in a Chicago slum. Yet he never came to regard the city, as Mumford has, as a "time-structure" that itself is a formative factor in civilization. Fuller, the inventor, has sought to create an utterly new urban environment. Mumford, the historian, has seen the city as an institution that is the expression of social as well as physical forces —"history made visible"—and that transforms man as he transforms his surroundings. Yet by paradox Fuller is much more at home in contemporary America than is Mumford.

Nevertheless these two Americans share many of the highest values of the national heritage. Fuller, after all, is the grandnephew of Margaret Fuller, the great feminist and friend of Emerson who has been described as the high priestess of transcendentalism; Mumford is the chief heir of Emerson in American moral philosophy. Each of them thus retains deep affinities with an older, more spacious, less mechanized, relatively unspoiled, and in part wild and almost unpeopled America in which individuals counted for more than organizations, which industrial technology has now changed forever. Yet each carries on the American intellectual adventure today, headed for different destinations but really voyaging outward to the world at large, following the great circle course of nonconformity, self-reliance, and transcendental awareness charted by Emerson and Thoreau.

But here any resemblance, either in philosophy or its practical applications, ceases abruptly. Precisely because of the breadth and scale of their synoptic outlooks—which Fuller, characteristically borrowing a term from astronomy, would call "sweep-outs" but which Mumford would consider valueless if not complemented by a searching "sweep-in" to the psychic needs of individual men —the two are irreconcilably opposed in their interpretations of man and his place in the universe, just as they are in total disagreement concerning the role of science and technics in civilized life. The profound differences between their concepts of planning and architecture are part of these larger philosophical differences, and cannot be fully understood except in the broader context of their total thought.

Neither man has dealt at length with the other in any of his voluminous writings, but everything to which Mumford would object in Fuller's approach is castigated in a powerful chapter in *The Conduct of Life* entitled "The Fallacy of Systems," which Mumford has called "a key to my whole life and thought." Since the seventeenth century, he asserts, "we have been living in an age of system-makers, and what is even worse, system-appliers," the Procrustean mutilators of life who lop off its essential irregularities to fit "a single set of consistent principles and ideal ends." But life "cannot be reduced to a system: the best wisdom, when so reduced to a set of insistent notes, becomes a cacophony: indeed, the more stubbornly one adheres to a system, the more violence one does to life."

Against "system-mongers" who seek "to align a whole community according to some limiting principle," Mumford opposes his "philosophy of the open synthesis," which he also names "the affirmation of organic life," in which the valid features of one system or another may be invoked by turns "to do justice to life's endlessly varied needs and occasions." This would be above all a life of "balance," maintained in "dynamic equilibrium," with an open attitude toward change. "Those who understand the nature of life itself will not . . . see reality in terms of change alone"; and "neither will they, like many Greek and Hindu philosophers, regard flux and movement and time as unreal or illusory and seek truth only in the unchangeable." History offers proof of this lesson: "Actual historic institutions, fortunately, have been modified by anomalies, discrepancies, contradictions, compromises: the older they are, the richer this organic compost." And yet, "all these varied nutrients that remain in the social soil are viewed with high scorn by the believer in systems."

Among the many systems, including capitalism and Marxian communism, that he enumerates with such distrust, Mumford has taken care to include utilitarianism, with its crass mechanistic notions of "efficiency." Although the social crimes committed by industrial civilization in the name of utility and efficiency should by now have shorn us of any simplistic mechanical "idea of progress," nineteenth-century utilitarianism happens to be alive and well in the twentieth, under the guises of technocracy and scientism; and if Mumford, in the rare passages where he mentions Fuller, had not considered him merely as an ingenious housing prefabricator with a "Jules Verne–Buck Rogers" side to him, but had instead analyzed Fuller's thought, he might well have consigned him to one of the lower circles of an organic philosophical hell among the Benthamites.

Fuller cannot be categorized quite so neatly, however, for he is an authentic original. Like Thorstein Veblen, he is much more than a rudimentary technocrat who has greater confidence in engineers and machinery than in politicians and the present price-system. But certainly, as far as faith in the system of doing the most with the least is concerned, he is a true believer. He is also an indefatigable system-applier who seizes any opportunity to find fresh exemplifications of his general principles, with the result that the earth's surface is now dotted with some five thousand geodesic domes of greatly varying dimensions and materials, serving innumerable purposes in climates as diverse as the Arctic DEW-line and steamy Louisiana, but all based on the same fundamental structural concept. As a system-monger he has long been incorrigible, and will cheerfully spend hours selling his ideas to anyone who will listen, from Tahiti to M.I.T., be they kindergarteners or U.S. Marines.

As physical systems go, Fuller's is remarkably complete, and yet, like his domes, structurally lean. For all his prodigality of language, replete with arcane Latinisms of his own devising that put a substantial obstacle between him and his audience, Fuller's system rests on only a few grand concepts (from which he draws a wealth of inferences), just as his architecture is limited to a few basic forms.

Except for some baldly technocratic borrowings, such as the contention that we had better give up politics altogether and let technology order the world, his philosophy is derived almost entirely from post-Newtonian science and is as near to being an *absolute* system, based on "universal laws," as any yet postulated by a modern environmental theorist. Since he began formulating universalist concepts in the twenties, taking the whole world—including the oceans and the atmosphere—as an integral field of development, Fuller's energies, according to his biographer and friend Robert W. Marks, have been "centered in a single drive: to promote the *total use of total technology for total population*, 'at the maximum feasible rate of acceleration.'"

But this unremitting exploitation of technology is inseparable from science and is based on cosmic harmonies. Fuller's structures are all based ultimately on the triangle, or combinations of triangles, which he claims is the basic building unit of the universe, lending itself naturally to incorporation in spheres, on macrocosmic and microcosmic scale. If this sounds like latter-day music of the spheres, reminiscent of the trinitarian metaphysics of the Middle Ages that found the triangle both universally symbolic and exceptionally stable as a structural component of vast cathedrals—or again, reminiscent of the theological associations of the purely proportioned domes of the Renaissance humanists—Fuller replies that such grand, simple forms express fundamental truths of nature, which he asserts is never arbitrarily complex. On the contrary, nature is accurately described by equations of the purity of $E = MC^2$. If Fuller is right, we are about to learn that chaos is nonexistent: "all that was chaotic was in man's illiterate and bewildered imagination and fearful ignorance."

But certain things will remain unpredictable, at least for the time being, due to the phenomenon that Fuller has dubbed "synergy," which means that "the behavior of a whole system" is "unpredicted by the behavior of any of its components—or sub-assemblies of its components." An example of a totality adding up to much more than the sum of its parts is a metallic alloy such as chrome-nickel steel, which, as Fuller gleefully points out, is far stronger than the sum of the strength of its separate ingredients.

A rather more overwhelming example of synergetics, to be sure, is the release of atomic energy. Fuller in one of his great insights foresaw in the 1930's that, thanks to a new and unlimited source of energy, a revolutionary increase in the world's productive capacity was at hand. With somewhat less insight, he assumed a corresponding improvement in human welfare.

What followed of course was the Bomb. Fuller was undaunted, and not really surprised, for he had long been aware that the most far-reaching technological innovations of modern times, for better and worse, have often originated in weapons research and development. Hence his unashamed association with the Pentagon—to Mumford the pit of conscienceless scientific and technological perversion—which has led to the large-scale delivery of his domes, sometimes by helicopter, to military establishments in many parts of the world.

Meanwhile, as the Cold War continued, nuclear power stations—soon to be combined with the saline-water conversion facilities indispensable to Fuller's long-standing scheme to occupy the watery three-quarters of the globe—appeared in many countries. In 1958 Fuller told Nehru: "Science has hooked up the everyday economic plumbing to the cosmic reservoir." In other words, wealth is now nondepletable. It is really "universal energy," and therefore classical economics, like classical geometry, may be totally discarded.

Thus Fuller's search for a general solution to terrestrial problems has gone into celestial orbit. Unhesitatingly he has placed himself in the forefront of the effort to get out into space, in order to tap inexhaustible cosmic resources; and he is a consultant to the team of scientists and technicians who are designing the first moon colony. What Fuller hopes to bring back from the moon, for the good of mankind, is the first "little black box" containing a truly miniaturized mechanical system including tiny energy fuel-cells and a tiny waste-disposal system, which will revolutionize household management everywhere in the world—at a time when there is not even everyday plumbing in the hovels of India. Analogous reasoning has permitted him to take some comfort from the introduction of giant helicopters in the Vietnam war, a war that in other respects causes him pain but nothing like the outraged sense of horror and anguish that has made Mumford one of the foremost spokesmen for peace and disarmament in the United States. If these powerful aircraft were released for nonwar duty, notes Fuller (who as early as 1927 conceived a lightweight, ten-story apartment house of "wire-wheel" structure to be delivered by zeppelin, which first would drop a bomb to excavate a foundation crater), they could deposit still larger geodesic domes any place on earth, providing huge instant shelters for Eskimos or Zulus.

With deepening despair Mumford regards such "power-centered" infatuation with technics as pathological folly. It is not that Fuller's schemes, which Mumford once might have dismissed as science fiction, are unrealizable. It is that they are all too swiftly feasible in an age of unparalleled *technical* capabilities that are beyond effective human control; and not surprisingly Mumford likens the Space Age, or Nuclear Age (he bitterly notes that it is not called the Age of Man), to an automobile without driver, steering wheel, or brakes, but crammed with demoralized passengers hurtling full speed toward doom. To those who call him Jeremiah, Mumford replies that it was Jeremiah whose prophecies "so fatally came true." As for Fuller himself, if Mumford would trouble to single him out as a prototypical antagonist, he might describe him, as he once did Le Corbusier, as "deeply in harmony with the negative tendencies of our times."

For Fuller is probably America's most vociferous and energetic advocate of what Mumford denounces as "the myth of the machine"; the notion that technics, rather than man himself, is the central component of culture. By now this technological interpretation of human progress has a rather long history, dating from the early industrial period when Carlyle and others first called man a "tool-using animal." On the contrary, Mumford replies, man from his beginnings has been "pre-eminently a mind-making, self-mastering, and self-designating animal." Therefore, it is not the mindless machine (which, according to Fuller, works "more reliably than the limited sensory departments of the human mechanism"), but man in all the richness and complexity of his "symbolic" activities who must be the true center. Not technical advancement, but human development, which imparts *significance* to life, is Mumford's measure of social good; and he warns that the chief moral problem in every part of the world, regardless of "prevailing ideologies or ideal goals," is to clarify the tragically blurred distinction between good and bad.

Thus, in book after increasingly formidable book, from *The Story of Utopias* in 1922 to the early masterpiece *Technics and Civilization* of 1934 and last year's *The Myth of the Machine*, a great autumnal work of which only the first volume has appeared, Mumford has celebrated the "mindfulness" of man, whose supreme discovery—in all the history of invention—has not been tools, but his human self. Man's most superb technics has not consisted of material technology at all, but of his human ability to speak and to dream, to laugh and to weep, to sing and to love. Hence human development is scarcely confined to work, even though Mumford places considerable value on "joyful common toil" (which should not be mistaken for nostalgic agrarianism). The sum of man's rational and irrational activities includes "ritual, art, poesy, drama, music, dance, philosophy, science, myth, religion"—the list could be extended endlessly—which are "all as essential to man as his daily bread." The universe appears very different, Mumford remarks, once "the light of human consciousness, rather than mass and energy," is perceived to be the central fact of existence.

Then organic *growth*, rather than "inordinate power and productivity" and "purposeless materialism," emerges as the principal goal of a truly civilized society.

Mumford has never rejected the machine per se. He abhors only the "overgrowth" of technics at the expense of human needs and aspirations —like the overgrowth of inhumane and inefficient metropolises—because it has thrown modern civilization into perilous imbalance that cannot be righted by simplistic injections of more powerful technologies operating at higher and higher speeds.

Mumford is a spiritual Luddite who would break, and certainly cease manufacturing, many machines, especially the sinister engines that, governed by "invisible" electronic controls, can now virtually declare war by themselves. Even if the automated missiles do not put an end to human existence, other seemingly less menacing machines may wreck all that to Mumford makes life worth living, condemning men to "mandatory consumption" of the limitless array of products—not at all necessarily "goods"—poured forth from the technological cornucopia, and at the same time manipulating man socially and politically. If Fuller cheerfully suggests that the communications revolution has made it feasible for the entire population to cast its vote on any issue every day, Mumford asks: What are the issues, who is to formulate them, and how much will elections affect fundamental public policy?

For Mumford is more profoundly aware than Fuller that the impact of the mathematical and physical sciences upon technology in the past century, which has seen the rise of psychotic totalitarianism on every continent, has indeed caused "a radical transformation in the entire human environment." He further realizes, as Fuller in all innocence does not, that this great transformation—which has equipped man with so many marvelous "mechanical extensions"—also transforms man psychically.

"Alterations in the human personality" are produced, Mumford demonstrates, as indeed they have been throughout history whenever man has decisively changed the face of the earth. But the scale of modern technics is unprecedented and represents the most sweeping transformation of man since the Pyramid age. The age of "megatechnics" has begun, and it is perfectly capable of creating the very environment that a "dominant minority" (with which Mumford would surely associate Fuller) is striving to establish with the assistance of a "tentacular bureaucracy": "a uniform, all-enveloping, super-planetary structure, designed for automatic operation" that, Mumford fears, will reduce man to "a passive, purposeless, machine-conditioned animal." In the last third of the twentieth century Mumford, perhaps the last in the apostolic succession of the great Anglo-American environmental humanists—Ruskin, Morris, and Mumford's own master, Patrick Geddes—despairs of the now almost lost chance to build a truly "biotechnic order," based on human scale and human needs and employing technology only for the fulfillment of man. Thus he awaits the appearance of "Post-Historic Man"—the phrase is the title of Roderick Seidenberg's brilliant book—congealed in the icy fixity of a totally organized and utterly depersonalized technological age of "megamachines."

Yet this is a lesson Mumford has learned from his study of remote antiquity. Fuller's fantastic and exhilarating excursions into history have resembled raids, like those of the intrepid seafarers he so admires who adventured in "the outlaw area" on the high seas in the teeth of raw nature, where no bland social institutions hampered their expansion of human power as they took what they wanted and let the rest go. Mumford, on the other hand, is the greatest historian of urban civilization from its origins in the neolithic village to the "insensate" industrial metropolis; and in his grand historical synthesis he has traced the coexistence of two different technics: "one 'democratic' and dispersed," which found its highest expression in the authentic "polytechnics" of the Middle Ages; "the other totalitarian and centralized," whose supreme monument was the Pyramid of Cheops at Giza, the largest of man-made tetrahedral structures—Fuller's ideal assemblage of triangles. From the beginning, then, Mumford's "positive" and "negative," life-giving and death-dealing technologies existed side by side, although—in some cultures—one or the other might be overwhelmingly dominant. Mumford also points out that unchanging, "static" technology, as in the case of bowls and cisterns, dams and reservoirs, and other "containers" (even the city is described as a "container of power"), is fully as important as "dynamic," incessantly changing technology. To this Fuller might reply as he did in one of his poems, "Change is normal/thank you Albert!"

In considering the Great Pyramid, which even by modern standards was built with extraordinary speed and precision, without heavy lifting machinery, Mumford had one of his great insights into the nature of technics. For the Pyramid was built by a "megamachine," which until Mumford's discovery had been "invisible" to historians because its thousands of interacting components were human. Society itself had been mechanized into an enormous machine capable of swift performance of enormous but essentially meaningless physical tasks; and there is an inevitable analogy with the largely "invisible" technologies in which we have invested so heavily today. What are the Egyptian pyramids, Mumford asks, "but the precise static equivalents of our own space rockets? Both devices for securing, at extravagant cost, a passage to Heaven for the favored few."

With unerring consistency Fuller has just completed Mumford's argument by designing a pyramid greater by far than any dreamed of by the Egyptians: his "Tetrahedral City," two hundred stories high and two miles long to a side, which will be a metropolis in itself. The vast structure, surely one of the most astounding visionary designs in the history of architecture, can either float on a moat in Japan, the earthquake-ridden, land-short country for which it was designed; or else it can be towed out on the ocean, freed at last from the chaos of history, with its nuclear power plant providing the energy to work its innumerable machines and its fresh-water distillery, and with supersonic airliners, giant ocean-going vessels, and electronic communications connecting it to the rest of the world and to outer space, where a Fuller-influenced settlement may by then be in operation on the moon. Here, as in the Great Pyramid, posthistory may begin.

Fuller's megastructure, by far the most ambitious project of its kind ever seriously proposed, weighing only a small fraction of the enormous tonnage of materials that would have been required, say, for Frank Lloyd Wright's "mile-high" skyscraper, is to Mumford nothing more than an "urban hive," better fit for social insects than for men. Rather, it might accommodate the superb robot that Fuller described, only partly tongue in cheek, in his answer to the question "What's a man?":

Man?

A self-balancing, 28-jointed adapter-base biped; an electro-chemical reduction-plant, integral with segregated stowages of special energy extracts in storage batteries, for subsequent actuation of thousands of hydraulic and pneumatic pumps, with motors attached; 62,000 miles of capillaries; millions of warning signal, railroad and conveyor systems; crushers and cranes . . . and a universally distributed telephone system needing no service for 70 years if well managed; the whole, extraordinarily complex mechanism guided with exquisite precision from a turret in which are located telescopic and microscopic self-registering and recording range finders, a spectroscope, et cetera. . . .

All that is omitted is the *purpose* for which this most beautiful mechanism exists; and not surprisingly, Mumford asks instead: What is the human brain? It serves:

as a seat of government, a court of justice, a parliament, a marketplace, a police station, a telephone exchange, a temple, an art gallery, a library, a theatre, an observatory, a central filing system; and a computer: or, to reverse Aristotle, it is nothing less than the whole polis, writ small.

Only the telephone exchange, the complex communications system that both men have used with such courage, is mentioned in both quotations.

Yet the opposition of Mumford and Fuller is not quite that simple. If Mumford's generous philosophy theoretically accommodates incessant change while retaining the usufruct of the past, he himself has not accepted the largest part of the magnificent liberating innovations of the past generation. *The City in History* of 1961, in its recommendations for remaking the environment, did not differ in its essentials from *The Culture of Cities* of 1938. In an era of abundance Mumford called for the same program as in an era of scarcity; and although the program was handsome, proposing deconcentration and decentralization on the model of the remarkably prescient New York State regional plan of the late twenties, the British and Scandinavian new towns, and TVA, it took cognizance, for the most part, only of negative change during the interval between the two books.

Like the angry students at Berkeley, Mumford cried out, with reason, that our immediate need is peace, and that the human soul is not an IBM card. But the computer is inherently no more evil than the abacus, just as the jet plane is for no fundamental reason a less desirable form of transportation than the railroad. The value of machines depends upon the use to which they are put by men. In this respect history, on which Mumford has built one of the most complete philosophical syntheses of the modern age, may have escaped him. For the innumerable appliances and gadgets produced in the past thirty or forty years—which, together with birth-control pills, for instance, have opened an altogether new and almost incredibly more dignified life for women—have *not* thus far resulted in what Mumford calls "a dismally contracted life, lived for the most part confined to a car or to a television set."

Thirty million people, in this nation alone, remain impoverished, but the majority of Americans know that machines, besides bringing air pollution and devastation of the landscape, have brought them their new leisure, their release from age-old drudgery, their improved education, health, and cuisine, their ability to travel and to sail in their own boats, their symphony orchestras, galleries, and museums, their growing awareness of the necessity for privacy and solitude, their fresh awakening to the majesty of the wilderness, their educational television stations, and their millions of inexpensive paperback books, including Mumford's and Fuller's.

Fuller has ridden this wave of the future, remarking that "the old-fashioned square-shooter is today's square." If his puristic simplifications are oversimplifications, if his prefabricated houses and bathrooms are not as good as fine traditional dwellings as yet, if his domes and space-frames impose standardized solutions where a fully industrialized technology would provide limitless variety for personal choice (as it does in our machine-made clothing), Fuller has nevertheless been open to the future.

And the future remains open to us. To adventure truly upon the future as civilized beings we need new criteria for action: an unprecedented philosophy capable of solving unprecedented problems that neither would be linked indissolubly to the past (for it is conceivable that on positive grounds we may wish to relinquish much more of the past, which, after all, has landed us in the present predicament) nor would be stained with the philosophical sin of pride that Bertrand Russell called "cosmic impiety." The world, as Mumford knew from the start of his career, is a single complex entity, but it must be ready for change on a scale that few men, Fuller among them, have dared to contemplate. What each of them has done, really, has been to write philosophical poems celebrating a world that does not truly exist, and perhaps can never exist, even though the poems are true. Mumford is an epic poet, as grave, as moral, as grandly tragic, as John Milton; Fuller is a lyricist, and his bright, luminous structures had best be taken as lovely technological songs. Someday, from somewhere on the unified earth, a new poet may emerge to combine their gifts; but that supreme poet, as Santayana wrote at the end of his appreciation of Lucretius, Dante, and Goethe, is in limbo still.

Allan Temko, an architectural critic, is presently at work on a study of urban civilization in the technological age for the 20th Century Fund.

Lewis Mumford, lifelong apostle of humane environments, raises a cautionary hand to an encroaching bulldozer

Roger Revelle, a former oceanographer who now studies human population problems, is shown submerged in a populous sea

MAN AT WAR WITH NATURE

III · Too many born? Too many die. So says Roger Revelle

If population growth is the root of ecological evil, how can it be stopped? A demographer finds a clue in a paradox: the birth rate is out of control because the death rate is out of control

Among demographers, Roger Revelle is a middle-of-the-roader. Demographically speaking, that means he stands somewhere between pessimism and optimism about controlling the population explosion. On the one hand, he calls "poppycock" those prophecies that contend that the human race is already doomed to be suffocated by its own fertility. On the other, he rejects the view that somehow everything will work out. Revelle believes that man *can* do something to keep the world from being overwhelmed by people. He simply is not convinced that man *will*.

Revelle is head of the Center for Population Studies at Harvard, one of perhaps a half-dozen institutions set up within universities in recent years to find answers to the problems raised by man's great proclivity to reproduce. He is a giant of 6 feet 4 inches who at fifty-nine retains a robust physique that serves him well on his frequent excursions to the Asian subcontinent, Africa, and Latin America—the real trouble spots of the population boom. But whether in his modest offices at Harvard dealing with tables of statistics or on the Indus plain seeking new food sources for unborn millions, Revelle is constantly searching for ways of persuading the individuals who are creating this boom to modify their behavior. He is tough but not dogmatic in his quest, except in insisting that humanity, to survive, must be ready to accept fundamental changes in time-worn patterns of life.

"This situation will not yield to romanticism and nostalgia," Revelle says. "The world will never again be the same. A willingness by man to innovate is the first condition for resolving the population dilemma." Revelle's own willingness to take a fresh approach has led him to one rather startling conclusion: in the underdeveloped countries, where birth-control programs have had such difficulty making headway, the best way to lower the birth rate may be, paradoxically, to keep lowering the death rate—the very thing that brought about the population explosion.

Only through a chance undertaking that helped bring a basic innovation to the pattern of life in Pakistan did Roger Revelle become a demographer. All his life he had been a student of oceans, not people. As director of the Scripps Institution of Oceanography on the La Jolla campus of the University of California, he had acquired a world-wide reputation. (He is, in fact, one of the few men living who has a college named after him—a new school in the rapidly expanding La Jolla complex.) It was not until Secretary of the Interior Stewart Udall appointed him science advisor in 1961 that he began to contemplate a new profession. His decision was precipitated by an expedition he led, at the request of President Kennedy, to study the deterioration of agriculture in the Punjab region of West Pakistan, where famine threatened a population of thirty million people.

It may seem incongruous that an oceanographer was sent as head of a team to deal with an agricultural problem. But the problem was exactly in his element—water. Much of the arable land in the Indus valley, a vast plain created by a great river and five of its tributaries and cleft by an extensive network of irrigation canals, was threatened by a rising water table and a resulting excess of salt accumulation in the soil. As an oceanographer Revelle had long been interested in the conservation of natural resources and the development of new sources of food. More important, he was an expert in the characteristics of water flow and salinity. So he came to be given responsibility for devising a plan to restore fertility to the Indus plain.

Revelle and his colleagues concluded that the valley did not have too much

By MILTON VIORST

water, as most experts before them had assumed, but too little. They recommended that deep tube wells be drilled throughout the region to bring to the surface enough fresh water to wash the salt from the soil. Since much of this water would evaporate, the level of the underground water would drop below the danger point. Revelle and his associates also urged that fertilizers, high-yielding seeds, insecticides, and other improvements in farming methods be introduced.

The Pakistani government adopted the proposals and began at once to implement them. Revelle was astonished at the response. When the first tube wells proved effective, the people approached the next steps in the redevelopment process with vigor and ingenuity. New industries sprang up to manufacture the drilling and operating equipment for the wells. Enterprising Pakistanis learned how to derive nitrogen fertilizer from local natural gas. The government built roads and marketing facilities. Auxiliary industries were founded to make bicycles, sewing machines, soft drinks, and other personal amenities.

Pakistani farmers found new incentive for increasing their crop yield. They could now market their products and make major purchases with the money they earned. Contrary to the standard notion of peasant conservatism, they eagerly adopted the new kinds of seed and the new cultivating techniques that were being introduced to them. "Once relieved of the fear of starvation," Revelle says "they demonstrated a willingness to experiment. We helped them to have the confidence to shift from traditional subsistence farming to genuine market agriculture. They did the rest." In recent years food production has been increasing throughout the region at a rate of 5 to 6 per cent a year. If this rate holds up, Pakistani farms will be doubling their yield in fourteen years or less, far exceeding the growth rate of the population.

Revelle returned from his experience in Pakistan a confirmed student of population, if not yet a professional demographer. In 1964 Harvard established the Center for Population Studies, and Revelle was offered the directorship. He accepted, gave up the sea, and moved across the continent to Cambridge.

At Harvard Revelle started from a premise contrary to that popularly attributed to Thomas Robert Malthus, the celebrated early-nineteenth-century economist and theoretician of population. In his *Essay on the Principle of Population* Malthus argued that man, characterized by the capacity to reproduce geometrically, would one day outstrip the world's food supply, which could grow only arithmetically. Though Malthus later modified this deterministic view significantly, the neo-Malthusians of demography still have a tendency to deal with man as an impersonal object whose patterns of behavior are predictable. Revelle rejects the view that man is not the master of his destiny, that he is somehow the victim of immutable law. "The direct constraints on population growth are social ones, not, as Malthus thought, starvation and disease," Revelle has written. He insists that man, being reasonable, has the ability to control his own social conduct and that, if he tries, he can indeed bring population into balance with food resources.

Revelle points out that for all but a fraction of the million or so years that man has been on earth, population has been relatively stable. Not until the invention and spread of agriculture did the first major change come. In the eight thousand years before Christ population soared from five million to three hundred million. The second population explosion began about 1650 with the development of Western technology and has not yet run its course. According to estimates, the present world population of some 3.3 billion will double by the year 2000. But, Revelle continues, in these two periods of great population growth a decrease in the death rate rather than an increase in the birth rate has been chiefly responsible. Overall, history suggests that man behaves not as the neo-Malthusians say but, consciously or unconsciously, in a fashion designed to keep population at a relatively unchanging level.

Although it is unclear how societies decide to control their numbers, the evidence is persuasive that throughout history they have adopted any number of means to do so. Demographers trace a line between Leningrad and Trieste west of which there has been measurable population control since the beginning of the technological revolution. In some parts of this area evidence suggests the practice of *coitus interruptus*. In others large numbers of women marry late or not at all.

But western Europe has not been alone in its efforts to control population. Japan has traditionally sanctioned abortion, while some parts of India in the past have given approval to the neglect of female children. In many societies prolonged nursing is practiced, which tends to delay ovulation and thus lengthens the time between pregnancies. In some cultures infanticide has served as a cruel but effective form of population control. Revelle argues that no society has let its population run amuck over any long period, to the point where its very existence has been threatened.

Even today, Revelle maintains, societies everywhere take steps to limit births. Demographers calculate the maximum annual birth rate to be about seventy per thousand. Since the birth rate in India is no higher than forty or forty-five per thousand, it must be assumed that prospective parents take conscious or unconscious steps to limit the number of their offspring. If the birth rate does not drop further, Revelle argues, it is not necessarily because of ignorance or the unavailability of contraceptive devices. Parents have children because they want them, and birth-control techniques, no matter how sophisticated they may be, will not succeed unless people choose to use them.

Revelle is personally convinced that the chief factor behind the high birth rates of the less developed countries is the desire to have surviving sons. In one society sons may have a special religious importance, in another they may bring secular status. Some parents want sons to help till the fields, others to care for them in their old age. What is significant is that most families in backward countries expect at least one of their children to die before reaching adulthood. (Revelle even defines the less developed countries as "those in which, for every thousand live births, more than fifty children die before the age of one.") Therefore, to be certain of having one living son parents feel they must bear an average of four to five children. But with present rates of mortality, a society in which the average family has as few as four living children will double in population about every thirty-five years.

"Though the population problem of our time is the consequence of lowered death rates," he maintains in what is his central thesis, "we are faced with the paradox that, to cure it, we must lower death rates still further—concentrating, of course, on infant and child death rates. It is possible that if we get these death rates down to the level of the Western world, we will have reached the crux of the issue. I suspect that the pace of population growth will then begin to level off."

Revelle points to a Harvard study of birth rates in the Punjab that he regards as particularly instructive. There farmers reproduced at the rate of thirty-one per thousand, less than the average for the subcontinent; they were apparently unwilling to divide up their land holdings among too many heirs. In contrast, leather workers in isolated villages gave birth at the rate of fifty per thousand, presumably because more children could earn more rupees. The birth rate among army veterans was lower than among those who had never left the land. Finally, reproduction among the urban middle class, with its low rate of infant mortality and high living standards, stood at the Western level or below. Revelle believes that there is no natural predisposition on the Asian subcontinent toward reproduction on a massive scale. If anything, this study and others like it sustain the contention that birth rates are closely related to social goals.

What societies must do, Revelle says, is to shift cultural patterns to minimize the benefits of having large numbers of children and to reduce, where possible, the dependency on surviving sons. He suggests such changes as these:

¶ Institute compulsory education for eight or more years. This would mean that children, who require parental support during their school years, would become productive only at a much later age.

¶ Provide jobs for women. Their earnings would give them an incentive to work instead of incapacitating themselves by bearing or rearing children.

¶ Make consumer goods available. The opportunity to raise living standards would deter many parents from spending whatever money they have on larger families.

¶ Establish a strong social security system. By reducing the fear people have of being abandoned without support in old age, there would be less need to have children, particularly sons, as a form of insurance.

¶ Shift more of the population from agriculture to industry. In most instances industrial workers produce fewer children. This is probably because in an urban society, where skilled labor is in demand, there are fewer opportunities for children to work—as compared to rural areas, where unskilled labor is the rule. Too, wage earners must learn to plan for family support within the limits of known income.

"Birth-control instruction, by itself, changes social patterns, too," Revelle claims. "It teaches people that they can plan for themselves. It instills some confidence. It helps overcome fatalism among those who feel that because they are poor, they are destined always to be poor."

But if Revelle's notions about the desire for surviving sons are right, then the best way to reduce birth rates is to provide the means to make children healthy. "The principal killers of children," he says, "are the diseases that result from a combination of infection and malnutrition." He reasons that if food supplies were adequate, both in quantity and quality, birth rates would not—as the neo-Malthusians insist—rise to consume them but would instead drop to much lower levels, thanks to the assurance that children would survive.

"I think agriculture over the next twenty years is an essential key to the population explosion," Revelle says. "You must realize that because of the dramatic drop in the death rate since World War II, most of the population in the underdeveloped lands has not yet reached child-bearing age. Even if our birth-control teachings succeed tomorrow beyond our wildest dreams, the next generation will still be larger than the last. We have not yet reached the point where we can foresee a leveling off. We need the food to nourish the millions of bodies that are currently and soon to be with us. But we also need food, I am convinced, to lay the foundation for greater population control."

Revelle is not afraid to say that the underdeveloped world must be willing to westernize if it is to avoid chronic starvation. He points out that by embracing only one facet of Western civilization—modern medical and public-health technology—the underdeveloped peoples put themselves on the road to devastating overpopulation. "You can't accept Western ways piecemeal," Revelle cautions, "and expect only unmitigated good to come of it." He does not mean that underdeveloped societies must adopt Western dress or political systems or food or religious practices. He does mean that they must make the transition, within a framework suitable to themselves, to Western methods of production and distribution of goods. Whatever psychic satisfactions the old ways bring, they are scarcely defensible if they serve as obstacles to restoring the balance between food and people.

The process of change is exceedingly complex. It could break down at almost any stage through poor execution or want of motivation. In the Punjab, for example, where economic growth has been so encouraging, the whole system is threatened by a shortage of agricultural credit. "Of course, it's asking a great deal to achieve a transformation of this magnitude," as Revelle says. "But there have been success stories already, in Mexico and Pakistan. Unfortunately we still don't see signs of a declining birth rate in either of these places—but there has not yet been a decline in infant and child mortality either. In Korea and Taiwan the economy has grown, and a decline in infant and child death rates has followed. In these places the birth rate has dropped. I am reasonably confident that if Mexico and Pakistan can lower their death rates, we will see a drop in the birth rate as a consequence."

The difficulty of achieving this range of economic development cannot be underestimated. It will take at least two generations to reach a satisfactory level in most countries—after they have begun to try. Past efforts, he maintains, have been characterized by "short-term, quick payout programs, or by gimmicks of various kinds." Large-scale, long-range programs are what is most needed now. And such programs require the investment of money, a commodity more scarce than food in the underdeveloped world.

Revelle challenges the contention that the underdeveloped countries themselves have shown little will to begin performing the tasks, many of them unpleasant, necessary to bring food and population into balance. He is impressed by the success of Taiwan and Korea and by the efforts of Pakistan and India. But even in India, he concedes, traditional family relationships and the caste system remain virtually untouched as obstacles to progress. Still, a large number of countries help themselves far less. He cites Egypt as a particularly troublesome example, because so much of its capital resources are spent on arms. Throughout much of the globe national leaders entertain the people with demagogy and overburden the budget with irrelevancies, while population spirals upward. On the whole, the pattern of effort in the vast underdeveloped regions of the world gives small cause for optimism.

The underdeveloped world is not alone, of course, in contributing to the population explosion; the United States and other industrial countries are also growing in numbers. In the developed societies, however, the characteristics of population growth, as well as the problems, are much different. American parents, for example, are sophisticated about birth-control techniques and on the average tend to have precisely the number of children they want. Revelle—who himself has four children—feels that the sustained growth of American population comes about because Americans want it that way. He concedes that demographers have a hard time explaining the big baby-boom after World War II, which is responsible for most of the current population swell. But he blames continued growth on America's equation of bigness—in just about anything—with virtue. Our government, our businesses, our labor unions, all tell us that America's greatness depends on relentless expansion. Unless Americans begin to believe otherwise, he insists, the United States will become more and more crowded.

Fortunately, Revelle says, this country's growth rate has declined in recent years to a little more than one per cent a year, a half to one-third of the growth rate in much of the underdeveloped world. Compared to the doubling time of about thirty-one years for India, American population will double in about sixty-five years, according to current estimates. Western resources, both agricultural and industrial, are clearly sufficient to absorb a population increase of this magnitude for the foreseeable future. Revelle rejects the notion that there is an "ideal" population for the United States. He personally believes that the society would be healthier if the population curve declined to an annual increase of zero—which would require a birth rate of fifteen per thousand, equal to the death rate, instead of the current seventeen per thousand. But determining the size of the population of the United States involves a value judgment that the American people must make. Revelle is not persuaded that recent studies showing the harmful effects of crowding on laboratory animals are applicable to humans.* But he does foresee declining wealth and comfort, diminishing diversity in all aspects of life, and a less wholesome relationship of people to their environment. The problem in the United States is not survival; it is the quality of life.

In most of the Western world, population growth and technology have already combined to debase the quality of life. They have polluted the air and the water, covered beautiful countryside with unsightly ribbons of concrete, destroyed forests and seashores, transformed charming cities into unlivable slums. They may even threaten the long-term outlook for democracy. As Revelle has written: "One has to ask whether juvenile delinquency, student alienation in the universities, and unemployment among untrained youth, are not also partly related to our rapid population growth, and, if

---

* See "E. T. Hall and the Human Space Bubble" by William Kloman, HORIZON, Autumn, 1967.

so, how this should affect our national thought and action." But he rejects the contention that the country lacks the money to repair the damage. The funds exist, he says, to restore a high level of education, to rebuild the cities, to create new national parks, to end air and water pollution. What troubles him is that the country has not yet made the commitment to spend that money.

The search for recreation is a good example of the problems we will face and of what might be done about them. "Thirty-five years from now," Revelle predicts, "average incomes will have doubled. The average working week will have declined to around twenty-eight hours . . . From an average of one week per year vacations will lengthen to four weeks or more." But where will they all go? "By the end of the century some one hundred and fifty to two hundred million people may be struggling for places on the beaches and in the narrow coastal waters. With our present length of shoreline this would mean about two people per foot, even if the entire coastal strip were a public beach." The number of visits to national parks may rise to a billion visitor-days annually.

Revelle suggests that "the shoreline can be stretched by building spits and peninsulas, offshore [sand] bars and islands, and by dredging and improving estuaries." In the most crowded of the national parks, like Yosemite, wear-resistant paths can be built. "A desperate, but perhaps necessary step would be to ration visits among the applicants and to stagger visiting times. . . . Perhaps in the future most of the United States will find its highest use in recreational space. The land taken out of agriculture can be used in this way. The marshy islands of the Mississippi delta and the rocky barrens of the Nevada desert are obvious candidates."

Over the long run, however, the commitment that the United States must make to bring world population under control is even more significant. "This crisis can only be met internationally," Revelle states, "and experience shows that no international program works unless the United States takes the lead."

Revelle does not conceal his discouragement over America's current contributions to international economic development. The share of America's gross national product devoted to assisting the underdeveloped world has in recent years become negligible. With American assistance, public and private, fallen to less than one half of one per cent of our national income, the rest of the Western world has found ample excuse for following suit. To make matters worse, because of shifts in the global terms of trade, the underdeveloped world has recently been earning two billion dollars a year less than before. It also repays a billion a year for loans previously granted. Furthermore, experts have computed that the annual "brain drain" to the industrial countries costs the underdeveloped countries half a billion dollars a year. In all, Revelle says, the technologically advanced West is taking about as much out of the underdeveloped world as it is putting in.

Revelle readily admits to uncertainty about whether man, in both technological and underdeveloped societies, will rise to the challenge that overpopulation presents. At Harvard he is doing his best to help, culling ideas from historians, politicians, philosophers, architects, engineers, economists, physicians, biologists, nutritionists—anyone who might have some wisdom to share. The center he directs spends some six hundred thousand dollars a year. Much of it goes to teaching, to preparing a cadre of experts in population. Another substantial proportion is devoted to research in reproductive physiology. The center gives advice and assistance to India and Pakistan and is conducting experimental projects in Chile, Haiti, and Greece. Other energy is devoted to research on resources, genetics, reproductive psychology, and the ethics of population control.

Revelle concedes that he and the others who deal with the population problem have scarcely gone beyond the point of "feeling our way" for answers. But he does not accept ignorance as an excuse for inaction. For enough knowledge is now at man's disposal to confront many of the root causes of the problem.

Though there has been far too little confrontation as yet, Revelle is not ready to surrender to the popular feeling of doom. In the developed countries, at least, some progress has been made. Japan, Sweden, Hungary, and Italy have all essentially stabilized their populations; birth rates are declining in France and Russia.

Meanwhile, in the underdeveloped world little changes for the better, and much for the worse. At present growth rates, Egypt will double its population by 1988—just twenty years from now. But the country can feed itself at present levels, meager as they already are, for no more than another ten or twelve years. In India, where vasectomies are performed in the Calcutta railroad station and IUD coils are inserted by the thousands, 45 per cent of the population is under fifteen years of age. Calcutta could grow to sixty million within the next fifty years. Such runaway urban expansion is a world-wide problem, of course. By the middle of the next century the total area covered by cities could be one hundred times larger than today, and equal to perhaps one-fifth of the entire land surface of the planet.

Still, as Revelle indicates, there is nothing immutable about these astronomical rates of growth. Men and women can stop them—if they want to. "I'm hopeful," he says, with some resignation. "That's all I can say. I'm hopeful."

Milton Viorst wrote on the new town of Reston, Virginia, and its plans for accommodating our growing population, in the Autumn, 1967, HORIZON.

The Population Dilemma

Two horns of the painful dilemma of expanding population: right, the sprawl of Los Angeles is checked only by the rugged hills in the distance. (And how long, one wonders, will it be before they, too, succumb to the bulldozer, the split-level, and the mega-diaper service?) Above, President Lyndon Johnson tenderly busses his first grandchild, Patrick Nugent. Looking for space and a private piece of earth, men crowd in upon each other in dreary rows of monotonous streets, while urbanists predict such vast future conurbations as "Boswash" (Boston to Washington) and "Sansan" (San Francisco to San Diego). Looking, too, for a small share of futurity, men take pride in parenthood and see in the numbers of their grandchildren satisfying evidence that they have not spent their lives vainly. To control the growth of our population means, inevitably, curbing our wish for satisfactions that are, in themselves, essentially good.

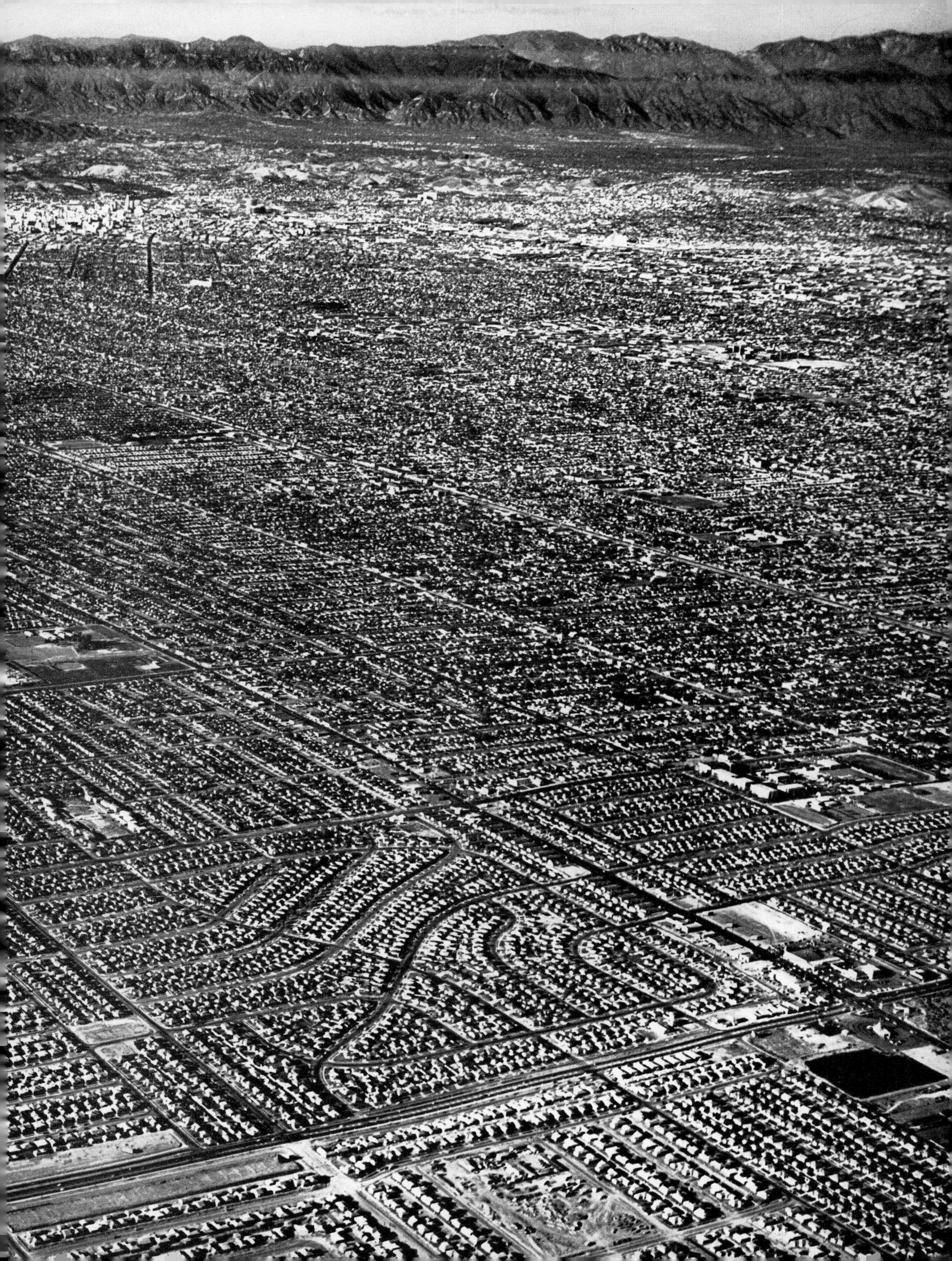

ON THE RAISING OF ARMIES

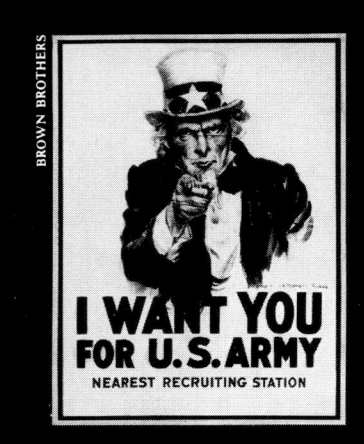

Militias are fine for defending the homeland, and conscript armies can be raised for wars of survival. But no world power has ever found it practical to depend on drafted soldiers for fighting distant border-wars

By CORRELLI BARNETT

Send for the boys of the Girl's Brigade
To set old England free,
Send for my Mother, my sister or brother,
But for God's sake don't send me . . .

This British soldiers' song of the Great War sums up in four crisp lines the problem of military manpower down the centuries. Not all men of military age wish to exchange the comforts of home and family for a roofless lodging in the field, a sodden bed, food to daunt the strongest digestion, the oppression of NCO's, the extinction of individuality on the parade ground, and ultimately the terror and the horror of a far-off battlefield, wounds, or death.

The essential point about volunteers in major wars is that there have rarely been enough of them. Only some great patriotic cause, some dearly held —if poorly understood—principle, draws a mass of volunteers from the whole social body of a nation: thus the citizen armies of France in the Revolution, the Union and Confederate armies of 1861, and the British "New Army" of 1914–16. Even the spur of great principles is of limited duration. Wars last longer than anyone expects; mud, dust, and disease dim the enthusiasm; the possibility of death or mutilation becomes increasingly apparent. The flood of volunteers dries up; the demand for men does not. Compulsion in some form follows: compulsion sanctioned or condoned by national opinion.

Small wars constitute an entirely different problem, and it is this problem that the United States now faces in recruiting for Vietnam. The war in Vietnam, like the earlier French war in Indochina or the British war with the Boers of South Africa in 1899–1902, is not a life-and-death struggle against a great power. It divides rather than unites home opinion. It is essentially a war on an imperial frontier, although "empire" has ceased nowadays to be manifested by direct annexation and rule by governors general, and the word itself is much out of fashion.

This description of the Vietnam war does not imply an ethical judgment; it is simply a military definition. It is the small wars in Korea and Vietnam and the continuing commitment they represent, rather than the great but brief crises of the world wars, that really mark America's emergence from isolation; the abandonment of the Founding Fathers' hope of an inward-looking nation of citizen farmers. Since 1945 America has faced for the first time the far-off permanent involvements of a great power, and the current agonizing over Vietnam and the draft are symptoms of a profound and painful adjustment.

However, the current American dilemma is by no means novel: draft boards, draftees, protesters, and evaders only tread where Greeks, Romans, Spaniards, English, Prussians, French, and many others have trodden before. For throughout history the acquiring of imperial frontiers beyond the homeland and the adoption of an imperial role have presented different societies with essentially similar problems of military organization and recruitment —problems usually solved only by profound military and social change. Parallel problems and changes have been caused in the modern era by the pursuit of power ambitions on the part of nation-states.

The experience of the great powers of the past and the evolution of earlier societies therefore serve to place current American problems concerning the draft in perspective; they also offer some clues to a solution. All military institutions are the product of particular strategic needs, particular patterns of political and social acceptability, and the particular state of military techniques at a given time. When any of these factors alters in character, changes occur in the pattern of military organization. History suggests certain generalizations about types of military organization and recruitment.

States that need to think only in terms of emergency home-defense depend on citizen militias—compulsory and universal military service, but only for brief periods. Foreign expansion and the acquiring of an imperial role lead instead to a smaller force of long-service professionals. Shortage of volunteers for such a force leads in turn to some kind of selective compulsory service to flesh out the ranks.

The modern age of mass political participation—from the French Revolution onward—brought a new version of the militia: the nation in arms, universal military service, but within the frame of a regular and professional army. However, universal military service was intended for—was only politically acceptable for—the contingency of a major war against another great power. No country has applied it to the maintenance of peacetime foreign policy or imperial rule—except the British in the aftermath of the Second World War, and then only as a continuation of the wartime call-up.

The oldest and commonest form of recruitment in settled communities is a militia. A militia rests on the obligation of the entire male population of weapon-bearing age to take the field in defense of the community and its territory. As long as it fits functional and strategic needs, a militia is the ideal moral and political solution to the problem of military manpower. It avoids the creation of a powerful military class, with the consequent threat to constitutional government and civilian predominance. It expresses the civic obligation of each man to defend his own society. It is cheap, since there is no unproductive military class. Upon a threat, the peasant leaves his holding, the smith his shop, the burgher his countinghouse, each with spear or bow and helmet. They join the host, prod or clump the invader for a brief time, and return to their homes again.

Militia service was indeed the original form of universal conscription; but not conscription *into an army*.

Traditionally militia service has been seen as a right and a privilege rather than as an infringement of individual liberty. In the Greek city-states it was the mark not only of a free citizen but of a citizen of some solid worth. In the Roman republic the right to serve was determined by a property qualification. In Anglo-Saxon England only freemen could serve in the fyrd. In the United States, where the concept of militia service was derived—via English common law—from the fyrd, the Second Amendment to the Constitution reaffirmed this sense of privilege and right and stated in addition that standing regular forces were a threat to constitutional liberties:

"A well regulated Militia, being necessary to the security of a free State, the right of the people to keep and bear Arms shall not be infringed."

In England the compulsory element in militia service, both in terms of service in war and training in peace, lapsed only in the long Victorian tranquillity after Waterloo; even then it was a lapse in practice, not in law. The "militiamen" called up for military training in the doom-laden summer of 1939 were not, as so many British people thought at the time, the first British peacetime "conscripts" in the Continental European sense, but were a revival of the ancient English common-law obligation to bear arms and train in their use.

The modern Swiss military system is based entirely on the ancient militia principle of a nation-in-arms and a universal obligation to serve. In Switzerland, indeed, there is no regular professional army other than a general staff and command organization and certain essential cadres; here in the modern world the ancient concept of military force as simply civil society with a weapon in its hand survives in its pristine form. All Swiss citizens must serve from the ages of twenty to forty-eight. They keep their uniforms, weapons, and equipment at home; they are ready for mobilization at any time; they must leave addresses or telephone numbers behind them when they make business trips or go on vacation. The paradox is complete: the life of this highly civilian and peaceful state is permeated by military duty.

Perhaps the most notable modern example of a successful militia system is furnished by Israel. Here, too, military service and citizenship are bound together; here, too, there is no sense of any gulf between civilian society and the armed forces, no sense that compulsory service is an invasion of liberty but rather that it is a privilege. Unlike the Swiss system, the Israeli armed forces have been tested twice by war, and twice have won epic victories. These victories prove the intelligence and efficiency with which Israelis are trained in their initial military service—two and a half years for men and two years for women—and are kept to a high standard thereafter by refresher training. It is also a tribute to the miraculous speed of Israeli mobilization, which can take men and women from farms, offices, and factories and turn them within the space of twelve hours into a deployed army, a fleet at sea, and an air force ready to fly.

Nevertheless, the Israeli experience illustrates a fundamental weakness of all militias. The Israeli armed forces cannot fight a long war, because if the mobilized manpower is retained in uniform longer than a few weeks, the entire economy is paralyzed. Militias have never been able to keep the field. Thus Marc Bloch, a historian of feudalism, writes of the Anglo-Saxon fyrd at the time of the Danish invasions of Britain in the eighth through tenth centuries:

"Compare, in the narratives of the English Chronicles, the spirited tactics of the *here*—the Danish Army—with the clumsiness of the Anglo-Saxon fyrd, the heavy militia which could not be employed in even the shortest operation save by permitting each man, under a system of reliefs, to return periodically to his farm."

The English militia of the sixteenth century was subject to similar disabilities; it could be got together long enough to put down a revolt or beat the Scots but soon tended to go home in answer to the urgent calls of agriculture or trade. The American militia of the eighteenth century faced the same problem. Since the bulk of the North American population were farmers, they too disliked being long from their fields and animals; they, like their Anglo-Saxon ancestors, wanted to take down their weapons from the hearth, do some nearby enemy in, and push off home to tell the story. So it was in 1776. Washington observed of his militiamen: "There is no time to drill the men before they are gone, and discipline is impossible because if it was enforced they would go."

Despite the lesson offered by the painful evolution of a field army that could stand for the duration of the War of Independence instead of militias able to fight but one skirmish before dispersing, the opening of the Civil War in 1861 illustrated afresh this limitation of the militia. Lincoln at first called on the states to furnish militia units for *three months*. And once again a field army capable of fighting for years had to be created.

There is another and crucial limitation to militias: they are essentially home-defense forces. The moral basis of universal obligation to military service in a militia lies in the individual's duty to join in the communal defense of his own home and family and those of his neighbors. And it is for this limited purpose that well-organized militias are militarily effective. Foreign wars, long overseas campaigns, the general pursuit of power ambition, lie outside both the military capability and the moral principle of militias. An invasion, limited in both space and time, of a neighbor's territory in order to forestall attack is as far as a militia can go toward foreign wars: the Israeli strokes against the Arabs in 1956 and

1967 are illustrations of such operations.

Throughout history it has been difficult to budge militias from their own localities. The commanders of Elizabeth I's forces, gathering against the threatened Spanish invasion in 1588, had to face the heartfelt groans of county authorities who argued that their men were needed more at home than with the field army at Tilbury. In the English Civil War commanders found it not always easy to get units raised in one locality to march off on a long campaign elsewhere. Washington, too, had to struggle with this immobility of militias.

Of all the militias of modern times that have actually seen action, only the Israeli forces have possessed the skill to achieve outstanding success in battle. The Israelis are a particularly intelligent and highly educated nation, and they have the constant spur of desperate national danger. Lacking these attributes and this incentive, militias of the past—especially those of the common Anglo-American heritage —have not generally been inspiring performers. Elizabethan England made a gigantic administrative effort to organize, arm, and train the militia during the war with Spain. Yet in 1588, the year in which the Spanish attempted to invade England, Sir John Norris, an experienced professional soldier who was sent around the country on a tour to inspect the militia wondered that he could see no man in the kingdom afraid but himself.

Half a century later the London Trainbands were effective, and stopped Charles I on the outskirts of London in the first campaign of the English Civil War; but otherwise neither side relied much on the militia, preferring to raise new armies. And a century and a half later still, George Washington expressed views on the combat efficiency of the American militia that echoed those of commanders of the English militia in the past.

"To lean on the militia," wrote Washington, "is to lean on a broken reed. Being familiar with the use of the musket they fight under cover, but they will not attack or stand in the open field." Washington's sagacious opinion was borne out again in 1861 at the beginning of the Civil War, in the sanguinary comedy of the First Battle of Bull Run.

Indeed, it was always hard enough in Britain and the United States to induce the militia to take seriously its small peacetime obligations of training. The following picture, given by an English officer, of militia training in the early seventeenth century would fit in general terms National Guard training in the United States in the late nineteenth (and, some would say, the mid-twentieth):

As trainings are now used, we shall, I am sure, never be able to make one good soldier, for our custom and use is, nowadays, to cause our companies to meet on a certain day, and by that time the arms be all viewed, and the muster master hath had his pay (which is the chiefest thing many times he looks after) it draws towards dinner time: and, indeed, officers love their bellies so well as that they are loath to take too much pains about disciplining of their soldiers. Wherefore, after a little careless hurrying over of their postures... they make them charge their muskets, and so prepare to give their captain a brave volley of shot at his entrance into his inn: where after having solaced themselves for a while after this brave service every man repairs home, and that which is not so well taught them is easily forgotten before the next training.

But the decisive limitation of all militias in history lies in their inability to keep the field for long periods or serve far from home. Over and over again in history a long war, even near home, or continual foreign wars and territorial acquisition have seen the replacement of militias by professional long-service forces.

In the era of Greek expansion into Asia and Africa that followed Alexander the Great's attack on Persia in 334 B.C., the citizen armies that had served the earlier city-states were replaced by cosmopolitan professional soldiers drawn from most parts of the known world. Greek expeditionary forces were recruited by methods that were to be time-hallowed: mercenary bands hired complete under their own captains, individual mercenary volunteers, military agricultural colonies.

The Romans, too, found that as soon as war got beyond drubbing the Samnites the militia would not do. A permanent army, not just a levy of citizen farmers for each campaign, was needed. At the same time the increase in the number of Roman citizens meant that not all able-bodied citizens had to be called up. Only a few had to bear the burden of long service. The Romans therefore hit on the system of military selection later adopted by the British in the eighteenth century, by the French between 1815 and 1870, and by the Americans in the Civil and the two world wars: a ballot, choice by lot.

Nevertheless, in the later Roman republic the citizen element in the army diminished. The selected citizens disliked leaving their farms for long periods of army service or garrison abroad. It was Gaius Marius who finally changed the basis of the Roman military system by opening the army to volunteers without property qualifications; the army became a standing force of mercenary career-soldiers, drawn not so much by the pay (about that of a laborer) as by hopes of plunder. The levy henceforward was used much as the United States today uses the draft—to fill out the regular forces in case of an emergency. Augustus finally abolished compulsion (though not in law), and Rome came to depend no longer on her citizens for defense but on standing professional forces. Empire and a professional army came together. The legions could march to the Scottish Highlands or to the Euphrates or sit it out on the Rhine, without crops and olive presses going untended back in Italy.

43

Similarly it was the foreign wars and colonial conquest marking England's rise from a second-class island kingdom to a world power that forced the expansion of the British regular army. Even the most passionate defender of the militia as the ideal military defense of the home island could not argue that the militia could have fought at Blenheim and Minden or won Canada and India. Indeed, under English law the militia could not be required to serve outside the kingdom. Attempts to get it to do so by sending individual militiamen rather than units abroad excited spirited resentment.

The British, like the Romans, discovered that conquests required garrisons; that restive tribes beyond the imperial frontiers, often stirred up by other great powers, required punitive expeditions by ever-ready field forces. Although the militia did in fact garrison Mediterranean bases and serve in South Africa during the Boer War, the British global commitment to garrison duties and minor wars could only be met by a professional long-service volunteer army, a large part of which was permanently stationed overseas.

The British Empire forced the British army on an army-hating nation. Compulsory service in this professional army was utterly unacceptable to the British people. Indeed, it may be wondered whether the British would have acquired their empire at all if the British citizenry in general had been obliged to go and fight its small wars. The British mercenary army spared the British nation the pains of imperial power, as the Roman army had spared the citizens of Rome.

In Continental Europe it was the rise of the great national monarchies during the fifteenth and sixteenth centuries and the continuing clash of their power ambitions that led to the evolution of the modern kind of institutionalized long-service professional army. The sixteenth and seventeenth centuries were eras of almost perpetual war. In such circumstances the late medieval royal army, which consisted of an *ad hoc* combination of royal household troops, noble retainers (sometimes raised and hired for the king's service under "indentures"), and mercenary bands, gradually evolved into permanent state armies. Since compulsory service could only be legally required of the home defense militias, the new royal armies had to rely on other methods of recruitment.

Ideas of national loyalty were not so narrow or tightly defined as they are today; nothing was thought of hiring out your sword in a quarrel, first to one side and then to the other—or even of fighting against your own country in the cause of your religion. The great military monarchies could therefore draw on all men of military inclination who could find no employment at home. English and Scottish regiments fought in the service of The Netherlands throughout the seventeenth century; other Scots valiantly served the Danes and King Gustavus Adolphus of Sweden. The French army before 1789 included at one time or another Scottish, Swiss, English, Irish, German, and Italian regiments. The small states into which seventeenth- and eighteenth-century Germany was divided built up a thriving export trade in troops; as with all German exports, the product was good and the organization efficient. An essential element in the rise of the British Empire was the fiercely whiskered Hessian mercenary (among others). The contract of hire specified numbers, cost, and duration.

Despite the foreign mercenaries, the monarchies of the seventeenth and eighteenth centuries still had to raise most of their troops at home. It was not always easy to do so. Until well into the eighteenth century, recruitment, like all else that related to the economy of the individual regiment, was in the hands of the regimental colonel. Regiments were private enterprises belonging to their officers rather than integral parts of a royal organization. It was the colonels' responsibility to keep their units up to strength by sending round recruiting parties. A military career held few attractions for the ordinary citizen, since the pay was low, the living conditions appalling, the discipline horrendous, and the chance of dying of disease, exposure, or wounds well known. It was also evident that too many colonels made a fine private income by diverting into their own large pockets money intended by the state to buy equipment and clothing or provide pay for the soldier.

Military life thus being held by respectable citizens to be little if any better or more creditable than prison, the recruiting parties could not afford to be as finicky about standards of physical fitness or intelligence as a modern American draft board. In the British army of the late seventeenth century there were one-eyed or squint-eyed men, semi-cripples, the old, and the shattered. The French army of the same period also had to lower its standards to get the men; in 1685 Louvois, the minister of war, wrote to his inspectors: "The King does not wish at all that the soldiers be measured, and it is not at all necessary to chase away an old soldier because he is too small, nor a young man of good spirit."

Even though they accepted any man with arms and legs enough to march and level a musket, however depraved or criminal or idiotic he might be, the armies remained hard up for recruits. So private methods of "conscription" were often employed. In the eighteenth century Prussian recruiting officers kidnapped all over Europe. In seventeenth-century England there was a famous house in London where shanghaied recruits were incarcerated; it took an act of Parliament to end the worst of the abuse.

In addition to such private-enterprise methods of forcible recruitment there was, even in constitutional England, government-condoned "impressment," a technically illegal form of selective conscription adopted at times of national emergency when the army had suddenly to be expanded. Shakespeare has given a living portrait of the sixteenth-century press at work in *Henry IV, Part 2*, where Falstaff and Justice Shallow pick likely draftees from the militia rolls by pricking their names with a pin.

FALSTAFF. Is thy name Mouldy?
MOULDY. Yea, an't please you.
FALSTAFF. 'Tis the more time thou wert used.
SHALLOW. Ha, ha, ha! most excellent, i' faith! things that are mouldy lack use: very singular good. In faith, well said, Sir John; very well said.
FALSTAFF. Prick him.
MOULDY. I was prick'd well enough before, an you could have let me alone: my old dame will be undone now, for one to do her husbandry and her drudgery: you need not have pricked me; there are other men fitter to go out than I.
FALSTAFF. Go to: peace, Mouldy! you shall go. Mouldy, it is time you were spent.

What would now be called the "guidelines" on which these precursors of modern draft boards operated were definitively stated by an English professional soldier, Barnabe Rich, in the reign of Elizabeth I:

... the petty Constable when he perceiveth that wars are at hand, foreseeing the toils, the infinite perils and troublesome travails that is incident to soldiers, is loth that any honest man ... should hazard himself amongst so many dangers, wherefore if within his office, there hap to remain any idle fellow, some drunkard, or seditious quarreler, a privy picker or such a one as hath some skill in stealing of a goose, these shall be presented to the service of the prince.

The defenseless and the shiftless long nourished the British and other armies: more battles were won in the cells of Newgate jail than ever were gained on the playing fields of Eton. The methods so accurately reported by Barnabe Rich achieved fresh success in the hands of American local authorities during the War of Independence and the Civil War. Contemporary accounts describe Union army recruits in terms that would have been true of most armies hard up for men over the previous three centuries: "... branded felons ... blotched and bloated libertines and pimps ... thieves, burglars, and vagabonds ... cripples from birth; men partially blind; idiots ... puny boys ... escaped prisoners ..."

British and American antimilitarism and belief in a militia preserved all the varied devices, illegal and semilegal, for gingering up "voluntary" recruitment long after European nations had adopted straightforward conscription. In their geographical isolation from other nations the British and Americans had no need for great armies to insure survival; nor did British and American expansion call for massive wars of conquest against neighboring powers.

It was Prussia that first managed to transform the principle of a universal obligation to serve in a militia into a basis for systematic conscription for a regular army. In 1713 Frederick William I abolished the militia but declared that any man who left the kingdom in order to escape military service would be a deserter; in other words the obligation to serve had been neatly transferred from the defunct militia to the king's army. No British king or government or American president would have got away with that. For twenty years Frederick William developed his new system, capping it with the decrees of 1732–33, which laid down its legal and organizational framework. Each regiment in the army was assigned a canton from which to draw conscripts. Every canton kept a general roll of all males, and the captain of companies and the local headman picked the men jointly from the roll. This was Falstaff and Shallow erected into a universal and legal system.

The Prussians, too, invented the concept of exemptions for men more useful to the state in their own trades and professions than as soldiers; the Prussians also selected conscripts according to Barnabe Rich's scenario. The Prussian system of selective service in the eighteenth century thus manifests classic features repeated in other such systems down to the current American draft. Men useful to the economy—the bourgeoisie, the skilled tradesmen and craftsmen—were exempt. The Prussian system tended to spare the middle classes from service—for the best of national-economic reasons, of course—but probably the best of all reasons was that the middle classes were better placed to raise hell than the poorer peasants who in fact got drafted.

The British militia of the eighteenth century and the French selective compulsory service of the early nineteenth also fell lightly on the bourgeoisie as a vociferous political element worth sparing irritation; selected young men of respectable provenance were allowed to furnish human substitutes from the poor and needy. American draft legislation during the Civil War followed the same pattern. Perhaps the griping in the United States today would be less articulate if the neat suburban homes and the university campuses were still entirely exempt from the threat of the draft. However, it would hardly be possible to return to the open class-discrimination of the Civil War draft, although there are those who darkly allege that draft boards practice covert class-discrimination along the classic principles enunciated by Barnabe Rich in 1587. Whether the allegations are justified or not, an unacknowledged bias toward the Negro and the white dropout (balanced against an open system of student exemptions) is probably as far as a modern American administration could go under a selective service system in sparing the articulate middle classes what Barnabe Rich referred to as "the toils, the infinite perils and troublesome travails" of war.

Universal, as opposed to selective, military service—the nation in arms—was the creation of the French Revolution. It was an aspect of the new principles of equality and democracy. It was born in a time of desperate national danger in the course of the first modern war to be fought on the basis of passionate ideology, and the midwife was a regime of ruthless revolutionaries. The Prussian system had merely expressed a universal *obligation* to serve, while actual conscription had been selective. Under the new French system, *every* French citizen, upon reaching military age, served as a soldier for a stipulated period.

The new system took shape over a period of six years. In 1792 generals were authorized to requisition recruits for a single campaign; these recruits were dubbed, with exquisite felicity, *volontaires forcés*. The next year the Committee of Public Safety decreed a levy of 300,000 men—a colossal figure by the standards of the *ancien régime*. In 1798 these expedients were crowned by a straightforward conscription law aimed at producing 80,000 recruits a year: all Frenchmen were made liable for four years' military service upon reaching the age of twenty. Not even the absolute monarchies had been able to tap their national manpower so completely and simply.

Universal conscription altered the whole basis of war: troops were no longer scarce commodities to be husbanded with care and committed to battle as rarely as possible; they were a human wealth to be poured out to purchase quick and decisive victories. Field armies grew astoundingly in size. It only needed railway networks and the telegraph to make it possible to move and control these huge armies with a speed and precision hitherto unthinkable.

It was Prussia, in the 1860's, under Bismarck, that gave the definitive form to modern universal conscription as a phenomenon of peace as well as war. Year in, year out, complete age groups of young Prussians passed into the regular army to be trained and militarized and later returned to civilian life as part of a massive reserve of trained manpower. This accumulated reserve was recalled to the colors upon imminent danger of war. The telegraph, the railway, and modern staff-work permitted more than a million men to be recalled, kitted out, and concentrated for war in some three weeks. Mobilization became the key to military planning, its speed the looked-for answer to swift victory. The enormous body of trained reserves furnished by universal military service were the essential ingredient of the Prussian successes over Austria in 1866 and France in 1870.

After 1870 all the great European powers and, in the Far East, Japan, depended on universal military service. Nevertheless, the underlying moral and political principle was clear; it was, indeed, the same as that underlying the militia system—the obligation of all fit men to defend the national territory in a great war. A partly Continental and partly imperial power like France did not employ conscripts for purposes of colonial garrisoning or colonial wars. For the imperial role France continued to rely on long-service professionals or foreign mercenaries —the Foreign Legion.

By 1914 only Great Britain and America among the great powers, apparently secure behind their moats of the Channel and the Atlantic, relied solely on miniature professional armies with almost no trained reserves. Both countries acknowledged the ancient common-law obligation of all fit men to serve in the militia (in America now called, after the French term, the "National Guard"); both regarded compulsory service in the *army* as an intolerable invasion of a citizen's rights and the straight road to the militarization of society à la Prussia. In France, too, universal military service in the army, under professional officers, was attacked as undemocratic. The great French socialist Jean Jaurès advocated the abolition of the regular army and its reactionary officer corps, and their replacement by a militia on the Swiss model—but to no avail. France, like Germany, went to war in 1914 with a professional regular army that was swelled to millions by universal military service.

When the Western Front hardened into stalemate after the Battle of the Marne, it became clear that the British would also have to turn their small professional expeditionary force into a mass army. Yet even now national hatred of conscription was so deep that the Liberal government made no attempt to introduce universal military service. Instead Lord Kitchener, the Secretary of State for War, called for "the First Hundred Thousand" volunteers for his "New Army." By the middle of September, 1914, 500,000 Britons had volunteered; by February 23, 1915, a million; by September 3, 1915, a million and a half. By April, 1916, the British army, navy, and flying corps comprised nearly four million men—all wartime or prewar volunteers and far and away the largest volunteer forces ever raised in history. But despite this astonishing response, not enough fresh volunteers were coming forward by the end of 1915. On October 8 Lord Kitchener warned the Cabinet: "The voluntary system, as at present administered, fails to produce the number of recruits required to maintain the armies in the field."

With utmost reluctance and often against bitter opposition, the British government moved step by step toward conscription. In January, 1916, the Military Service Act deemed all single men as enlisted for the duration of the war. In April it was decided to extend conscription to married men: universal military service at last. Lloyd George, then Minister of Munitions, told the die-hard Liberal opponents of conscription: "Is this Bill inconsistent with the principles of either Liberalism or democracy? Is it inconsistent with the principles of democracy that the state should demand the services and help of every man to defend its life when it is at stake?"

The bill was passed at the end of May. Yet the results of conscription in Britain in 1916–18 were almost as disappointing as the results of the draft in the United States in 1863–65. That portion of the manpower reservoir not already emptied by the enormous volunteer movement of the past three years was found to be needed as much in war industry as in the field. Once again in history there was a system of exemption for essential skilled men, and once again there was scope for abuse. Yet exemption was necessary and inevitable: the French had found in 1914–15 that the call-up of all men, without exemption, had crippled the expansion of their war industries.

When the United States entered the war in 1917, it profited from the painful experiences of recruiting and drafting during the Civil War. The Selective Service Act restated the ancient common-law obligation to serve, which thus became—and remains—the basis of American conscription. The new draft system avoided all the old errors of the Civil War: there were no substitutes, no bounties, and the administration of the draft was placed on a civilian and local basis. Thanks to the draft, America was able to avoid the indigestible rush of volunteers that had thrown British military expansion into confusion in 1914–15.

Nevertheless the American system, being selective, was—and is—different from the *universal* military service operated by the European powers and by Britain in the two world wars. Neither in war nor in peace could any European or Briton ask, "Why me?" because *every* man of his age was going. Hence there has been very little resentment of conscription in Britain or Europe. Surely the element of luck, discrimination, or worse, favoritism, in the American draft must account in part for the protests. Again in Britain, from 1945 until the end of universal military (or national) service in 1960, there were far fewer exemptions or deferments than is the current case in the United States. Young men joined the forces straight from school, completed their military service, and then went on to college. This sequence had an additional, personal advantage: men went to the universities older and maturer people, and when they graduated they were free to embark without interruption on their own chosen career.

The British experience in the years after the Second World War probably constitutes the nearest parallel to the present American situation. A combination of the Cold War and colonial unrest kept the British army at full stretch all over the world. During that time there were, in particular, the terrorist troubles in Palestine, Kenya, and Cyprus, the long struggle to smash the communists in Malaya, and participation in the Korean War. National servicemen saw active service in each of these military involvements, and no public disquiet or resistance to call-up was evinced.

However, none of these emergencies much stirred or divided British public opinion; on the other hand, had the Suez operation of 1956 developed into a long campaign involving drafts of national servicemen, there would have been the bitterest opposition in Britain. In France, for example, the employment of national servicemen in the unpleasant conflict in Algeria aroused very similar reactions to those now on view in the United States—violent political protest, demonstrations by young men earmarked for the fray. Yet it is to be noted that French national servicemen were only employed in Algeria on the grounds that constitutionally Algeria was an integral part of metropolitan France. In Indochina, truly "overseas," the French used only professional troops.

How, then, do the experiences of other nations, the lessons of the past, illuminate the current American dilemma over Vietnam? The essential difficulty is that the United States is trying to apply a system of manpower procurement formulated to meet one situation—a great national war—to quite another situation: an episode in power diplomacy or imperial rule. It would be foolish to count on Vietnam's being the last of such episodes. But however much the *Pax Americana* may serve the general cause of liberty, its maintenance is not the same kind of issue as a great national war.

And only great national danger and a generally united national opinion have ever justified and sanctified large-scale conscription. Compulsory military service to make possible a general foreign or imperial policy has never, anywhere, been otherwise than extremely unpopular. Therefore the great powers of the past either relied on volunteer professional forces or took pains to see that the burden of conscription fell on those least able to resist it effectively, least politically important. If the American administration wishes to avoid a new tide of isolationism partly impelled by the draft, it might consider the expansion of the regular army to a size where it would be capable by itself of fighting a war like Vietnam. Then the American middle classes would be troubled not as mothers and fathers yielding up sons, but merely as taxpayers yielding up dollars that would make a military career rewarding enough to attract volunteers.

A professional long-service army, much of it permanently away from the homeland, often partially composed of foreign mercenaries, was, after all, the Greek, Roman, British, and French answer to the problems of global commitment—why not the American?

Correlli Barnett is an English military historian and a member of the Institute for Strategic Studies. A veteran of the British army, he has written The Desert Generals *and* The Swordbearers.

A Modern Bestiary

Drawings by DOMENICO GNOLI

Man's imagination, it seems, has always been haunted by monsters. They appear in his earliest legends and his primeval art. In the Middle Ages they were gathered together in bestiaries that soberly mingled lions and foxes with unicorns, gryphons, dragons, and all manner of flying, swimming, fire-breathing creatures. The age of reason thought them dead, but they are with us still.

One herd of these monsters dwells in the imagination of Domenico Gnoli, a talented artist whose portfolio of fanciful Italian cities we published in July, 1959. At HORIZON's invitation Signor Gnoli has drawn the modern bestiary that appears on these pages. His creatures are not the fierce dragons of the ancient forests but beasts of our own times, fond of luxury and adapted—though not always happily—to living in his villa on the sunny island of Majorca. But let the artist describe them:

"First, naturally, I imagined these animals in the open. Then, little by little they followed me all the way to the sitting room, to the bathroom, to the bedroom. Visions? Hallucinations? Not at all. I would hate them if they were—if they owned me and barged into my life at their whim. No. These are polite monsters. They come only when called.

"There is a large zoo full of them, built since the beginning of time. They prospered in mythology; lost a lot of weight, but none of their presence, in the Gothic period; grew fat again in the Baroque. The eighteenth century tried hard to domesticate them; the surrealists returned them to the dark recesses of the subconscious. Why do I want to bring them out again? Maybe because they still roam around us, impressive and horrid as always."

We found Signor Gnoli's explanation charming but not exhaustive. To illuminate the subject further we therefore asked the artist's friend and neighbor on Majorca, Robert Graves, to explain monsters in general and Gnoli's creatures in particular. In addition to being one of the world's finest poets, Mr. Graves is a learned mythologist who has his own personal (and often controversial) interpretations of ancient legends. His article begins on page 50; the captions for Gnoli's pictures are also his. Whether they accord with the artist's own interpretations we are not in a position to say, but in this dark sphere a poet's guess at the meaning may be as good as the artist's—or your own.

OPPOSITE: **Gnoli's impatient cock with the rhinoceros horns and crow's tail is about to visit the occupant of Number 13 in a hotel. Rhinoceros horns proclaim its irresistibility; the cock body implies that it has come to rouse some sluggard from sleep; the crow tail portends death. We are sorry for the occupant of Number 13, though indeed Number 13 is a rarity in hotels—I have never come across one in America, myself.** —R.G.

1·2·3·4·5·6·7·8·9·10·11·12·13·14·15·16·17·18·19·20·21
OTIS
UP
DAWN
OTIS
D·G·67

What is a Monster?

By ROBERT GRAVES

What is a monster? In modern English the word can be used in two very different senses. As a rule, it means something of remarkable size, such as a monster pumpkin or a monster wedding cake or else a creature of remarkable savagery: as most husbands, if not worms, tend to be monsters; and most children, if not little angels, tend to be little monsters. Millions of years ago, of course, huge natural monsters roved the earth, among them the harmless vegetarian diplodocus, whose skeleton dominates an immense hall in the Natural History Museum in London; also the flying pterodactyl, the ichthyosaurus, the brontosaurus, the fearsome saber-toothed tiger and mammoth—some of these coeval with man.

Whether or not we inherit dream-memories of these beasts is arguable, but they can at any rate be distinguished from the equally zoological but grossly enhanced monsters of legend. Legendary cats, for example, such as the Irish Irusan, who lived on the banks of the river Boyne: he could carry off a plow-ox in his claws and is said to have once run off with Seanchan Torpest, the master poet who claimed the faculty, mentioned by Shakespeare in *As You Like It*, of rhyming rats to death.

Yet a monster cat remains more or less a cat; so also a hundred-foot giant is no more than a man blown up by unrestrained fancy. Such enhanced, though otherwise normal, zoological monsters seem to have been born from psychotic visions or under the influence of drugs, mostly fungal hallucinogens. The predicament of Alice, who, in Wonderland, nibbled a piece of mushroom and found herself shooting up to monstrous height and then diminishing to so small a size that a mouse became a monster for her, has recently been explained. Lewis Carroll had been reading M. C. Cooke's *A Plain and Easy Account of British Fungi*, which relates that when the Koryak of Siberia eat fly agaric (a red toadstool with white spots that grows under birch trees and is associated with dwarfs and Santa Claus), "erroneous impressions of size and distance are of common occurrence, a straw lying in the road becomes a formidable object, to overcome which a leap is taken sufficient to clear a barrel of ale or the prostrate trunk of a British oak."

Some years ago I ate the Mexican mushroom *psilocybe* and at one point in the resultant trance felt myself fourteen feet high. These strong, strong natural hallucinogens, which account for many divine visions, include the fungus found on manna, the taste of which seems to have confused Moses' Israelites into enlarging its quantity by a hundred thousand times. But gods are made in man's image, rather than contrariwise. Ancient storytellers have invented still more grossly exaggerated monsters to pretend that they were speaking oracularly; each outdid the other in hyperbole. The prize, I think, can be awarded certain early medieval Jewish embroiderers on the Book of Genesis. Not only was Leviathan, an enhanced crocodile, said by them to grip his tail between his teeth and form a ring around the entire ocean, but, to quote *Hebrew Myths*, ". . . once Rabh Saphra, as he sailed in a ship, saw a two-horned beast lifting its head from the waters. Engraved upon the horns he read: 'This tiny sea-creature, measuring hardly three hundred leagues, is on its way to serve as Leviathan's food.'" Their Behemoth, likewise, was an enhanced hippopotamus with bones like brass conduit pipes and a tail bigger than the trunk of a cedar; it could crop the Thousand Mountains bare in a single day, and all the water that flowed down the Jordan in a whole year barely served for Behemoth's single gulp. The Ziz, an enhanced crane, was king of the birds. Rabba bar Bar-Hana "on a voyage once saw the Ziz standing in mid-ocean, yet the waters wetted only its ankles. 'We judged that the sea must be shallow and thought to disembark and cool ourselves. But a heavenly voice warned us: "Seven years ago, a ship's carpenter dropped his axe at this spot and it has not yet touched bottom!"'"

Enhanced legendary monsters are often confused with fabulous or mythological monsters, which are pictorial devices explaining man's relations with nature. The school of Plato either misunderstood, or pretended to misunderstand, the language of myth; and their view was adopted by the practical Romans. The poet Horace, for example, satirized such "unnatural" forms as centaurs and satyrs, though these simply represented totemic Pelasgian Greek tribes who disguised themselves in their ritual dances as horses and goats. Similarly, after the Semitic conquest of Crete, the bull-headed Cretan Minotaur, which Theseus the Greek killed in the middle of a sacred labyrinth, stood for the king of Knossos while he was impersonating the Semitic bull-god El. Bible readers will recall how once the prophet Zedekiah, son of Chenaanah, speaking with the mouth of El, bound iron horns on his forehead and told King Ahab: "With these shalt thou push the Syrians."

OPPOSITE: **The woman flatfish in the old-fashioned bath, though a less urgent monster, is a warning of what may happen if one tries to domesticate even a shallow-water mermaid; she will find the bath narrow and sandless, and the fresh water will choke her.**

OVERLEAF: **An even sadder monster is the narwhal-snail stranded on the lodginghouse sofa. The true narwhal is a terrible beast. His twisted ivory horn has been known to pierce the oaken timbers of a first-rate battleship and can measure up to eleven feet; his tail propels him at a fantastic speed. He, not the whale, is the true king of the ocean. But in Gnoli's drawing this formidable creature has been reduced to a flounderlike fish with a small, blunted horn, a sea-snail shell to hamper his locomotion, and a stuffed but loveless sofa, not green depths, for his abode. His eyes are agonized. Like the woman flatfish, he is out of his element.** —R.G.

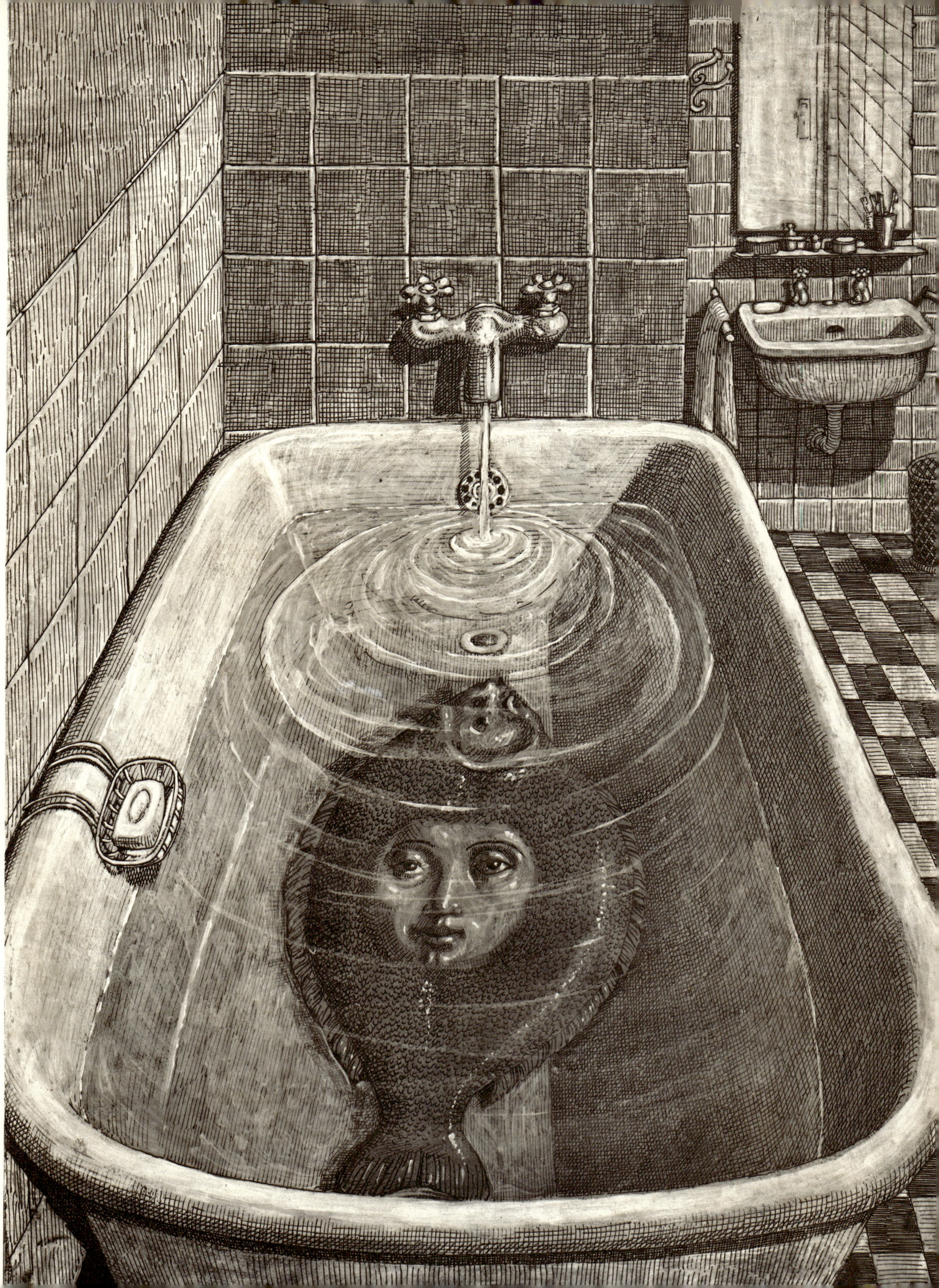

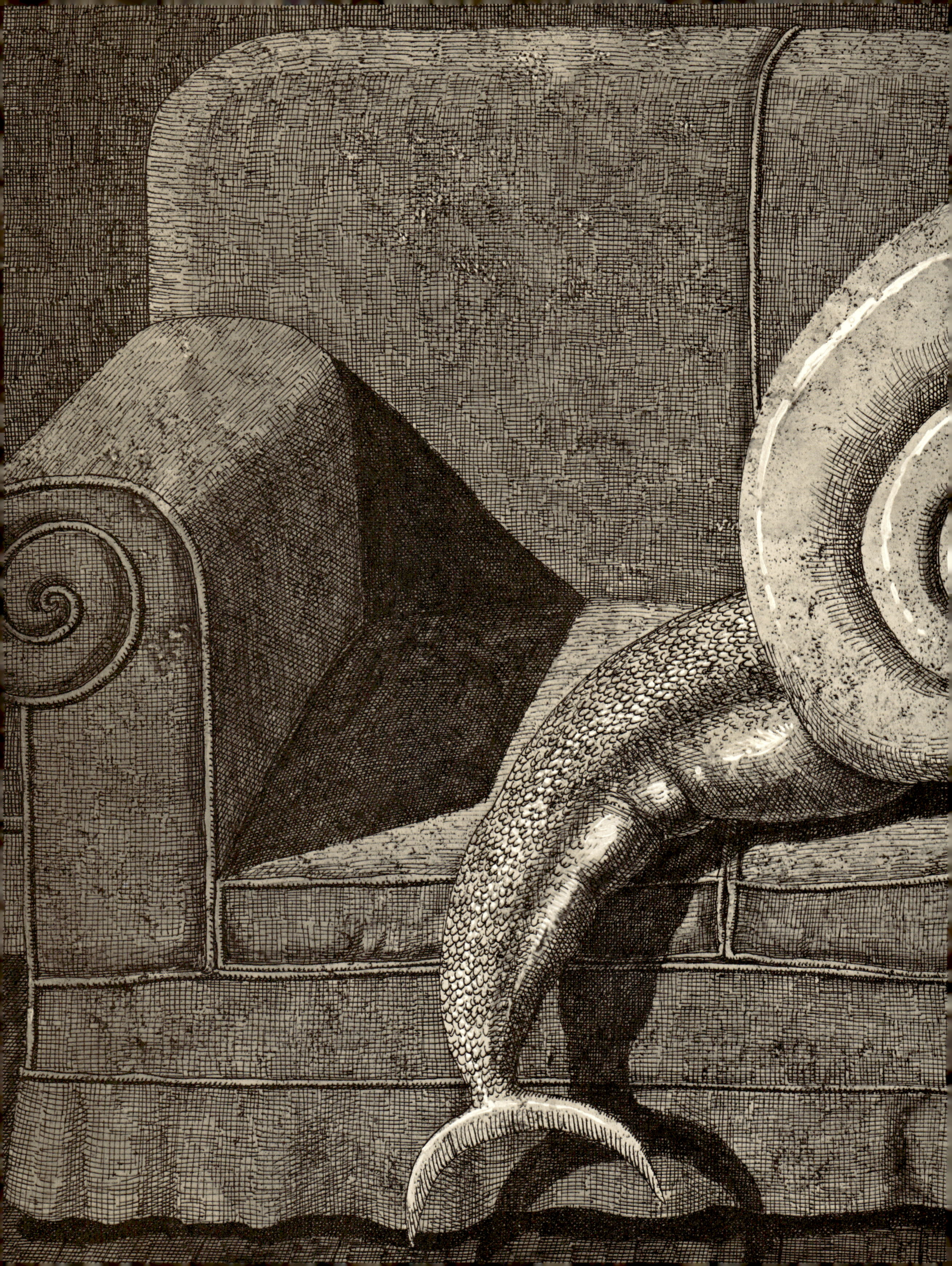

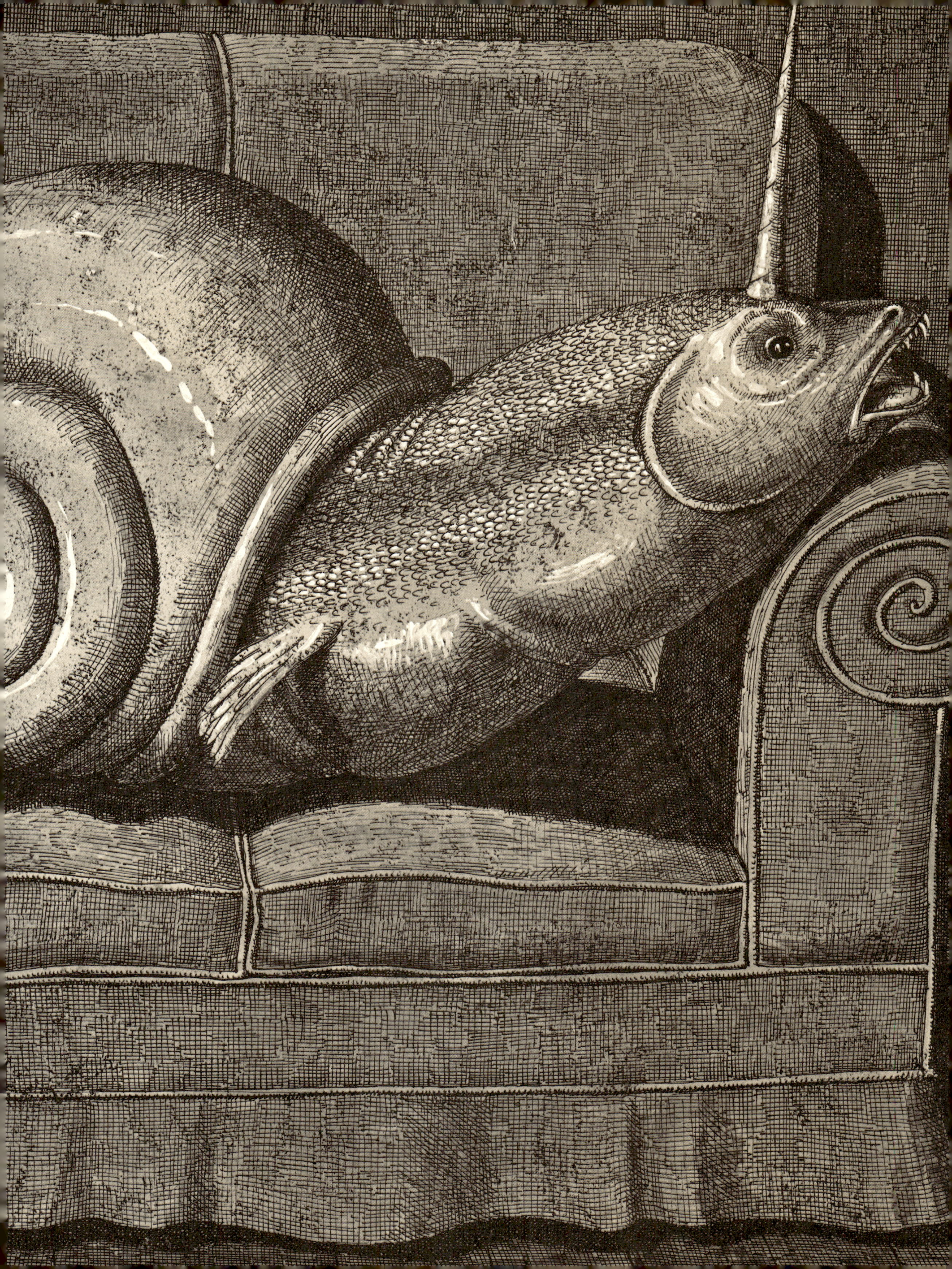

Greek mythographers accounted for the monstrous Minotaur by saying that Queen Pasiphaë of Crete indulged a depraved sexual yearning for a bull and was punished by bearing it a bull-headed child. But they were saying no more than that the original matrilineal nobles of Crete, immigrants from Libya, had worshiped the moon-goddess Neith and that their queen, Neith's high priestess ("Pasiphaë" was a royal moon-title meaning "She who shines for all"), was unhappily forced to acquiesce in the Semitic conquest and to accept patriarchal rule and patrilineal marriage with the invading chieftain. Her union with this bull-god's representative disgusted and horrified all true Cretans as much as the act of bestiality with which they compared it. As well as a Minotaur, by the way, there was a Cretan Minotrage, meaning a king who impersonated a Semitic goat-god. There were also ass-centaurs.

More complicated mythological animals, such as the Chimera and the Unicorn, began as simple pictographs of astronomical concepts. Plato and his followers treated the Chimera as a ridiculous or insane fancy. Yet Homer, who recorded that this monster had a lion's head, a serpent's tail, and a goat's body and was killed in Asia Minor by the Corinthian hero Bellerophon, suffered from no chimerical delusions. He knew that the Lion (*Leo*), the Goat (*Capricornus* in Latin, but *Chimaira* in Greek), and the Serpent (*Draco*) were constellations, and therefore he understood that Bellerophon had dethroned a sun-king, whose emblem was a combination of Leo, Capricorn, and Draco in a single pictograph.

The original Unicorn was described by the mythographers as having the horn of a rhinoceros, the head of a deer, the body of a horse, the feet of an elephant, and the tail of a lion; it began, it seems, as a calendar pictograph of the five seventy-two-day seasons in the Pharaonic calendar. The phoenix was another calendar pictograph. Since the ancient Egyptians had no leap year, their calendar of exactly 365 days, including a five-day intercalary period, grew yearly more and more out of touch with the solstices and equinoxes, because of the troublesome extra few hours occurring annually. After each spell of 1,460 years these extra hours added up to an extra year. The phoenix was portrayed as an eagle, the royal sun symbol, and was said to have been born in the form of a small worm on the palm tree (*phoinix* in Greek), sacred to the great goddess Isis. The worm symbolized these extra hours, which after about four years amounted to a whole extra day—the phoenix chick thereafter gradually maturing into a full-grown eagle. At the end of the 1,460-year phoenix cycle the bird returned to its palm-tree nest for the inauguration of a fresh cycle and was burned alive in a nest of palm branches. From the ashes, it was said, a new worm hatched that grew to a chick again, and so a new phoenix cycle, or "Sothic year," began. The Jews and early Christians, however, continued to believe in a literal, zoological phoenix even after 30 B.C.—the year in which the emperor Augustus killed it when he abolished the long line of Pharaohs and imposed the intercalated Julian calendar on the Egyptians. In late Jewish legend the phoenix figures in the Noah's ark story not only as the sole beast without a mate but as the one that gave the least trouble to Noah and his sons when they were perpetually busied with the task of feeding and watering their comprehensive menagerie.

The Sphinx, another mythological beast, had a woman's head, a lioness's body, and an eagle's wings. She stood for the great goddess who claimed domination of the air as an eagle, queen of birds, and of the earth as a lioness, queen of beasts. "Sphinx" means "the throttler"—a throttler of men. When Oedipus overcame the Sphinx at Boeotian Thebes, his victory represented the same patriarchal triumph over matriarchy that the Minotaur had gained at Knossos.

Mythological birds and beasts often change their semantic associations as society changes. Thus the unicorn became confused in the Vulgate translation of the Bible with the solitary wild ass of the desert. The poet Darley writes of the unicorn:

> Lo! in the mute mid wilderness,
> What wondrous Creature, of no kind,
> His burning lair doth largely press,
> Gaze fixt and feeding on the wind,
> His fell is of the desert dye,
> And tissue adust, dun-yellow and dry . . .

In medieval times this unicorn was associated with the male pride that can be chastened only by a woman's love. A unicorn would lay his horn in a pure virgin's lap and allow her to lead him tamely away with a halter about his neck. Until the Reformation the unicorn's actual existence was everywhere accepted, and "unicorns' horns"—either those of the desert oryx or of the narwhal ("sea-unicorn")—fetched immense prices because, when dipped in a drinking cup, they were held capable of detecting poison.

Still more confusion was caused when James VI of Scotland became James I of England and used the royal unicorn of Scotland and the royal lion of England in his coat of arms as supporters of the Crown. The famous nursery-rhyme occasion when the unicorn fought the lion for the Crown took place in 1651. The Scottish army had invaded England under James's grandson, Charles II, recently crowned at

OPPOSITE: **The mirror-entranced cat-bat that flits above a bedroom chair must be read as a morbid emblem of narcissistic female obsession. The woman's dress lies discarded on the bed; she herself has turned into the cat-bat.**

OVERLEAF: **Almost more distressing than the narwhal-snail is the swan-tortoise. The swan, which had been awarded the noblest constellation in the sky, was sacred to Apollo, god of music, and drew the flying chariot of Venus herself. Almighty Jupiter did not disdain to court Leda in swan disguise. The tortoise, on which Venus often used to pose, illustrated the slowness and sureness of love; the tortoise is also reputed in Indian myth to bear the whole weight of the universe on its back. Yet it is here combined with a swan as an inglorious back-seat driver in what looks like an expense-account Cadillac.**

—R.G.

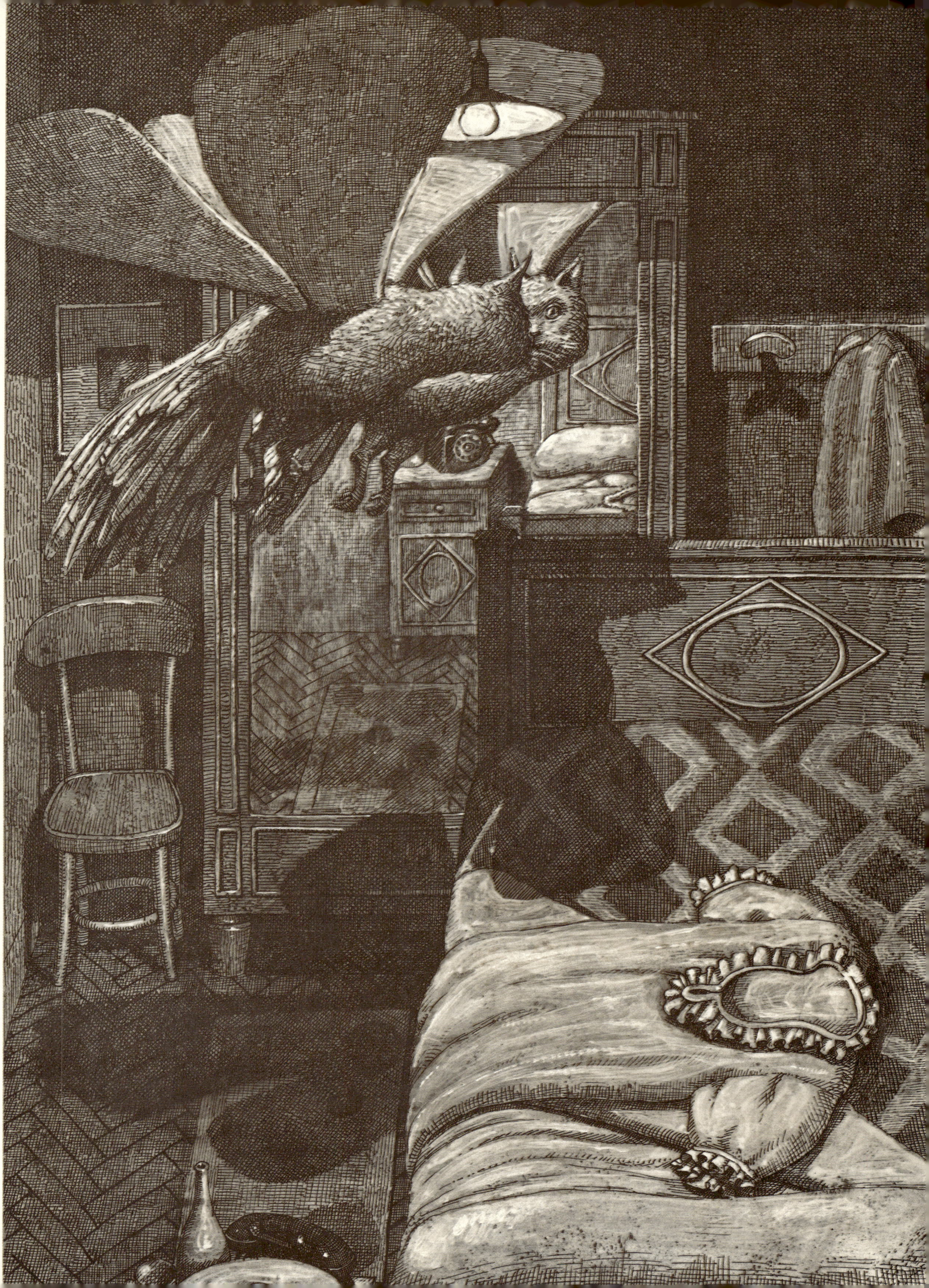

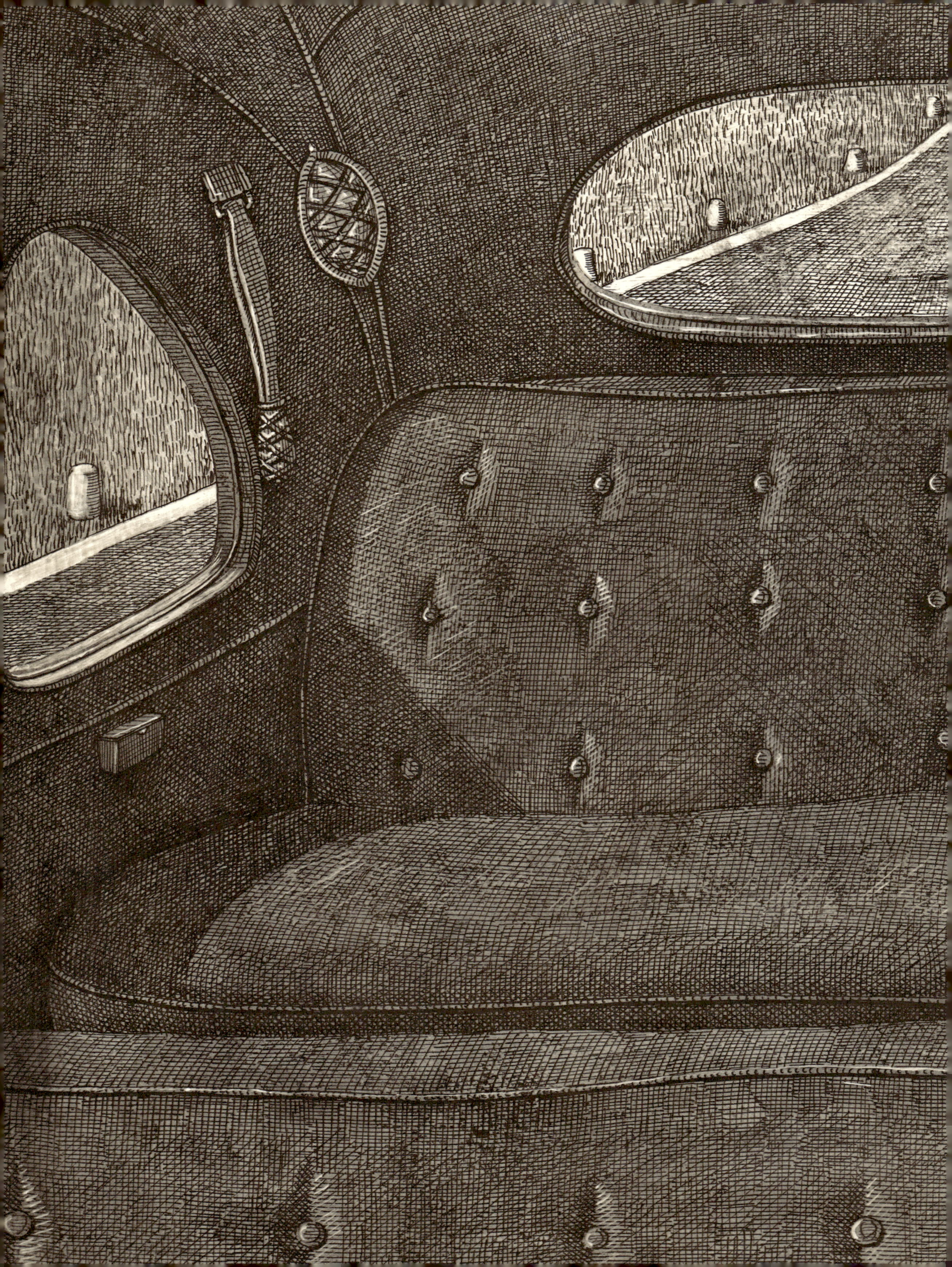

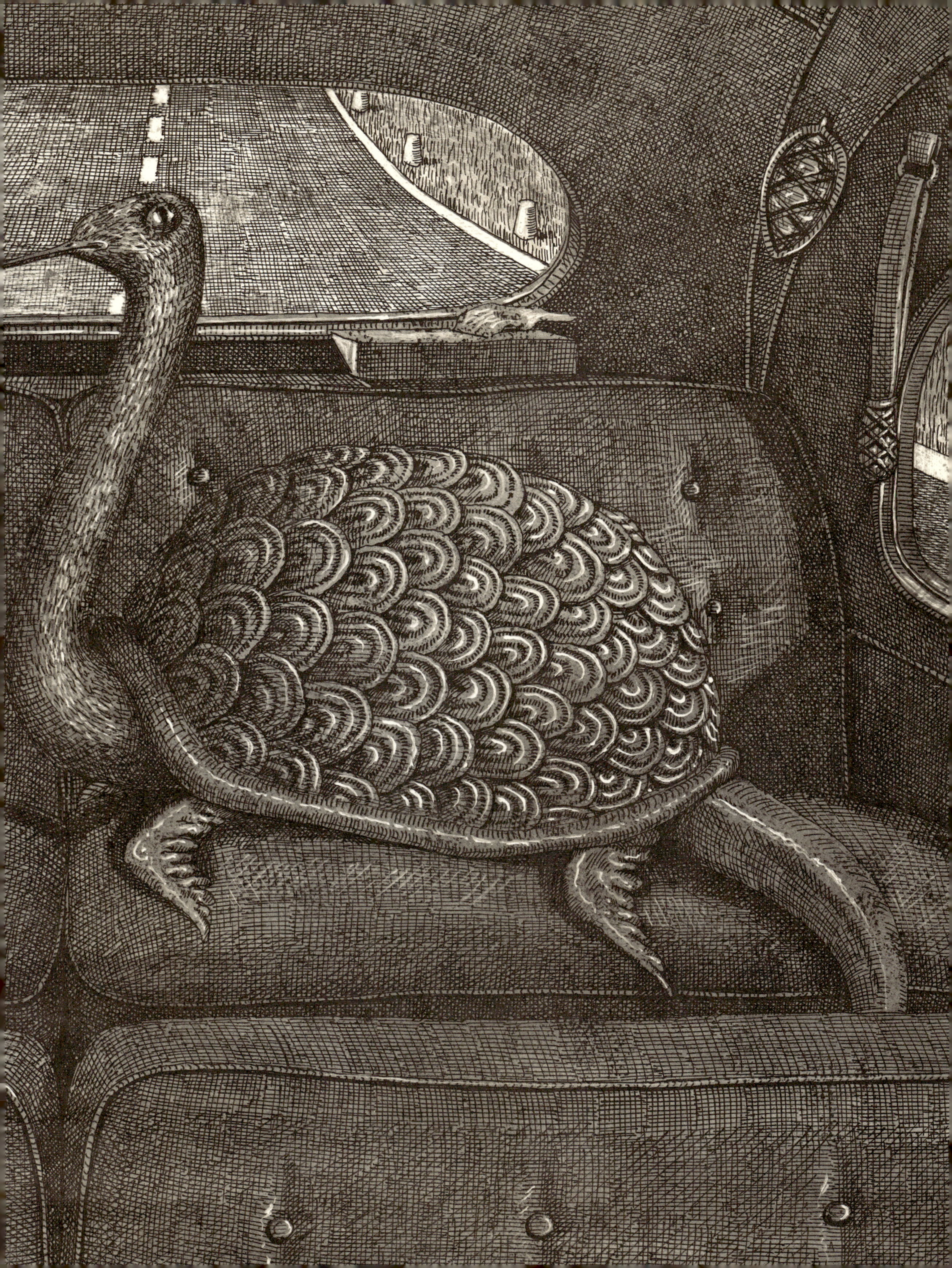

Scone, but the lionhearted English Commonwealth forces drummed the unicorn out of Worcester town.

The dragon represents sometimes a huge legendary red-colored serpent—the Greek word *drakon* means just "serpent"—sometimes a lizard. Saint George, who killed the dragon, is a Christianized version of the Babylonian god Marduk, who similarly killed a sea serpent, the goddess Tiamat. Pope John XXIII, aware perhaps that the killing of the sea serpent had been attributed by the prophet Isaiah to Jehovah himself, demoted Saint George in the historical hierarchy of saints but allowed his worship to continue in those places where he was still honored.

The lizard type of dragon comes from China: the Chinese, impressed it seems by the gigantic lizards found on the East Indian island of Komodo, had told travelers' tales about them. Thus the *Dra Goch*, the lizardlike red dragon of Wales, has a very different origin from Saint George's dragon. The *Dra Goch* was brought to Britain from China by way of Constantinople several centuries before Saint George's arrival, because a red silk dragon shaped like a wind sock had long been used as a banner by Byzantine generals. The archers watched the dragon to see from which quarter the wind was blowing and with what force, and were thus able to correct their aim. By the time of King Arthur, a sixth-century A.D. Roman British cavalry leader, the red dragon had come to be the banner used by successive commanders in chief of Rome's British allies. King Arthur's father, King Uther, held the title "Pendragon," or "chief dragon." Thus Arthur inherited the banner and fought behind it against the invading Saxons; and after his death, when Saxon hordes drove the British back into the hills of Wales, the red dragon remained the British emblem.

As far as I know, the only new mythological monsters that have been invented in Europe since Christianity displaced the old Greco-Roman religion are the products of heraldry. Most of them are based on the medieval bestiaries—fanciful zoological compendiums that drew morals from the natural, or unnatural, histories of animals. For instance, the lion, as king of beasts, was credited with kingliness, courage, honor, generosity, and the other royal virtues; the fox was a shrewd, sly politician or bandit; the bear was a fierce, stupid, blustering soldier with a sweet tooth and a sore head. A proud prince might choose his crest by combining the eagle, as king of birds—with its sharp eye, remorseless swoop, and inaccessible eyrie—with the lion, as king of beasts, naming the combined animal a "gryphon." The same Alice, it will be recalled, met an unusually somnolent gryphon in Wonderland.

Uneducated men-at-arms believed in the actual existence of gryphons; also of allerions, which were beakless, clawless, heraldic eagles—symbols of pacific royalty; and of warlike wiverns, which were winged dragons with eagles' legs and barbed tails.

Domenico Gnoli, an Italian of old family, remains true to the European heraldic tradition. His monsters develop naturally and without conscious thought when the old language of the bestiaries is applied to modern circumstances. Most Americans, though laughing at the quaint result, are unlikely to be interested in the significance of his terrifying monsters—an attitude satirized by Hilaire Belloc some seventy years ago in *The Modern Traveller:*

> Just north, I find, of Cape de Verd
> We caught a very curious bird
> With horns upon its head;
> And—not, as one might well suppose,
> Web-footed or with jointed toes—
> But having hoofs instead.
> As no one present seemed to know
> Its use or name, I let it go.

The Romans, who invented the word *monstrum*, put monsters in the same class as portents and prodigies, being, according to Cicero, signs pointing out that something sinister was afoot, just as a portent *portended*, and a prodigy *foretold*, a usually evil event. The birth of a two-headed calf, a typical monster, demanded from its owner a ritual sacrifice to avert disaster; so did Siamese twins, or a cock with hen's plumage. The colt foaled on Julius Caesar's farm with each of its hooves divided into five toes was a monster; but, by breaking it in and riding it to victory after victory, Caesar determined to make it an evil sign for the enemies of Rome rather than for himself. Yet its monstrosity in fact portended fresh civil war and the Roman republic's eventual extinction. The Old English word for any monster of this sort was *baeddel*, something that *boded* ill, from which the word "bad" comes.

Thalidomide babies are typical *baeddels*, or monstrous births. The particular warning that they convey is one against rash scientific experiment and against putting drugs on the market before all possible side effects have been investigated. The thalidomide baby warning has unfortunately been disregarded: although the firm that first supplied psychiatrists with LSD no longer manufactures the drug, its formula has been widely published and thus become available to junior assistants in every college chemical laboratory. There is now little hope of stopping its secret manufacture, though LSD bears chemical resemblances to thalidomide and may produce equally significant monsters. It may, however, be soon superseded by still more disastrous compounds of the same sinister drug. And the eventual result will then be monsters of the mind that dim the horror of any monster portent or prodigy hitherto known to even the most luckless of mankind.

OPPOSITE: **The hedgehog-owl peeping from the clothes closet is a warning that witchcraft, of the sort used for cursings and blastings, has not yet by any means been stamped out in either Europe or America. For the owl is sacred to the infernal goddess Hecate, adored by the Scottish witches in Shakespeare's *Macbeth*; and the hedgepig, or hedgehog, was the familiar that whined to announce their "Sabbaths."**

—R.G.

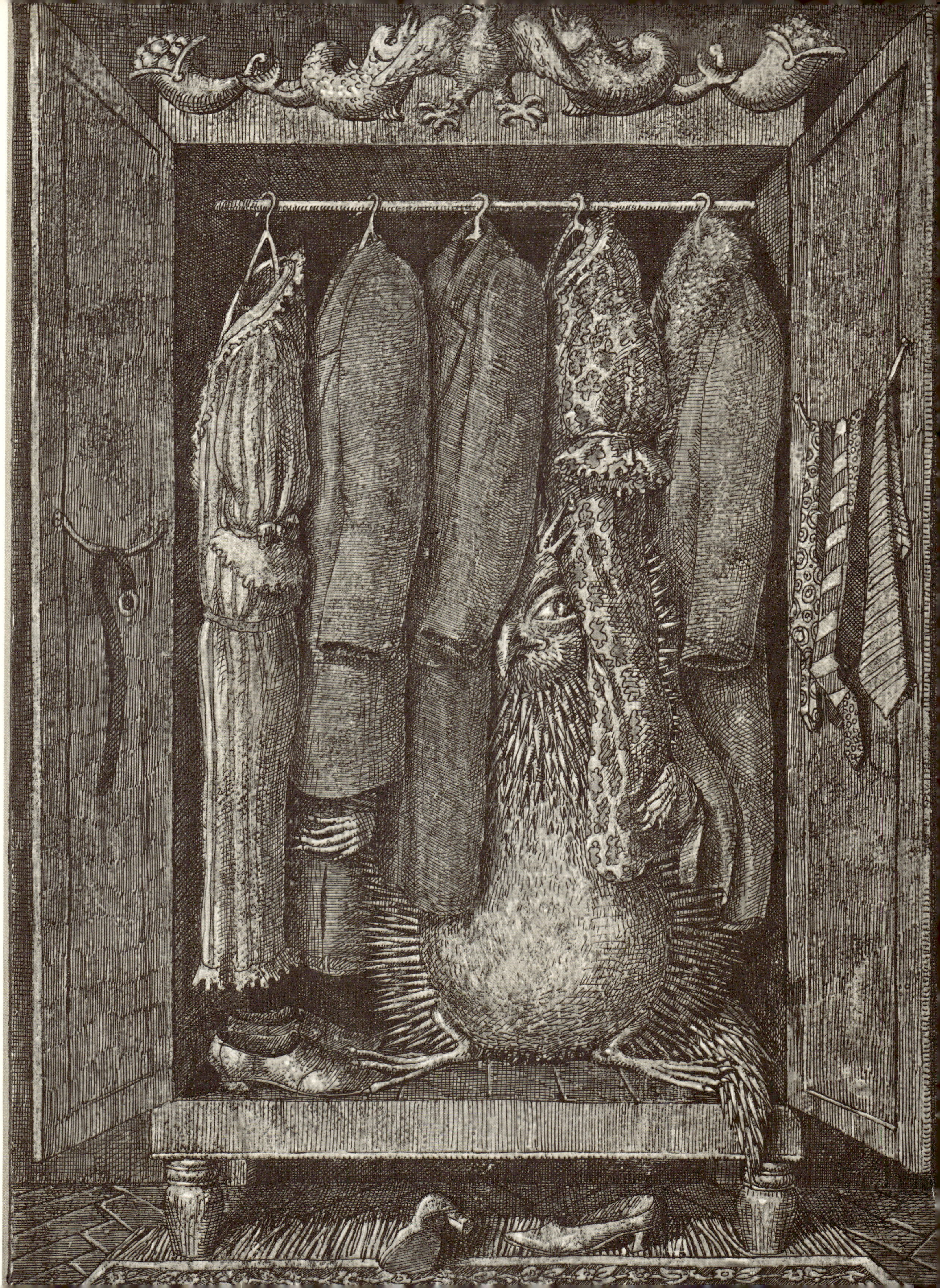

Johnson (?) on Johnson

No, not Lyndon, but Samuel, LL.D. (honorary)—lexicographer, biographer, satirist, critic, wit. A series of brief lives of English poets was commissioned from Johnson late in his life, and a number of corrected galley proofs of this were recently discovered in the home of Lord Vestige (a British peer not famous for his literary interests, as fellow members of the London Playboy Club will know). Attached to these proofs was a yellowing manuscript in no known hand—evidently an intended addition to the Lives of the Poets. *Its authorship can only be guessed at. The manuscript came to* HORIZON *via one of its contributors, the English novelist Anthony Burgess, whose longtime admiration for the great lexicographer, coupled with his known linguistic versatility, have aroused suspicion in certain quarters as to the manuscript's authenticity. It is, in any event, reproduced here without emendation.*

The illustrious subject of the ensuing pages will, as is to be presumed on the anticipatory evidence, receive so large a treatment, not less candid than encomiastick, in the projected *Life* of Mr. Boswell, that the present proposed summation must seem alike insufficient and supererogatory. However, it was considered by the booksellers who were its sponsors, that the *Lives of the Poets* would be deemed wanting by its readers unless the author himself, in respect of both his life and his productions, were accorded the due of inclusion. To determine the scale of such exhibition, whether to honour with the enlargement proper to a Milton or dismiss with the brevity apt for a Cibber, must always set nice problems of judgement when posterity, whose adjudication alone is final, cannot be consulted as an aid; the author, in his joint office of biographer and critick, must accept with frigid resignation that he has said both too little and too much. And yet the sun is not reviled for an excess of effulgence nor the candle for the paucity of its light. Who seeks luminosity will always be thankful to find it.

Samuel Johnson was born in 1709 in the town of Lichfield in the midlands of England. That, when he had long elected to be considered a Londoner, he thought with kindness on his birthplace, may be adduced from the entry in his Dictionary under "Lich," where he interpolates the gratuitous apostrophe "*Salve magna parens.*" His father was a bookseller, and it may be conjectured that the propinquity of works of both learning and delight determined the future preoccupations of the son. But, in such circumstances, inclination must precede opportunity: he who lives among sheep is not preordained to a gust for mutton. That the bookish inclination was strongly present in the young Johnson cannot, however, be doubted. He read voraciously, though not always with commensurate understanding, from the variety of his father's stock, nor was appetite matched more by the selective faculty than by the power of digestion. That he retained much of what he read, however, seems certain, possessing as he did an inherent capacity for incontinent memorization: what he got by heart he got without effort.

Large-framed and sturdy from his earliest days, he was yet afflicted with certain corporeal infirmities that physick could not alleviate. At the age of three years he was taken to London to be touched by Queen Anne for the king's evil, or scrofula, a belief in the thaumaturgick properties of the royal person being still superstitiously prevalent. Additionally to this ailment, of which the queen's condescension provided neither cure nor palliative, he was afflicted with near sight, of such a morbidity that, when on his way to school, he would crouch down in the street to ascertain whether he was in danger of involuntary precipitation into the gutter. On one occasion, so it is credibly recorded, his nurse was dispatched after him to forestall such an eventuality, but he turned in rage to beat her, being then, as thereafter, both jealous of his independence and physically equipped to defend it. His sole bodily endowment was strength; his father had failed to transmit to him a comeliness that had, without the elder Johnson's immediate knowledge, so inflamed a young woman with love that she had literally languished and died. The son was neither damned nor blessed with a patrimony of such tragick propensities; no female heart was doomed to shipwreck on his shore.

It is proper, though painful, to add other, less palpable, afflictions. Johnson was always subject to a profound hypochondria, or melancholy, so intense as intermittently to deprive him of the ordinary faculties of sensation, or even of visual recognition: he would pass a whole hour unable to read the time on a publick clock. This infirmity could also take a religious manifestation, inducing a conviction that he was eternally damned, but this was doubtless fed by an awareness of genuine culpability: he was given, which is not venial in one of declared philosophick bent, to the practices of Onan. He also suffered from a number of spasmodick impulses, such as unpremeditable and

60

uncontrollable jerks of the limbs and head, which must strike all who did not know him well as, at best, distractive oddities and, at worst, the marks of idiocy. The habit of gulosity, despite his invective in *The Rambler*, was a controllable failing which he did not wish to control, though it may, in charity, be referred back to a morbid predisposition. He was not over-clean and had, on his own admission, no love for fresh linen; in his life of Dr. Swift he seems, with his term "Oriental scrupulosity," to castigate the Dean's predilection for washing as unnatural and eccentrick. Johnson's aversion to the habit may be called a fault of character more than an innate morbidity, though charity again may relate it to an indolence that is one of the sad fruits of hypochondria. But I digress, or anticipate.

Johnson was educated at Lichfield Grammar School and, in 1728, was accepted for Pembroke College, Oxford. When introduced to the latter, he was at first shy and awkward in the presence of the erudite, but he suddenly struck into the conversation by quoting Macrobius, thus giving evidence of a scholarly precocity rare in a freshman. It was generally acknowledged among his preceptors that he was better fitted for the benisons that the university life could bestow, than any they could recollect being committed to their instruction. But aptitude can no more burgeon in conditions of indigence than a rose can flourish in Arabian wastes, and the penury that had overtaken the father rebounded on the son. A poor scholar, he exhibited his poverty in the very nakedness of his toes, though his innate independence rebuffed the gift of shoes from a fellow student, anonymous in his charity. A year after his admission, he was obliged for lack of funds to suspend his courses, and he went down but little advanced up the ladder of a degree.

So often is genius betrayed by circumstance, and aspiration revealed as the bondman of subsistence.

His father died in 1731, and the destitution of his family was his sole, though unpurposed, bequest. Johnson worked as an usher of a school in Market Bosworth but found in the instruction of careless youth little sustenance for the body and none at all for the spirit. It appears that he then secured literary employment of a degraded kind, contributing essays to a Birmingham newspaper. In 1735, he published his first book, though this was no original composition but a translation from the French of Father Jeronimo Lobo's *Voyage to Abyssinia*, a mechanical task that wholly merited its anonymity. Yet no work is wasted, and it is certain that the scenery of *Rasselas* was derived, however partially and inchoately, from his drudging perusal of the worthy priest. In this same *annus mirabilis*, he fell in love and married, the bride being Mrs. Elizabeth Porter, a widow twenty-one years his senior. Fired by the uxorious ambition proper to his new station, he started a school at Edial, near Lichfield, but the enterprise languished for lack of pupils. One of these, however, if a proleptick view be admissible, attained such distinction in his subsequent career as to bring retrospective honour to the establishment. This was David Garrick, the lustrous ornament of the English stage. His zest for the observation of life, as well as his gift for the mimesis of its passions, were, it must be confessed, but meanly employed in this phase of his youth; for he would watch through the keyhole of the marital bedchamber the caresses his master bestowed awkwardly on his bride, and subsequently entertain the small audience of his fellows with impertinent mimicry of those intimacies.

It was with this forward pupil as travelling-companion that Johnson and Mrs. Johnson set out, in 1737, to engage the vaunted opportunities of the metropolis. For a poor scholar with no connexions and small hope of patronage, London had little to offer but, at best, the derisory rewards of Grub Street and, at worst, the sloping path to rags and the debtor's jail. Yet the confidence of the one will always prevail against the experience of the many, else history had long ago come to an end; what men learn from others is that they must teach themselves. Johnson entered the service of Mr. Edward Cave, the printer and founder of *The Gentleman's Magazine*, in whose columns the young aspirant displayed his facile ingenuity in the modes of literature that a periodical then accommodated, contributing essays, odes, occasional poems, Latin verses, biographies, and the reports of parliamentary debates. These last were neither verbatim transcripts nor close paraphrases, but original compositions founded on speeches actually made, in which current issues of policy were treated with an eloquence of which the discutants in the Chamber must, with rare exceptions, be considered hardly susceptible. With genius, it is always easier to create than to copy, and the hues on the canvas of a Reynolds may, with some justice, be accounted superior to their correspondences in nature. Who would not choose to be exalted with the ideal, than merely to be informed by the actual?

In 1738, Johnson published his *London*, a poem written in imitation of the Third Satire of Juvenal, wherein the vice and degeneracy of the New Rome were castigated, as well as the oppression of the poor and the insolence of the rich. The "Thales" who speaks his disgust has, by many, been identified with the unfortunate Richard Savage, who was the companion of Johnson's own penurious drudgery, and it was perhaps no accident that a life of this struggling poet, in whom the expectations of a gentleman were thwarted by an unnatural mother's unremitting persecution, should appear as Johnson's next notable composition. The literary labours continued, but the material rewards were coyly withheld. Yet ambition will, with a kind of perversity, flourish most when least sure of fulfillment. It was in 1747, while still a stranger to fame, that Johnson issued the plan of a work that must, if realized, infallibly procure it. Planting his pennant high, he addressed to the Earl of Chesterfield the proposal of a Dictionary.

This eminent nobleman had represented himself as an arbiter of manners and a friend to literature. To a project that should settle the flux of the English language and determine for a whole age the principles of lexical correctness and stylistic elegance, it might be expected that he would respond with an exemplary ardour. Its proponent he indeed flattered with promises of help, and a retiring scholar, unacquainted with the ways of the *beau monde*, might be forgiven for a credulousness that men sophisticated by disappointment would not so readily conceive. The Tory principles of the lexicographer were disposed to a faith in the rectitude of the aristocracy, and here was aristocracy's most exquisite bloom. And yet the term "patron," which first connoted the condescensions of help, assumed, as the work progressed, ever more pejorative tones. The indifference and even insolence of one who was but a paragon of exterior forms, pusillanimous in substance beneath the mask of speciousness, bred in the nominal protégé the postures of stoicism and the dispositions of bitterness. The appearance of the *Dictionary* in 1755 was celebrated by the tardy laudations of his lordship. But years of neglect could in no wise be exculpated by belated gestures of facile praise, and Johnson very properly repudiated them in a letter compact of stoick dignity and frigid politeness.

While the *Dictionary* proceeded, the man of words did not forget that he was a man of letters, and philology intermittently yielded to his primary avocation. In 1749, he published *The Vanity of Human Wishes*, an imitation of the Tenth Satire of Juvenal, in which Johnson illustrates the futility of ambition, whether in the field of war, learning, or statesmanship. It is a powerful but melancholy dissertation, and the reader does not have far to seek for its causative springs. In the same year, Garrick, having achieved fame ahead of his old mentor, and mindful of the obligation of a former pupil, produced the tragedy *Irene*, which Johnson had written at Edial, in the days of a less equitable relationship. The play was not much liked, being little more than a parcel of moral disputations in the exotick setting of the Mussulman, but it yielded £300, a not inconsiderable sum at that time, and was thus the occasion of mitigating straits that had too long continued. In 1750, Johnson commenced *The Rambler*, a demihebdomadal magazine which he wrote practically without assistance, and in which grave moral essays were variegated with humorous flights hardly less grave. Levity was not easily associable with either his frame or his disposition.

The Rambler ceased publication on the death of Mrs. Johnson, in 1752. Whether the conjugal state was one to which this philosopher was naturally suited, is a question perhaps too delicate for publick consideration, and it is proper to respect Johnson's own reticence on the intimate conduct of matrimonial life. Whatever the moral virtues and intellectual endowments of the lady, these were not matched by corporeal beauty: she was excessively corpulent, and a preternaturally high complexion was exacerbated by the liberal potation of cordials. No record of her dicta lends credence to a compensative mental acuity. And yet her posthumous memory was consistently revered by her relict, who, as her living memory receded, was heard often enough to ejaculate on her putative charms. Whether Johnson's failure to remarry was due to his unwillingness to desecrate a bed of felicity with a new incumbent, or else to satiety with a state whose pleasures are rarely augmented by prolongation, must stay in the decent shades of ignorance, or be left to idle speculation. Johnson once described second marriages as the triumph of hope over experience, and *The Vanity of Human Wishes* admits no exception to the vacuity of hope.

Johnson eventually partook of the heady brew of fame, or rather of the regard of the learned, though this was never to be complemented by the acquisition of wealth. Unlike Pope, he achieved no swelling parterre or Twickenham grotto. His fiftieth year saw the solace of a competence still unattained, and he found it necessary to dash off the tale of *Rasselas* to defray the cost of his mother's obsequies. In 1762, he received a pension of £300 a year from Lord Bute, and this was to suffice for needs that long indigence had schooled to moderation. With the securing of manumission from the tyranny of the pen, the pen ceased to exercise even the sway of a limited rule, and the habits of indolence were quick to supervene. With the founding of the Literary Club, the pleasures of converse soon usurped the place long given to the pains of authorship. Convivial friendship pleased more than solitary study, and the drawing room afforded easier gratifications than the library. Moreover, in 1763, Johnson first grew acquainted with Boswell, the young Scotsman who was to propose the eternization of a biography, and here was as certain a passport to posterital notice as the continued labour of his own hand. He who has written to live, will generally scorn those who live to write, and if immortality be the aim of the literary endeavour, this may sometimes be conferred by easier means than the sweat of application. Johnson doubtless preferred to enter a book in prospect, rather than write a book in fact.

Notwithstanding, he continued to give to the world, though more sparsely than hitherto, and with a ponderous reluctance, such fruits of his genius as the publick hunger demanded. His edition of Shakespeare, which appeared after long delay in 1765, had been subscribed for much earlier, and it might not have come to birth at all had it not been for the Caesarean knife of Mr. Charles Churchill's satire. These present *Lives of the Poets* were, however, commissioned in the time of his independence, though it must be thought that only the united pressure of his friends attained what inclination alone could never have accomplished. A number of fugitive pieces accommodated the requests of his friends or the needs of the times, or else, as with the elegy on the death of Mr. Levett, the obligations of sad affection. Otherwise Johnson basked in the autumn of achievement remembered, or awaited, in the symposial sodality of his admirers, the closing of the crepuscular shades.

The residue of his days may be tentatively computed out of the common expectation, but it were presumptuous to set a term to them, or to anticipate the dispositions of the Almighty. To succeeding editors may be left the task of memorializing his consignment to futurity. [Johnson died in 1784.—Ed.] Those late years that had been irradiated by the hospitable friendship of Mr. Thrale, the brewer, and Mrs. Thrale, the beauty, were at length saddened by the demise of the one and the defection of the other, who must now be denominated Signora Piozzi. That innate melancholy, exacerbated by events, sought alleviation in the composition of meditations and prayers, which, to those granted the grave privilege of access, must impress with the eloquence of their terror of mortality, and of their deprecation of condign perdition. But all men must die, and all men must be judged, and the evasion of the common lot is accorded not even to a Johnson. *In die illa, fonte pietatis aspergetur.*

Of his character, it may be said that he hid a sufficiency of sweetness beneath an exorbitant rugosity, that he could love without the extravagance of constant asseveration, and that his prejudices were but the obverse of his convictions. If he hated Whiggery, it was not out of the spite of personal disappointment, but from a philosophical awareness of its being intrinsically pernicious, since it was, in the very declaration of its principles, inimical to the established order and dedicated to its destruction. If he abominated Americans, it was because they were a sort of aggravated Whigs, in whom repudiation of loyalty excused itself in the canting avowal of a plausible libertarianism. If he despised the Scots, it was because of their betrayal of ideals of national rectitude, their apostasy from the true religion, their neglect of agriculture, and their murder of the English tongue. What many, indeed, termed prejudice, he would term a just and reasoned hostility, whose complement was an infrangible faith in a monarchy from which he could expect nothing, a social order that had failed him, and a system of religion that had bred a fear of damnation.

As a friend, he was just, candid, and forgiving. In the forms of amical intercourse, it was accepted that he must lead, and that his voice must prevail; that he must have the right to censure insolence and overrule unreason, though it may be admitted that his love of argumentative conquest would deafen him to the rationality of an opponent: he must win, by fair stratagem if possible but, in the main, by whatever stratagem seemed expedient. He asked nothing more than that his *mots* should be applauded, his excesses of expatiation condoned, and his dogmatisms accepted. Such indulgence of the drawing room must be matched by both an exquisiteness and an amplitude of table hospitality, for, though he could eat grossly, he was yet sensible of the charms of culinary delicacy, and fierceness of appetite could yield to the niceness of gustatory discrimination. With wine, he was capable of abstinence but not of temperance, and where the latter could not be encompassed by philosophick self-control, the former could always be induced by fear of the devastation of excess.

His piety was genuine, and his generosity notable. This latter virtue was exercised as much to the animal or, to be strict, feline order, as to the human. His house was never without retainers, and his purse was as liberal as his means could accommodate. Of courage he was granted an heroick endowment, whether it were opposed to the pains of the body, or to the desolation of the spirit. By disposition inclined to pessimism, he yet displayed, when occasion called it forth, a contagious cheerfulness or even a controlled hilarity. Sage in precept, he could be extravagant in jest, as apt for the apophthegm as for the shaft of fancy. Whatever posterity may judge of his works, of his life it may find little to censure. Yet the exterior man is but half of the totality, and the interior must face the severer test of futurity, whose sentences no human lenity can abate. In this regard, his friends can but pray that one human wish shall not be informed by vanity.

It remains to deliver a general opinion of his works. What Johnson wrote in Dr. Goldsmith's obituary, viz. that he touched nothing that he did not adorn, cannot in fairness be predicated of his own compositions. In the fields of the drama and the romance, it must be held that he was deficient, possessing no power to animate his personages or inform their shells with aught but sententiousness. To read *Rasselas* is to be instructed, but rarely to be delighted. We carry from that book a variety of maxims that hold the memory and attain the force of proverbs, but never a sense of human passion. Who does not know by heart such sentences as the following? "Human life is everywhere a state in which much is to be endured, and little to be enjoyed"; "Marriage has many pains, but celibacy has no pleasures"; "Example is always more efficacious than precept"; "Integrity without knowledge is weak and useless, and knowledge without integrity is dangerous and dreadful." Yet who ever formed a distinct impression of Imlac or of the Abyssinian prince himself, and who ever cared for the outcome of their acts or the unwinding of their destinies?

In the moral essay, however, he must be considered supreme, whether in the prose of *The Rambler*:

There are minds so impatient of inferiority that gratitude is a species of revenge, and they return benefits, not because recompense is a pleasure, but because obligation is a pain;

or in the verse of *London*:

This mournful truth is ev'rywhere confess'd:
Slow rises worth by poverty depress'd.

And, even in the fugitive pamphlet, as "Taxation No Tyranny," on the unrest in the American colonies, true sense informs the most ephemeral apophthegm:

How is it that we hear the loudest yelps for liberty among the drivers of negroes?

As a poet, he rarely produces harsh numbers, but there are times when, looking for melody, we find only correctness and, seeking the enlightenment of fancy, discover only the strictures of precept. And, it must be admitted, he is not above the redundancies of *The Vanity of Human Wishes*:

Let observation with extensive view,
Survey mankind, from China to Peru;

where he would seem to demand of observation that, with extensive observation, it observe mankind extensively. Such tautology he condemned in others, but missed in himself. But a tendency to swollen ventosies may be attributed less to want of ear or of care, than to habits of Latinate balance that prevailed above the demands of sense. Yet the *chiasmus* frequently triumphs:

And, bid him go to Hell, to Hell he goes.
—*additions to Goldsmith's "Traveller"*

and:

Hides from himself his state, and shuns to know,
That life protracted is protracted woe.
—*The Vanity of Human Wishes*

What has been argued against this poet's claim to excellence is that, pursuing the general, he too often betrays the particular, so that he appears to impose on the diffused experience of mankind the contracted vicissitudes of his own life; as in the following:

There mark what ills the scholar's life assail,
Toil, envy, want, the patron, and the jail.
ibid.

where "patron" must not be supposed to be a legitimate term of disparagement in all vocabularies, but bears a private bitterness of very particular signification.

Poetry is less harmed by such disclosures than is the impersonal art of the lexicographer, which should inform without prejudice and enlighten without reserve. In his Dictionary, Johnson too frequently admits the gratuitousness of implicit or explicit animosities, as in the definition of "excise": "A hateful tax levied upon commodities"; or of "oats": "A grain, which in England is generally given to horses, but in Scotland supports the people"; or of "patron," which, as may be anticipated, bears a load of wholly personal acerbity: "Commonly a wretch who supports with insolence, and is paid with flattery"; or of "Whig," in which elucidation is forbidden by contumely: "The name of a faction."

Of his vocabulary, it has been objected that it prefers the exotick Latin to the indigenous Saxon, much to the harm of clarity; as may be exemplified in his definition of "network": "Anything reticulated or decussated at equal distances, with interstices between the intersections." Even in his private conversation, he seemed to evince a prejudice against the plain, and a correspondent predilection for the ornate, so that he would sometimes emend the one to the other in a single utterance; as when he observed of Buckingham's *Rehearsal* that "it had not wit enough to keep it sweet," and then corrected himself to: "I mean it possesses insufficient vitality to preserve it from putrefaction." Such a predisposition to the locutions of learning cannot always escape absurdity, and it is capable of translating a pithy proverb into a pretentious aphorism, so that "Birds of a feather flock together" must become "Ornithological bipeds of identical plumage invariably congregate in the closest proximity." The truth is, that there is a time for the Latin, as there is a time for the Saxon, and to confuse the two argues no niceness of discrimination: where we doubt the judge in one capacity, we infallibly doubt him in others.

Yet Johnson could contrive, on occasion, a style as easy as Addison's, as trenchant as Swift's, as dignified as Gibbon's; witness his letter to the Earl of Chesterfield, in which we introduce his word of most particular opprobrium for the last time:

Is not a Patron, my Lord, one who looks with unconcern on a man struggling for life in the water, and, when he has reached ground, encumbers him with help? The notice which you have been pleased to take of my labours, had it been early, had been kind; but it has been delayed till I am indifferent, and cannot enjoy it; till I am solitary, and cannot impart it; till I am known, and do not want it.

Of his obiter dicta it would be premature to speak, until those meticulously recorded by his friends have been exhibited to the publick. Let it suffice to say, that his power of conversation was unmatched in this age, and his gift of the apt riposte, the epigrammatical summation, the pleasantry homely but never indecent, and the rebuke just but never obnoxious, was as diligently cultivated by art, as it had been lavishly imparted by nature. It may happen, that he who sought immortality by what he did, may more readily attain it by what he was; that the words he spoke, may instruct more than those he has written; and the example of his character may elevate, where the precepts of his work may fail to instruct. Happy the man who may reach posterity by two roads, of which, if one be blocked, the other will be open.

His excellent good friend Sir Joshua Reynolds painted this portrait of Sam. Johnson in 1756

WALTER A. CURTIN—NATIONAL PORTRAIT GALLERY, LONDON; COURTESY *Life*

At the Sorbonne, a college of the medieval University of Paris, students hear a theology lecturer in a fifteenth-century miniature

Accept, if you please, that in the mid-thirteenth century twin brothers, Pierre and Paul, were born to a peasant family in central France. Very soon they began to talk and not long after to argue. They attended the little song school of the village church, promptly learned their letters from a hornbook, and memorized the Mass and a repertory of Latin hymns and chants. They talked to each other, mostly in their private language—Latin. Though lavishly beaten by their parents and cuffed by their elder brothers, they were the darlings of the curate and were even kindly noticed by the noble lordling in his castle. They were clearly apt for the church, being born in wedlock, physically whole, well voiced, with true pitch, and possessed of near twenty-twenty vision (for spectacles were not yet, and myopes and astigmats had little chance of a churchly career).

When they were fourteen, the curate summoned them to the sacristy for a serious talk. "My dear boys, you have a rare zeal for learning and the wits to rise in the world. But unless you want to spend your lives as half-starved village priests, like me, you must attend the university. I have a promise of a purse in aid from the bishop and another from our local lord, whom God preserve. True, the fulfillment is likely to fall short of the promise."

"Gramercy, Father. But which university?"

"You, Pierre, have an almost alarming delight in exploring the holy mysteries of our faith. Theology, the queen of the sciences, has her favorite seat in Paris. The way is long to the doctorate, but the outcome and the rewards are glorious.

By MORRIS BISHOP

Scholares Medii Aevi

In principio apud studium generale gaudia minima, maximae angustiae, labores infiniti: at quid vita, nisi meditatio aeternitatis?

"And you, Paul, have less of the spiritual flame but more practical and worldly wisdom. For you I counsel the study of the law, whether canon law or civil law. We see in the modern world prelates, popes, princes, and kings surrounded with legal counselors who readily become magistrates, treasurers, even ambassadors. Now the home of law, as all the world knows, is Bologna."

The boys needed no convincing. To gain the legal and social privileges of the cleric they received the tonsure. Properly their bishop should have been present to command the shears and razor, but the bishop was far away and very busy; the village barber did his work. Their mother confected cassocks, black gowns of coarse homespun wool with a hood that usually hung down the back and contained food and travel necessities. Tonsure and gown served as tickets of admission to roadside monasteries for free food and lodging. They were also protection: highwaymen, even if they did not respect the cloth, recognized it as a sign of poverty. The boys parted, with many tears and embraces, to take their separate ways. They soon fell in with other college-bound students, gaily trudging the roads. Such associations were not without their perils, for brigands often adopted clerical dress, the better to ply their trade.

Pierre came thus to Paris, which he found very crowded, dirty, and smelly. Since he could not understand the Parisians' French, nor they his Latin, he oriented himself by the towers of Notre Dame and thus reached the Petit Pont, which joined the Ile de la Cité to the left bank, already the Latin quarter. On the bridge, the preserve of philosophers, he noted a pair of gowned elders shouting and hammering fist on hand,

67

to the pleasure of a gaggle of students. Two of these, crying, "A *bejaunus!*" (*bec jaune*, yellow-bill, freshman), detached themselves and accosted Pierre, politely offering to show him suitable lodgings.

"I had hoped to gain entry to a *collegium*, a hospice for poor students."

"Those few places have all been taken long since. No chance for a *bejaunus*. Anyway, in the colleges the rules are strict and the food terrible. We can show you much better quarters. And the landlord doesn't care what you do or whom you bring in, provided you don't make too much noise about it."

The quarters turned out to be a tiny attic room under a gable, with a glassless window open to all weathers. The furnishings consisted of a rude table, a stool, and a straw-stuffed truckle bed, tipped against the wall during the day. But Pierre was roughly reared and asked nothing better. The landlord explained that he housed a dozen students and provided two meals daily in the *salle*, which even boasted a fireplace!

Pierre's new friends loudly praised their own master and urged Pierre to sign up for his lectures. When he demurred, they cried, "Just give him a trial! Attend three lectures, and if you aren't absolutely satisfied your fee will be refunded!" Only later did Pierre learn that his friends were touts, and received commissions from the professor for auditors they brought in.

His next act was to matriculate. He visited the rector, a magnificent elder who examined him briefly in Latin and declared that his preparation was insufficient to enter the school of theology. "You will enroll in the faculty of arts. The arts are seven; you will study the trivium—the major arts—grammar, rhetoric, and logic, or dialectic; and the quadrivium—the minor arts—arithmetic, geometry, as-

Student duties at Ave Maria College in Paris during the fourteenth century included, top, lighting a lamp to the Virgin, doling wine to the poor, and, at bottom, the sweeping out of the chapel.

tronomy, and music. In two years you will take the examination for the baccalaureate; you will become a bachelor, or practice teacher. In five or six more years, if all goes well, you will receive the degree of master, with all the rights, privileges, and honors pertaining thereto, including the license to teach. Then it will be time to think of the faculty of theology or another graduate school."

"But that will take forever!"

"What is life but a school for eternity? You cannot, by our rule, become a Doctor of Theology until you are thirty-five. How can one better spend one's days than by studying in Paris for twenty years or so?"

More than a little sobered, Pierre returned to his lodging. He found in the *salle* a band of older students.

"What is that horrible smell I smell?" cried one.

"There is a monster, a wild beast among us!"

"He must be dehorned and detusked! His claws must be clipped! He must be metamorphosed into humanity!"

Pierre was seized and deposited on the table. Kitchen tools were brought, and with much banging and prodding, hair clipping and face black-

ening, his rusticity was removed. Then, in a burlesque of the graduation ceremony, he was received into honorable student fellowship. And finally he was permitted to provide a banquet, for scholastic functions always ended, and still do end, with a banquet.

Meanwhile brother Paul had made his way over an Alpine pass and across the Lombard plain to stately Bologna. He found there something very different from Paris. For the University of Paris was a guild of masters; Bologna was a guild of students.

The Paris university and others formed on the Paris model imitated the structure of craftsmen's guilds. The student served his term as an apprentice; the baccalaureate made him something like a journeyman artisan. At length he presented his thesis, which corresponded to the craftsman's "masterpiece," or *chef-d'oeuvre*, gave a specimen lecture, and was formally admitted to the society of Masters of Arts. He might then continue to the doctorate and a professorship. The doctors ruled their institution, choosing their own rector. They were very high and grand. They wore special gowns, long gloves of chamois, gold rings, and brilliant, varicolored toques.

Bologna, the student guild, was originally no more than a group of serious students who hired competent authorities to instruct them, particularly in law and medicine. The students left to their professors the conduct of examinations and the granting of degrees; all other administration they kept in their own hands. They elected a student council and a rector from their own number. The rector represented, with considerable pomp, the student body in all its dealings with the faculty, the city authorities, and private citizens. He and his staff rented lecture rooms, approved or disapproved student housing and rents, supervised the book trade by fixing prices for purchases and rentals, enforced student discipline, and exerted civil and criminal justice, except in major cases.

The condition of the subject professor was pitiable. He had to swear obedience to the students' rector. If he wished a leave of absence for a single day, he had first to humbly request it of his students, then have the permission approved by the rector and the student council. He could not leave town without depositing a security for his return. He was forbidden to create holidays at his pleasure. If he failed to get five students for an "ordinary" lecture or three for an "extraordinary" one, he was declared absent and fined. If his popularity waned, he might bribe students to attend his lectures. He had to begin his morning lesson before the last peal of St. Peter's church bell and stop with its next toll. The students were required to leave the classroom while the bell was ringing; there would be none of a professor's desperate afterthoughts. He was fined if he skipped a chapter or a decretal or if he postponed a troublesome question to the end of his lecture in the hope of submerging it in the bell's clamor. He was obliged to follow a schedule and to reach a certain point in his text by a certain date. At the beginning of the academic year he deposited ten Bologna pounds with a banker as a security for the payment of his fines. A committee of students, the *Denunciatores Doctorum*, kept close watch on him "for his spiritual good."

The hireling profs swallowed their humiliations and courted student popularity, which was, on the whole, a good thing for a prof to do. His rewards in student fees could be very considerable; he could increase his income by buying houses and renting them to student groups—archaic fraternities.

The system was obviously an undergraduate's dream of bliss. It depended for its success on the presence of a large number of mature, sincere students, who would sit in sober judgment on their teachers with their long-term ends in view. The only modern parallel of which I am aware is the Art Students League in New York, wherein the students hire, discipline, and fire their teachers.

In contrast to Paris, with its emphasis on philosophy and theology, Bologna was practical. Its specialties were law, medicine, the training of notaries, and astrology, though the last was discouraged by the burning of Professor Cecco d'Ascoli in 1327 for making some mistakes. Its background was the democratic, commercial, realistic world of the Italian city-state. The course in arts was rather misprized as the refuge of triflers and dilettantes.

Medieval universities in general, having no buildings of their own, no property, no trustees or regents, and very little administration, were free to migrate if they thought themselves mistreated, and often they did so. The offshoots, such as Padua and Cambridge, frequently remained, to grow great in their turn.

The actual teaching routine did not differ much from Bologna to Paris or to Oxford, Salamanca, or Naples. In Paris the educational center was the left-bank Rue du Fouarre. Here and hereabouts the professors rented houses and classrooms. Large gatherings were held in churches and convent halls. The college, or charity dormitory, of Robert de Sorbon, established in 1257, boasted a large hall, the ancestor of the modern Sorbonne. In the classrooms the master had a high seat and a lectern; the pupils squatted on the floor. But in Bologna the student administrators rented the classrooms and, being concerned for their own comfort, installed benches and rude desks.

Classes commonly began at 6 A.M. For popular courses earnest students arrived even at 3 A.M., while the rich sent their servants to hold a place. At the appointed hour a beadle entered and called for attention. All rose, as in Europe they still do, for the professor's solemn entry. He took his seat behind the lectern, beside which burned a candle of fat. The rest of the room, during the northern winter, was nearly pitch-dark. No roll was called, but a beadle or proctor made sure that no interlopers were present, dodging the *collectum*, the teacher's fee. Students were always *mali pagatores*, complained the faculty; they wanted to learn without paying.

In the dark, note taking was impossible and even by day, difficult. Paper and parchment were too expensive for such a purpose, but wax-covered tablets, balanced on the knee and written on with a stylus, were commonly used. The prevailing educational theory held that the student should concentrate, fix the points of a lecture in his mind, without the distraction of writing notes. To this end the teacher was urged to talk fast and not dictate. By so doing he discouraged the underhand commerce in lecture notes.

A typical class lasted two to three hours—a long squat. It began with a *lectio*, the reading of a standard text; then a *quaestio*, or commentary; finally a *disputatio*, when teacher and students joined in criticism and debate—a quiz period, we should say.

Class discipline was ordinarily good. Ordinances forbade shouting, hissing, noisemaking, and throwing stones in class or deputizing one's servant to do so. There was a significant episode in a Bologna classroom. One student assaulted another with a sword; he was fined by the student council for wasting the time of the class.

The curriculum in different universities, different courses of study, different periods, varied too much to be considered here. Much old and new learning—Greek, Roman, and Arabic—poured into Christendom from the eleventh century onward. Mathematics, astronomy, classical literature, and particularly logic invaded the universities. Aristotelian logic was primarily a method of understanding, a reaching for assured truth by analysis, classification, and rational deduction. Its device was the syllogism. Its outcome was the exaltation of reason and order and a distrust of marvel and miracle.

The scholar's utensil, his weapon, is the textbook. By the thirteenth century, texts had become accessible, thanks to the generalization of paper, which, unlike parchment and papyrus, was both durable and comparatively cheap. (And the generalization of paper depended on the generalization of flax for linen shirts and underclothes, on the creation of a rag trade, with ragmen crying in the streets their eagerness to buy, with the organized shipment of their collections to paper mills beside pure mountain streams.) Bookmaking moved out of the monasteries and into the commercial world. A guild of professional copyists, laymen, arose who developed a swift, legible, compact Gothic minuscule. The universities commissioned and supervised them. The distribution of texts was in the hands of licensed stationers, *stationarii*, who kept a privileged station, or stall. Most of their business consisted not in the sale of books, far too dear for many students, but in the rental of pieces, *peciae*, usually eight-page signatures. At Bologna a board of six checkers, *peciarii*, collated and proofread the texts offered for sale and levied heavy fines for mistakes. (Half the fine went to the discoverer of the error.) The mass-produced textbooks were often surprisingly abundant. One wholesaler ordered four hundred copies of a popular manual.

The stages of a student's career were marked by examinations and the award of degrees. A candidate for the baccalaureate at Paris had first to rent a hall from his chief examiner. He then sent a present of little pies to the members of the board. If, on the great day, the attendance was sparse, his friends would drag in passers-by from the streets and distribute free wine—at his expense, of course. The professors questioned him through a long morning and, if he was successful, robed him with the bachelor's gown. He then invited all concerned to a fine banquet. This custom, unfortunately, has lapsed.

Much more serious were the ceremonies marking the award of the master's and doctor's degrees. The candidate for the Master of Arts announced in advance certain questions he proposed to discuss; for instance: Does every moral virtue moderate the passions and direct the operations of appetite? Are the actions of material subjects more related to their substantial forms than to their qualities? Is human felicity the final cause of all human acts?

The candidate defended his position with great play of syllogisms; challengers attacked, attempting to spear him in an undistributed middle or other logical weakness. The tournament might continue for days, with cheering and shouting from the audience at palpable hits. The examiners supervised the disputation and intervened at will. At Louvain frivolous or trick questions were forbidden, but the examinee might indulge in "*jocosas quaestiones ad auditorii recreationem.*"

Once accepted, the new master was formally admitted to the guild of teachers and given the *licentia ubique docendi*, the license to teach anywhere. He took the oath of obedience to the officers and statutes of the university. He was invested with a fur-trimmed gown and a tasseled cap, "a sign of the capacity of his brain and the breadth of his mind." He was seated in the high chair; a volume of Aristotle was placed in his hands. A ring, in token of his marriage to learning, was thrust on his finger. He was embraced by the examiners, now his colleagues. In Bologna he was triumphally paraded through the city, preceded by three university pipers and four trumpeters. Then he gave all the officials presents—robes, gloves, boxes of candy—and a splendid banquet. Sometimes he staged a dance or tournament, in Spain a bullfight. This was no time for economy. One new master who offered a mean banquet found his courses boycotted; he had to hire his listeners.

The high degree was the reward of the good student who always did as he was told, who always gave the right answers, who could endure. But most students could not bear the long years of study and hardship; they became dropouts.

Study, in fact, was not easy. There was the perpetual problem of light. Even by day one had often to close one's shutters against wind and beating rain. By night one had only tallow candles, and these were feeble, fitful, costly, and foul-smelling. There was the problem of cold. In Paris and Oxford the temperature often dropped below freezing, and chilblains were a universal affliction. There was no common study hall, no heating in student rooms. In Germany the college head was required to make periodic inspections to make sure the students had no improvised grates or braziers. At Oxford the undergraduates were forbidden to warm themselves in the kitchens. At Cambridge the students were ordered to run to and fro for half an hour before bedtime, "to get a heate on their feete."

There was also the problem of health. Epidemics were frequent, food poisoning and digestive troubles common, skin diseases and vermin ever present. The few practicing physicians treated only the noble and the wealthy. Students were cautioned to take plenty of exercise, to wash their heads once a fortnight in hot lye, and to beware of drinking water.

The great obstacle to study was poverty. Many students who were not well-to-do were supported by grants from their home monasteries. Student loan funds existed at Oxford and elsewhere. Some poor boys tried to "work their way through," against great odds. At Oxford they were known as "chamber-deacons." The great Roger Bacon tells of a youth who complained that "because he was obliged to serve those who gave him necessaries, during two years he found no one to teach him a word." A Bologna student alleged that it was two years since he had tasted wine, washed his face, or trimmed his beard.

Many lived by frankly begging, securing a mendicant's license from their institutions. Begging, to be sure, was made respectable by the friars; it did not debase as would manual labor. But it did not pay well either. Often a boy went hungry.

Nevertheless, for the average student the fare seems to have been adequate and tolerable for the times. The enormous kitchens of the English colleges must have served for something. At Oxford, where no breakfasts were provided, scholars organized surreptitious meals in their rooms. This is the origin of the "breakfast party," still important in English collegiate culture. Paris made a specialty of cooked-meat shops, *charcuteries*, with sausage, tripe, and chickens "to take out" and, as a between-meal snack, tartlets stuffed with pork, or eels, or eggs and cheese, all highly seasoned. Wine flowed freely. Minor misdemeanors were punished by an assessment of wine, to be consumed by masters and fellow students. This custom, known as sconcing, still flourishes in England. At the Sorbonne a young gentleman was fined a quart of wine for beating a servant. The wine was drunk by his mates—none, apparently, by the ser-

A student librarian at Ave Maria, top, inspects the books that fellow students return. Below, students feed the college goldfinches and ring the morning bell, the duty of the first man to wake up.

vant. On feast days a fire was permitted in the English college halls, a fine dinner was served, and the undergraduates sang canticles and listened to old histories and accounts of the world's marvels.

Sports were generally forbidden, even sports watching, as well as such indecent activities as gambling, dancing, gate-crashing, and interfering with the hangman at his work. Pet dogs were banned in the English colleges on the ground that they polluted the air. But in Paris there was the curious case of a student who owned a dog named Rose: he taught her to walk on her forelegs. Another student stole her, renamed her Violet, and taught her to walk on her hind legs. The case was brought to the bishop's court; the dog decided the case, contrary to all notions of justice, one would say, by walking on her hind legs and acknowledging only the name of Violet.

On the whole, life was grim for the typical student. In Europe, it can still be grim for the poor boy, ill-fed, shivering in a dark attic room. For such the romantic charm of Paris is imperceptible. But then as now the college years remained in memory as the time of freedom, adventure, and intellectual excitement. Friends of college days were likely to remain friends for life. Petrarch, in old age, tenderly recalled to a dear companion their youthful jollities at Bologna, the "order, vigilance, and majesty" of the teachers, the lovely girls dancing in the streets, the country walks afar, the return by night, and the climbing of the crumbling city walls. "I don't think any place on earth could have been happier and freer."

Often, to be sure, the compressed spirit found its compulsive discharge in wild gaieties, in burlesques of sacred mysteries. In Paris the Feast of Fools, on the first of January, became a scandal. Young clerks masked, put on women's clothes, danced in church, sang shameful songs in the choir, rolled dice before the altar. Then they paraded through the city, uttering immodest and scurrilous words. On other occasions drunken scholars accompanied by women of the town broke into classrooms, befouling and desecrating them. The record of student misbehavior could be prolonged forever, but as a picture of normal undergraduate life it would be as false as the roseate recollections of a fond old alumnus.

Occasionally tavern brawls between student groups of different national origins, or between collegers and the townsmen and police, developed into full-blown riots. These were likely to be sanguinary, with clubs and swords taking a toll of lives. Most famous was the Oxford Battle of Saint Scholastica's Day, or the Great Slaughter of 1355. It began with a dispute over payment for bad wine in a tavern; it developed into a civil war between town and gown, with many casualties on both sides. Twenty inns were pillaged, many college halls burned. The city was put under an interdict for a year. Thereafter the mayor, bailiffs, and chief burghers were obliged to attend an annual mass of reparation on Saint Scholastica's Day and to deposit on the altar each one a penny. This humiliation was not abrogated until 1825, perhaps as a result of monetary inflation.

Among the pugnacious swaggerers of the university world were some outright criminals. We remember François Villon, Master of Arts of the University of Paris, who killed a disreputable priest in a tavern scuffle and burglarized the faculty of theology for five hundred gold crowns, an impressive sum for the treasury of any faculty of theology. The Episcopal Court of Paris in 1269 inveighed against clerks and scholars who, under pretense of leading the scholastic life, atrociously wound or kill many persons, rape women, oppress virgins, break into inns, and repeatedly commit robberies and many other enormities hateful to God. In the following century an eminent bishop made a general indictment of students. "They attend classes but make no effort to learn anything . . . They frequently learn what had better be unknown—forbidden sciences, amatory discourses, and superstitions. On obscure points they depend upon their own judgment, passing over scripture and canonical science . . . They defraud their masters of their due salaries, although they are able to pay . . . They have among themselves evil and disgraceful societies, associating together for ill . . . Sometimes they contend against and resist the officials. On feast days they don't go to church. Or if they go to church it is not for worship but to see the girls or swap stories . . . They contract debts and sometimes withdraw from the university without paying them, on which account they are excommunicated, but little they care."

The accusation is too sweeping; it proves chiefly the bishop's bile. The students probably fell into a normal distribution curve. Among them were the fakers and the show-offs, who pretended a knowledge they had not worked to gain and hence were termed feline—for a cat likes fish but shuns the river. There were the wasters, the gamblers. One such, in Paris, diced away all his clothes. His friends found him naked in bed under a dirty, ragged quilt, racing fleas down the quilt to the winning post—his emerging toe. There were the libertines, who found plenty of opportunity in bawdy Paris. An observer remarked that when a student visits a woman by night, it is not to be presumed that they are reciting the Lord's Prayer.

Chiefly there were the idlers, the incompetents, the doomed, who sang:

*Le temps s'en vient,
Et je n'ai rien fait;
Le temps revient,
Et je ne fais rien.*

Escapees from the ordered life of society, they made a virtue and a boast of their failure. They enlisted in an informal fraternity, the *Ordo Vagorum,* or Order of Tramps, a parody of a religious order. Their patron was a mythical Bishop Golias, from whom they took the name of goliards. Their classrooms were the taverns, their homes what hovels they could find. They had their own literature—rebellious, mocking songs in thumping Latin rhythms and rhyme, celebrating wine and amour. ("*Mihi est propositum/In taberna mori . . .*"—"I've myself resolved upon/Dying in a tavern . . .") Many of these songs, preserved in the recording *Carmina Burana,* have had a new life in our own time. Most of the goliards quietly disappeared or let their defiance die into conformity. Some became wandering minstrels and jesters; others ended as beggars, petty thieves, brothel keepers. The Church decreed that they should be seized, their heads shaved to eliminate the tonsure and all benefit of clergy, and that they should then be clapped in the bishops' prisons. The modern parallel to this intellectual underworld is ready to hand.

The existence of an underworld helps to clarify and define the upper world. The medieval university, despite its shortcomings, was the intellectual center of the Middle Ages. It preserved traditional learning and welcomed the new. It taught the seven ancient arts, as we still do, though we have immensely multiplied their number. While it paid homage to orthodoxy, it taught the heterodox their critical methods. It encouraged, within its set limits, free inquiry, speculation, and invention. The innovators, from Grosseteste and Bacon to Wycliffe and Hus, were university men. And the students must seem to us very recognizable, very familiar. We could live their lives, though we would have complaints; they could transfer into one of our universities without complaint.

The university was a medieval invention. There was nothing like it before, in classical antiquity or in Islam. It remains essentially unchanged in its organization, purpose, teaching methods, class routine, and even formal costume. The medieval university was half modern, and we are half medieval—that is no bad thing.

And what about Pierre and Paul, whom we seem to have forgotten? Well, Pierre eventually took his doctorate in theology. He spent many years writing a monumental treatise on prevenient grace in Aquinas's *Summa,* which has not yet found a publisher. Paul became a *doctor utriusque juris,* a doctor of both canon and civil law. He entered the service of a German prince as legal advisor. When some of his advice turned out disastrously, he was sewn in a sack and thrown into the Rhine as a kind of surprise for the next ruler down the stream.

Morris Bishop is one of Horizon's *regular contributors and the author of the forthcoming* Horizon Book of the Middle Ages, *to be published this fall.*

Medieval Universities

A PORTFOLIO WITH PHOTOGRAPHS BY ERICH LESSING

Oxford

The great institutions shown on this and the following pages remain as an abiding link between the modern world and the Middle Ages. One of the earliest, Oxford, was the unintended byproduct of royal xenophobia. During the 1160's Henry II of England ordered all overseas clerics to return home; and Englishmen at the new University of Paris, unwilling to give up their studies, made their way to Oxford, where several church schools already existed. In a brief time a "*studium generale,*" or place of general instruction, sprang up. For undergraduates Oxford must have been a harsh place to live, and conditions were not helped by the fact that the original Oxford colleges, such as Merton and Balliol, were residences reserved solely for graduate students. At that, the colleges were far from splendid until William of Wykeham founded the New College in 1379 and provided it with a superb set of buildings. The miniature at right, drawn about 1461, depicts one of William's successors, Thomas Chaundler, with his scholars and, above him, the college's Front Quad, which is still as the founder designed it.

73

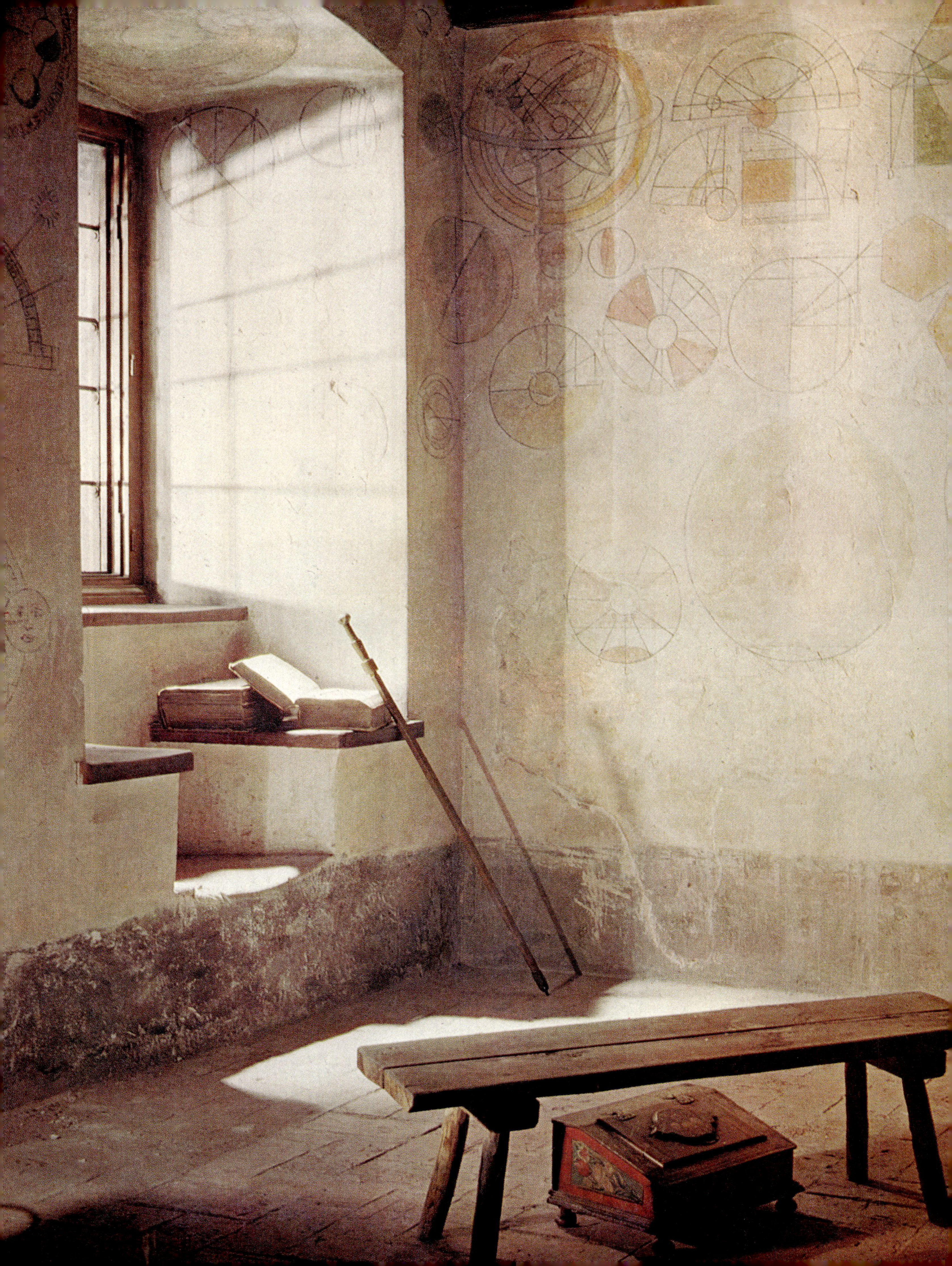

Cracow

Higher learning reached Eastern Europe in 1364 when Casimir III of Poland founded the university at Cracow, seat of the monarchy. It was called the Jagellonian University after a successor of Casimir's, a Lithuanian named Ladislas Jagello, who set it firmly on its feet in 1400 as a pious theological center largely for the benefit of Lithuanians, a people newly converted to Christianity. To this day, Madonnas are to be found in all of Cracow's old intact classrooms, including the room at left, where, in the absence of blackboards, geometry was taught from diagrams drawn on the walls. On a hard bench in a room such as this Cracow's most illustrious student, Copernicus, once sat, though the future monk may never have frequented the dim tavern below, where his fellow students caroused in the late fifteenth century.

Medieval tavern, resort of Cracow's scholars

Geometry classroom at the university

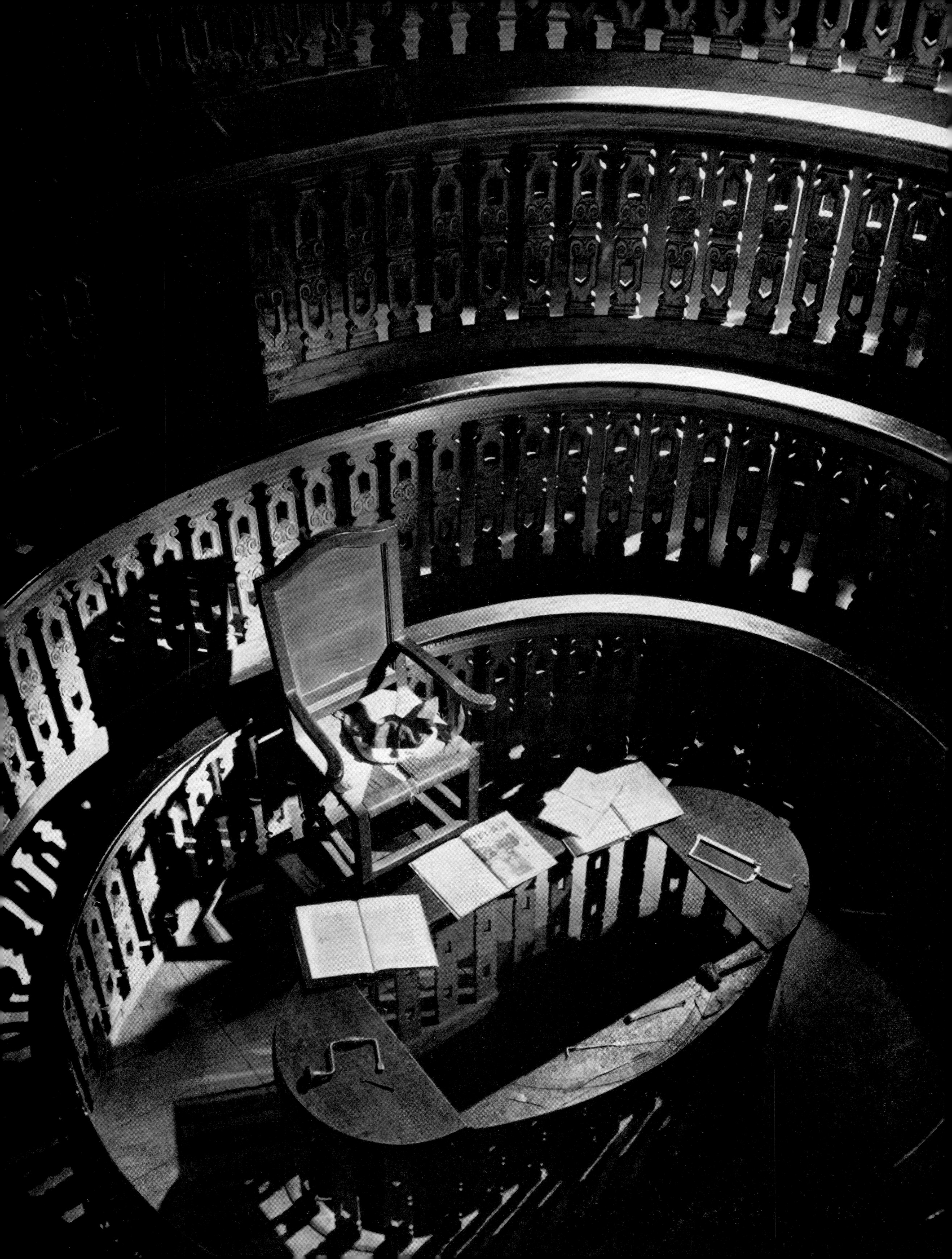

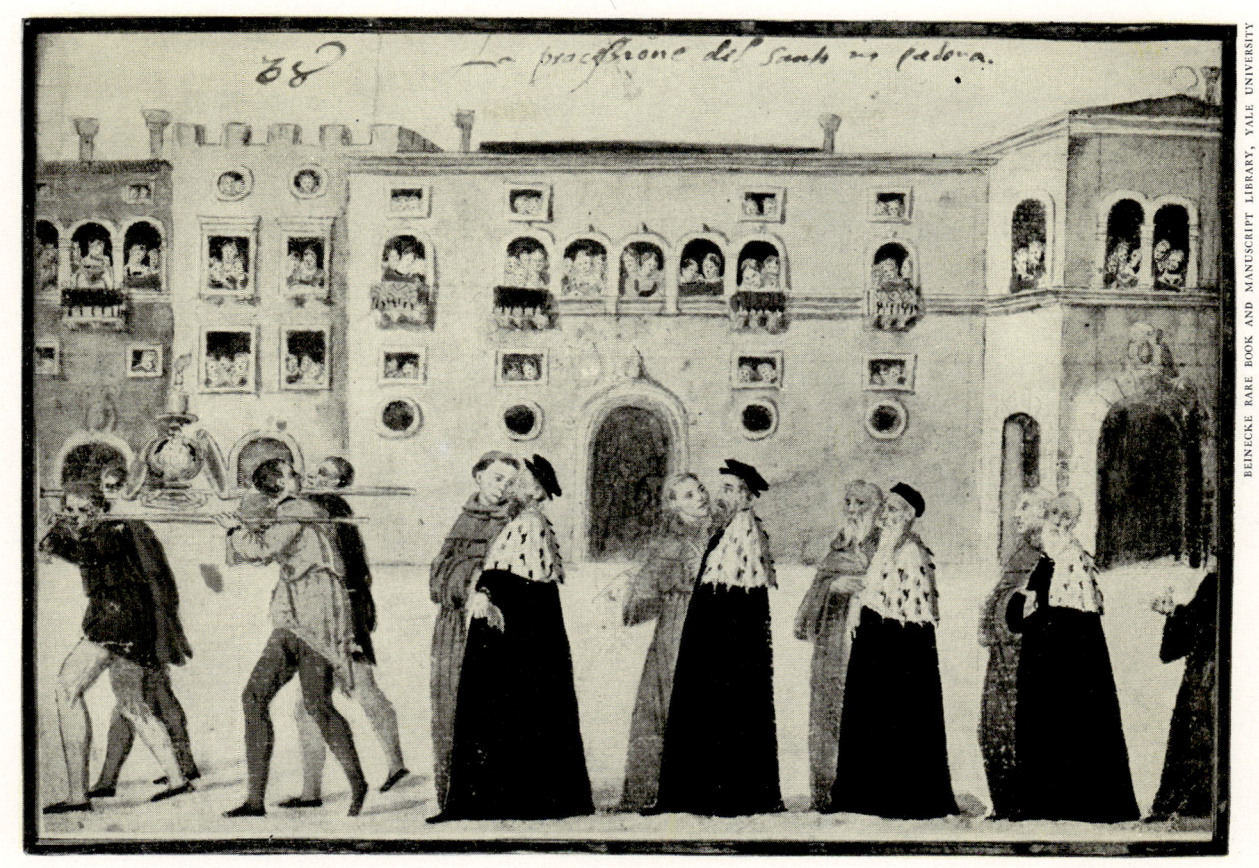

Padua's professors, with monks, in a saint's day procession

Padua

Like Oxford, the University of Padua was born with a student migration—from Bologna in 1222. Most of the migrants migrated again when they found the Paduans inhospitable, and the university did not begin to flourish until the middle of the century. Like its model, Bologna, Padua was governed by a rector (right) elected by the "nations," guilds composed of students from different national regions, such as Provence or Burgundy. Padua's heyday came in the sixteenth century when Galileo was made its professor of mathematics and the great medical amphitheatre (opposite) was built. The circular lecture hall with its deep, tiered well and its dissecting table is the oldest in existence. It has attracted, among others, such famous students as William Harvey, the discoverer of the circulation of the blood.

University rector in robes of the seventeenth century

Padua's anatomy theatre, built in 1594

77

The view from Bologna's old astronomical observatory

Bologna

Medieval students at a law lecture, probably at Bologna

The University of Bologna shares with Paris the honor of being the ancestor of all the world's universities. Both were born spontaneously, in the mid-twelfth century, of the same cause: the discovery of something esoteric to teach. The University of Paris grew up around the new study of logic; Bologna around the first medieval codification of civil and canon law. Its first students were not youths but established officials, which is perhaps why Bologna's students ruled their teachers—whereas the Paris students, being merely philosophical, were ruled by theirs.

The entrance to Padua's main auditorium, opposite, is festooned with plaques put up in honor of the leaders of student "nations"—the antecedents of modern fraternities.

AULA MAGNA

The Royal

*Patrons of porcelain:
At the top of this page,
Augustus II,
Elector of Saxony,
in red stoneware,
a material invented
at Meissen before
porcelain was perfected;
below, his son
Augustus III in true
Meissen, Madame de
Pompadour and Louis XV
(on horseback),
done at Vincennes*

Porcelain Craze

Started by Augustus the Physically Strong, it found its auctioneer in Louis XV. Rarely have useful objects displayed such beauty or commanded such prices

By J. H. PLUMB

"A porcelain factory," said Karl Eugen, Duke of Württemberg, "is an indispensable accompaniment of splendor and magnificence," and he thought that no prince of his rank could be without one, a sentiment that was echoed throughout Germany in the 1750's. Four electors —Mainz, The Palatinate, Bavaria, and Brandenburg—possessed flourishing factories, in output if not in profit, at Höchst, Frankenthal, Nymphenburg, and Berlin. The prince-bishop Heinrich von Bibra succeeded at Fulda, even though his brother ecclesiastics at Treves and Cologne failed; elsewhere dukes, princes, bishops, landgraves, and margraves were all in china, right down to the tiny principalities of Nassau-Saarbrücken and Pfalz-Zweibrücken. Most lost money, and all were overshadowed by factories supported by kings; but prestige demanded them.

The factories of kings, of course, were larger, more costly, more magnificent. The most famous of all, which belonged to Augustus the Physically Strong (his prowess derived from the boudoir, not the battlefield), Elector of Saxony and king of Poland, was established at Meissen in 1710. So famous were its wares, which for a time were unique, that it made a profit. This state of affairs did not last, because Louis XV of France sponsored a manufacture of china in Vincennes that put beauty before cost, even before the lives of its workmen, and for whose products the king himself was prepared to act as a salesman. No more magnificent and extravagantly expensive china has ever been produced in Europe than that made in France, but it had keen competition from the granddaughters of Augustus. When married off to their monarchs, they expected to have a porcelain factory near at hand; so the king of Naples set one up in Capo-di-Monte for Maria Amalia, and when they inherited Spain, they shifted it, along with their jewels and pets, to Buen Retiro, near Madrid. And Maria Anna, wife of the Elector of Bavaria, had her own factory at Nymphenburg, which was to produce some of the finest china figures of the eighteenth century. Only the English monarchy kept cautiously aloof and so avoided the appalling costs that drove Bow into bankruptcy, Longton Hall and Chelsea into closing, and Derby and Worcester close to ruin. George II, in whose reign most of these factories began, does not seem to have bothered to order either a dinner service or a suite of vases. The British royal family acted very much in character: they enjoyed their parsimony.

As with monarchs, so with their subjects, the craze bit deep. Aristocrats ordered fabulous services running to many hundreds of pieces; young English noblemen on the grand tour ransacked the fashionable Parisian china shops. They had pieces mounted in gold and silver and ormolu; they boxed their china picnic sets, even their knives and forks, in elaborate tooled leather cases lined with satin. By 1750 all Europe was in the grip of china-fever. No mania for material objects had ever been so widespread, so general to the rich of all nations; even the world beyond Europe was soon caught up in the obsession: Russians, Turks, Moguls, the emperor of China himself, wanted the porcelain of Europe.

Only once before, and curiously enough in staid, bourgeois Holland, had there been so wild a craze. In the early seventeenth century the Dutch had gone mad about tulips; bulbs soared to astronomical prices, rare specimens fetching the modern equivalent of a good Renoir. But tulip-mania rose and fell with the suddenness of a hectic fever, whereas the craze for porcelain burst like a thunderstorm that had been rumbling for days in the distant hills.

The making of porcelain began in China more than twelve hundred years ago—which is why its alternative and more common name has always been china. It was harder and more vitreous than other forms of pottery. It could be made thinner, molded into more delicate shapes, and given a more brilliant glaze. Its secret lay in the special clay from which it was made—kaolin.

A few pieces of china had crept into Europe in the late middle ages, but they were inconceivably rare and little appreciated. In the early Renaissance they became somewhat more common. Some of the brilliant blue-and-white Ming porcelain reached Italy, and it could be a piece of this superlative china that is depicted in Bellini's *Feast of the Gods*. The first clouds of the coming storm began to gather shortly after the Spanish discoveries of the New World had reached across the Pacific to the Philippines. Along with Inca gold and the bright feathered garments of the Aztecs, the Spaniards sent crates of brilliant Ming china in their great galleons going to Europe. Usually this was the common but very handsome blue-and-white ware that China exported to the East. Common in China, it was rare in Europe, rare and beautiful and desirable, fit for monarchs and noblemen but well beyond bourgeois dreams. The Dutch, precariously poised in Japan in the early seventeenth century, imported more, but not enough to meet the demand, and when they lost their foothold, the supply became uncertain for a time. But the demand grew insatiable. The Dutch at Delft made some splendid imitations in pottery, but pottery was not porcelain: it lacked the glittering whiteness, the sharpness, the splendid enamel glaze; also it chipped easily. The obsession for true china was becoming a mania. The holds of the great East Indiamen were crammed with it: one ship alone unloaded 146,748 pieces in 1700. Yet this was a mere sop. The market knew no bounds as the obsession to possess china seized the rich. Naturally men dreamed of making it, for a fortune awaited anyone who could rival the Chinese. Jesuits, keenly alert to Eu-

This lavishly decorated fountain bowl, painted at Meissen about 1727 in the manner of J. G. Herold, is an example of the chinoiserie *that owed its inspiration to imports from China. The bowl at right is in a silver-gilt mount.*

Seventeenth-century Chinese teacups

Sixteenth-century Ming bowl

rope's need, penetrated into Ching-tê-chèn, the great manufacturing center for exports, and sent back a report on how it was made, but mixed up the names of the clays—which did not matter so very much, since no one knew what the names meant anyway.

At this time there were throughout Europe alchemists seeking vainly to transmute base metal into gold. One of these, Johann Friedrich Böttger, was persuaded that porcelain, if he could make it, would be worth as much as gold, perhaps more. He joined forces with a scientist of repute, Walther von Tschirnhausen; luck favored them, for they found the most important of all the ingredients for porcelain—kaolin—near Meissen in Saxony, close to Dresden. By 1710 they had produced a hard china, indeed one so hard that it could be cut and polished like a jewel. The quest was over, and the storm burst. The factory under the patronage of Augustus the Physically Strong was established at Meissen, and its wares were soon intoxicating Europe.

Of all the monumentally self-indulgent kings and princelings of the eighteenth century, Augustus, hereditary Elector of Saxony and elected king of Poland, was the most fabulous. He was a short, square-shouldered, thick-necked bull of a man with a vast, powerful face. Immensely strong, he could crush iron horseshoes in one hand, jingling a bag of gold in the other, a feat that he often performed to impress the ladies; obvious and vulgar though it may have been, the trick paid excellent dividends, for toward the end of his life there were three hundred and fifty-five official bastards on the government books. A man of such formidable appetite could scarcely be delicate in the choice of food for its appeasement, and it might have been easy to write off Augustus as a tough stud-animal but for his obsession with china, which led him not only to patronize Böttger but also to create by his sympathetic interest much of the style of early Meissen.

Augustus, more pleased with his china than with his children, decided to create a porcelain palace, with rooms lined with porcelain as a setting for enormous vases, huge figures of animals, and life-sized figures of the Apostles—all in china. Almost certainly he had heard of the great porcelain tower at Nanking and wished to rival it. In order to cope with this challenge three first-class modelers were employed, the most distinguished of whom was Johann Joachim Kaendler. Some huge animals and birds, not entirely successful, and a vast quantity of Ali Baba-like vases of considerable merit were produced; but the value of the experiment was that it enabled Kaendler, a man of real artistic genius who was to prove himself to be the Bernini of porcelain, to explore the range and plasticity of the material. He discovered an individualistic style of modeling and the scale that was appropriate to his medium. Like many men of strong creative imagination, Kaendler's output was very large. He produced hundreds of models—peasants, miners, tyrolean dancers, groups of lovers, animals (almost a zoo of them)—but he returned time and time again to the tragicomic figure of Harlequin and the other characters of the *commedia dell' arte*, whose hold on the imagination of Europe at this time was like that of Charlie Chaplin in our own. It was Kaendler more than any other modeler who seized on the artistic possibilities of china and es-

83

tablished the porcelain figure as one of the minor decorative arts of the West. He has rarely been equaled.

These were the great creative years of Meissen, for besides Kaendler there was J. G. Herold, who began to paint naturalistic harbor scenes in silhouette, and Adam von Löwenfinck, possibly the most original of all china decorators, who developed a weird personal vision of Cathay in which fabulous animals gamboled with strange Chinese figures—Chinamen that existed only in the European imagination. The final achievement of this crucial period was the discovery of a magnificent range of ground colors—lavender, yellow, sea green, and puce; these were used with the decorative panels for the great vases that adorned Augustus's Japanese palace.

Much of the early production at Meissen reached a high level of taste, but there were times when imagination ran out and the plasticity of the material took control. Then strange monstrosities were born, like the absurd teapots modeled in the form of a cockerel being ridden by a Chinaman, or a monkey suckling its young; such excruciating lapses in taste occur again and again in the German factories but rarely in the French.

The triumph of Augustus's factory was the envy and delight of Europe: orders poured in from Edinburgh, Moscow, Stockholm, and Cádiz. Meissen china, usually called Dresden in England and *Saxe* in France, became the rage, and no aristocratic drawing room was complete without a vase, a figure, or a dish; the fabulously rich began to eat off it, drink from it, wash in it, even spit in it. Silver was banished as a commonplace. The market boomed, and jealous eyes grew beady: spies, *agents-provocateurs*, blackmailers, and seducers began to lurk about Meissen; in our own day only top-level nuclear physicists have been prone to such temptations as were offered the "arcanists" of Meissen. These men who knew the secrets of porcelain making proved human. As early as 1719 a runaway Meissen workman, Samuel Stölzel, had sold his secrets to Claudius du Paquier in Vienna. Paquier produced a glaze inferior to that of Meissen—it is so greenish-toned that some historians refuse to believe that it is based on the Meissen formula and regard it as a separate creation— but Paquier decorated his pieces with such panache that they now command staggering prices. After Stölzel's defection, security was redoubled, and all arcanists were carefully watched and rigorously disciplined. No further leakage of secrets took place.

Indeed, Meissen, and to a far lesser extent Vienna, had a monopoly of the market—their only rivals Oriental imports—until the 1750's, when, as in a cheap novelette, a wicked arcanist, Jakob Ringler, secured the friendship of du Paquier's daughter, persuaded her to betray the factory's secrets, then bolted. He tried to set up a factory at Künersberg, failed, and moved to Höchst, where he succeeded. Realizing he was in possession of a gold mine, he moved on to Strasbourg and sold the secrets to the great ceramist Paul-Antoine Hannong (who was afterward banished by Louis XV and took the hard-paste formula to Frankenthal). In the meantime, with the bit now between his teeth, Ringler moved on to Bavaria (Nymphenburg), then to Württemberg (Ellwangen and Schrezheim), and finally settled down at Ludwigsburg, where he remained manager for the rest of the century. Like some virus, he had spread porcelain factories throughout Germany; his associates completed what he had started, and by 1760 there was scarcely a waldgrave who had not got a porcelain factory under his patronage— and usually subsidized by his peasants.

This rage for a factory was not due to Augustus the Physically Strong, nor even to the beauty of Meissen; it was due to the fact that Louis XV, the arbiter of Europe's taste, had given the royal imprimatur to porcelain. Indeed, Louis had done more than this. He did not think it beneath his dignity to conduct personally an annual sale of his factory's products. At the end of each year, spread out on trestles in the splendid galleries of Versailles, were rows of plates, cups and saucers, soup tureens, *pots de chambres*, vases, eye baths, watering cans, ewers, and basins from his factory at Sèvres. The courtiers had to buy: the monarch acted as auctioneer. Nothing better indicates the reverence, the idolatry, that the European aristocracy lavished on china than that the Most Christian King, who could not socially meet a bourgeois, should have been willing to act as its huckster.

What he sold, however, was not the hard-paste porcelain from China or Meissen. It was more curious, more beautiful, much more expensive—not only in materials but in men who succumbed to the deadly diseases of silicosis and lead poisoning that its manufacture engendered. It was nearer to glass than Meissen was, the soft paste holding the clay in suspension. The softness of texture, however, absorbed colors more successfully than Meissen. Often it achieved a quite dazzling whiteness, and the glaze possessed an unmatchable brilliance. It easily went wrong in the firing, warping and cracking and breaking up in the kilns, yet the factory and the king insisted on perfection; in consequence the wastage was fantastic. It was, therefore, as it has remained, the most expensive porcelain ever produced in

Exoticism in porcelain: this white elephant bearing three soldiers with Roman helmets was created by Johann Joachim Kaendler, presiding genius at Meissen from 1731 to 1775. It is thirteen inches tall.
TUCK COLL., MUSEE DE PETIT PALAIS, PARIS

84

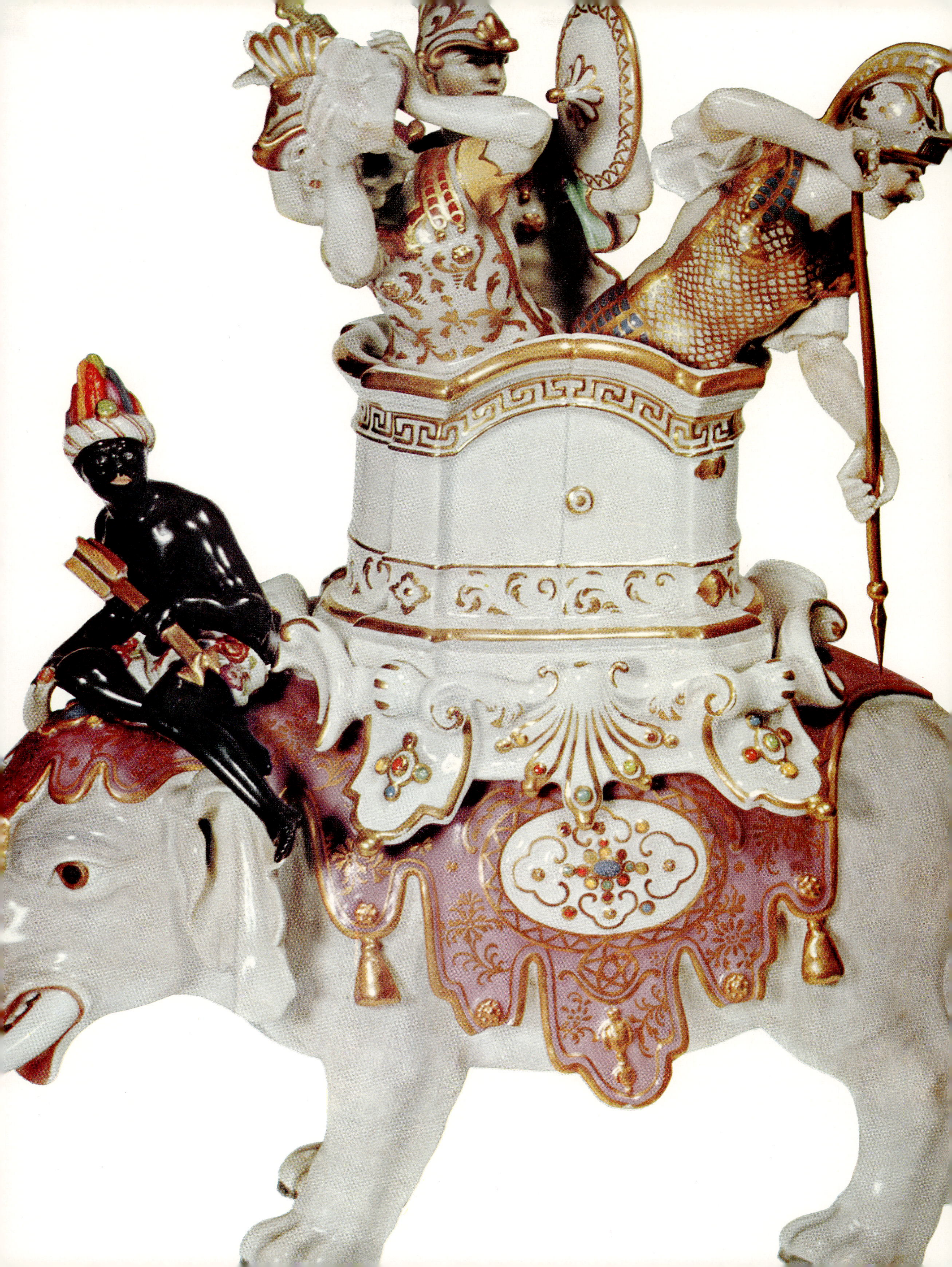

Porcelain in France

French porcelain, the pampered child of Louis XV and Madame de Pompadour, came into its heyday first at Vincennes and after 1756 at Sèvres, which was by edict the Royal Manufactory of Porcelain. In its elegance of decoration and the brilliance of its colors Sèvres surpassed all other porcelains. Louis himself owned the factory, and with his help Sèvres could claim such regal patrons as Catherine the Great, who owned the soup tureen shown opposite.

The bourdalou, a small oval-shaped chamber pot, was carried by a maid for her mistress when she went to church; it owes its name to a particularly long-winded preacher, Père Louis Bourdaloue.

Sèvres bowl with porcelain flowers

Coffer with Sèvres plaques, c. 1775

Europe. Known first as Vincennes, it was called Sèvres after the factory was moved to a royal château in 1756.

Of course the French had been trying to make porcelain for a long time. The proper clay, kaolin, eluded them for the best part of a century, but they had stumbled on soft paste, first at Rouen, then at Saint-Cloud, near Paris. But the paste was poor, the designs imitative. In the collector's eye they have a certain charm, but the products were primitive, in a sense amateurish. Under the protection of two great aristocrats, the Prince de Condé and the Duc de Villeroi, Chantilly and Mennecy did better. Many of their products have both charm and technical excellence, but they did not rival Meissen; indeed they never reached beyond the quality of a minor German factory.

That the French did in the end secure a factory that surpassed Meissen was due to Louis XV and his exquisite, sensitive mistress, Madame de Pompadour; cool, extravagant, far better at the decorative than the amorous arts, she dictated French taste. The manuacture of soft paste of high quality had already begun when Madame de Pompadour's interest was first aroused, but it was failing through lack of funds. The management was changed, royal funds soon flowed; the royal cipher, interlaced L's, was allowed to be stamped on the ware to proclaim Louis XV's interest. Great artists, including François Boucher, were persuaded to design for Vincennes, and the royal goldsmith was commanded to put all his technical knowledge at the factory's disposal. All other factories were forbidden to use gold. These Draconian measures produced immediate and startling success.

In 1747 Vincennes was producing rather indifferent imitations of Chantilly and occasionally even attempting an exact copy of Meissen. By 1750 it had found a style sophisticated, rich, and attuned to its material in a way that has scarcely been equaled. No factory ever achieved such beauty of color, and that includes those in China and Japan.

Vincennes took Europe by storm. The purity of its whiteness surpassed the famous blanc de chine of Fukien. Its glaze possessed a brilliance equal to that of Meissen, but its real triumph lay in the extraordinary way the body absorbed and held color, giving a softness and a depth that Meissen could never equal. And to proclaim its royal protection, Vincennes now used gold in superb profusion. Cups and saucers, even spittoons and chamber pots, were festooned with it. But Vincennes was fragile, very hard to make; the process was slow and expensive. Moreover, Vincennes, or Sèvres, possessed certain limitations—limitations that the collector has turned to great advantage. The clay, unlike that of Meissen, did not lend itself to large figures or groups of figures. They were attempted and made for some years in a brilliant white glaze—some of the most perfect objects ever made in china—but the wastage was so prodigious that often only two or three copies of these exceptionally beautiful objects were successfully made. Fewer survive, and competition for them is savage. As soon as the technicians succeeded in producing figures in an unglazed china, called biscuit, they stopped making the white glaze figures. This biscuit, which makes the china look much more like marble or stone, became immensely popular, and François Boucher designed a number of models that were afterward executed by Etienne Falconet. Though the Victorians collected biscuit with passion,

BOWL AND BOURDALOU: THE ANTIQUE CO. OF N.Y., INC. (INCORPORATING THE ANTIQUE PORCELAIN CO.); TUREEN: METROPOLITAN MUSEUM OF ART, GIFT OF R. THORNTON WILSON, 1950, IN MEMORY OF FLORENCE ELLSWORTH WILSON; CANDLESTICK, DINNER PLATE, AND WATERING CAN: MUSEE DE LA MANUFACTURE NATIONALE DE SEVRES; "RAISIN EATERS:" COLL. J. H. PLUME ESQ.

Catherine's tureen, Vincennes

Dinner plate, Sèvres, 1772

"Raisin Eaters," white glaze, Vincennes

Candlestick, Vincennes, 1753

Bourdalou, Sèvres

Watering can, Vincennes, 1755

Potpourri vase, Sèvres, c. 1760

modern taste turned away from it; only in the past two years has the tide turned once more, and the prices of biscuit have begun to soar.

But the glory of Sèvres lay in its useful wares—in its chocolate cups, its teapots, its toilet basins, butter dishes, soup tureens, and needle cases; indeed, every simple object that could be made in china was—even absurd little watering cans, so that a marquise might sprinkle a rose growing in a Sèvres pot. Never have men and women eaten from, or for that matter spat into, such exquisite china. Madame de Pompadour ordered an entire conservatory of china flowers. It cost nearly a million livres. Emperors, kings, and princes ordered colossal services. Catherine the Great's service cost more than three hundred thousand livres (in modern money, about nine hundred thousand dollars). Even Ch'ien Lung, the Chinese emperor, deigned to accept from Louis XV a vast service, and along with it some remarkable vases to be used as centerpieces. Rarely have objects of utility been either so expensive or so beautiful.

The ground colors surpassed all but the rarest of Meissen shades—lavender and puce. They possessed, moreover, a softness, a richness, a luster, that the Meissen lacked. The colors at first were simple deep blues splashed thickly and absorbed unevenly so that the result possessed the texture and highlights of velvet. The same effect was achieved a little later with apple green; but more sumptuous, and more expensive still, was turquoise, or *bleu céleste;* rarer and extravagantly difficult to achieve in pure color was yellow, the light daffodil yellow. But rarest of all was pink, made only for a few years and associated with Madame de Pompadour. Pink proved almost impossible to make—it so easily strayed into orange or purple, thus creating an unpleasingly harsh ground. The consequence was a dearth of pink. When it was successful, a color was produced that no other factory could rival. There was never enough, and collectors have sought it and paid wild prices for it. Today a pair of pink ice-cups fit only for midgets will cost with luck thirty-five hundred dollars at an auction and may be three times as expensive in a shop—if they can be found. A large piece will command as much as fifty to a hundred thousand dollars. And yellow, turquoise, and green are not far behind.

Colored pieces were usually inset with painted decorative panels that ran along a few popular themes. Birds —sometimes copied from beautifully printed plates of exotic (often just imagined) birds of South America— festooned cups, plates, dishes, vases of all kinds. Two painters, Aloncle and Evans, excelled at toucans, parrots, orioles, and birds of paradise, which were shown preening themselves or swooping improbably through the air. Flowers, of course, were the most common theme of all, developing from the rather slavishly copied botanical specimens that the artists at Meissen favored to splendid sprays of garden flowers scattered in stylized abandon across the surface of a plate or cup. But perhaps the most successful theme of decoration was children, drawn usually from sketches by Boucher—sometimes clothed, often naked. They sprawled on clouds, bottoms up, a wicked glint in the eye, playing the most improbable instruments; or, clothed like miniature adults, they chased birds, pushed wheelbarrows, watered flowers, bowled hoops—but always with a charm, a lightness, a gaiety, that removed them at once from the heavy and rather puddingy imitations that the Meissen factory was forced to make.

In brilliance of color, in splendor of decoration, in lavishness of gold, and in almost intolerable expense Sèvres outdistanced all of its rivals and in the 1750's and '60's dominated the taste of Europe. The great French cabinetmakers not only used it for table tops but also inserted plaques in the friezes of tables, *secretaires*, consoles, and corner cupboards and at times produced articles that seemed at first sight to consist of nothing but china set in ormolu.

But Sèvres, except for biscuit, could not make figures—the porcelain was too soft for the sharp, certain edges that figures required, and the factory never attempted to rival Meissen. However, the lesser German factories did, and many of them had their chance when the Seven Years' War hindered production at Meissen. Few matched the achievement of Kaendler, but Simon Feilner was successful at Frankenthal (a set of his Italian comedy figures was sold at auction a few years ago for forty-five thousand dollars). Only one modeler—Franz Anton Bustelli—surpassed Kaendler and Feilner. Bustelli, a Swiss from Locarno, has claims to be the only creative genius, apart from Kaendler, who has worked in china, the only one to realize completely both the possibilities and the limitations of the material and at the same time stamp it with his own unmistakable and remarkable style. His vapid, pinheaded creatures, of astonishing elegance, which he made simply with swiftly moving converging planes, linger in the memory as few other porcelain figures do. They lack the strength, the vigor, the humanity, of Kaendler at his best; but these very qualities of Kaendler's drive out of one's mind the fact that his pieces are of china; whereas with Bustelli one is always conscious of the fragility of the materials. About Bustelli there is a touch of Mozart—the elegance, the harmony, a hint of the tragedy that time holds for all men. Their success may be measured by the fact that since the day they were made they have never been out of fashion. They have been for nearly two centuries the prized possessions of museums and collectors. Now, like the impressionists, only millionaires can really afford them.

Bustelli came at the time when the great period of porcelain making was drawing to a close. The wonder and excitement of the new material grew stale with use: the severe standards of neoclassicism checked the exuberance of the rich, rioting, rococo style, which might have been invented for the wilder fantasies of porcelain. Also Josiah Wedgwood moved in: not only could he mass-produce but also his creation of jasperware was exceptionally well adapted to the neoclassic style with its formalized friezes of Muses or Grecian dancers. All too soon the modelers and painters of Sèvres were slavishly copying his models. With Wedgwood's technique pottery was thought to rival china in beauty, at half or a quarter of the expense. The result was that the mantelpieces, the occasional tables, and the dining rooms of the middle classes rivaled those in the mansions of the aristocracy.

The cult of porcelain persisted; indeed it has never died, but it has never achieved the ingenuity, the excitement, or the sheer exuberance of its early period. The circumstances of its development were curiously appropriate; at that time the fashionable world was enthralled by China—its mystery, its sophistication, its philosophy, as well as its crafts. Indeed writers and artists combined to create a vision of Cathay that first enticed, then seduced, the Western world. The triumph of porcelain manufacture occurred when Europe, particularly France, had reached a standard of excellence in the decorative arts achieved in no other time or place except in Mandarin China. The European aristocrats of the eighteenth century were closely tied together, certain of their taste, and possessed of an attitude toward the patronage of the arts that arose not only from their education but also from the very idea of themselves as gentlemen. That the cup that touched their lips should be an object of exquisite beauty aroused no thoughts of effeminacy, or even of connoisseurship or dilettantism; it was merely fitting, its expense a matter of pride. It would be useless to deny the self-indulgence, the indifference to poverty and to the pain and suffering of their fellow men, of the society that gave birth to porcelain, but as time passes, works of art disentangle themselves from their age and live serenely for other times and other men.

J. H. Plumb, HORIZON's *European Consulting Editor, has his own fine collection of Vincennes and Sèvres porcelain.*

The figurine of Leda above, a character from the commedia dell' arte, *was made by the great Franz Anton Bustelli, master modeler of lissome rococo figures. The Harlequin opposite is one of the masterworks of Kaendler, who created the art of modeling porcelain figures.*

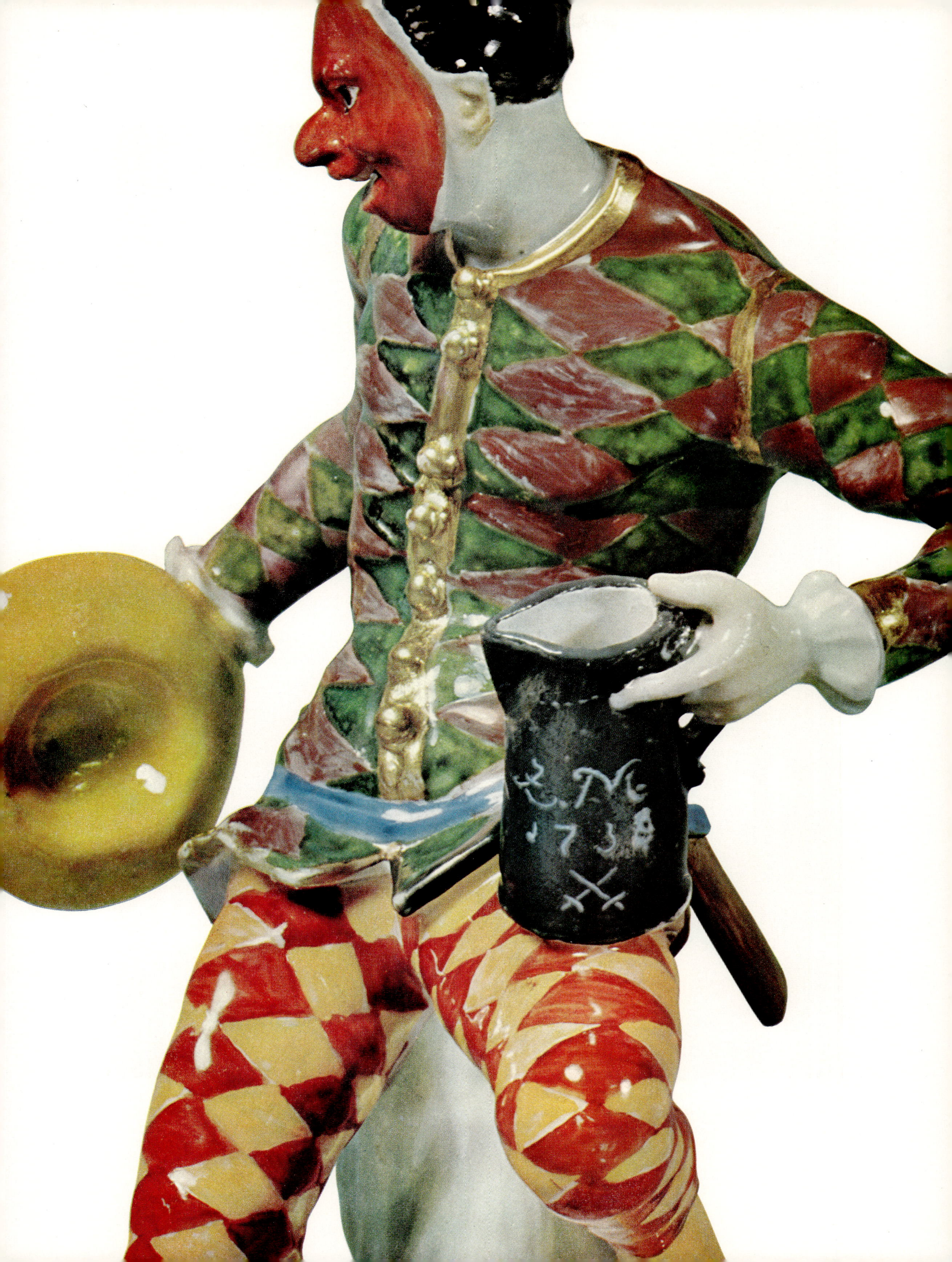

Goya painted this portrait of Don Manuel Osorio, son of a nobleman, about 1788. A serene epitome of childhood—and yet, what of the cats staring so fixedly at the magpie? Soon such disquieting effects would dominate his work.

GREAT ARTISTS AND THEIR WORLDS

GOYA AND HORROR

In his early, brilliant years as a court painter, hints of evil lurked
in the background of his rococo pictures. After his illness
they burst forth in a swirling, screaming apocalypse of Black Painting

Of all the great masters of the past to be claimed as ancestor by modern artists, Goya is easily the favorite. Romantics are nourished by his violence; realists point out that in a time of artificialities he found his point of departure not in formulas but in the streets; social rebels or painters of social consciousness feel that they are the descendants of Goya the liberal thinker, who drew and painted his indictments instead of writing them down; fantasists recognize a kinship with a master of nightmare. And even artists who have renounced the pictorial image, or at least one large school of them, can seize upon passages in his late work as approximations or prophecies of the abstract-expressionist aesthetic.

And yet Goya is also the antithesis of all these modernisms. He was a first-rate rococo decorator; in many portraits he revealed himself as the natural follower of Velázquez's baroque tradition. It is never safe to stand in front of a Goya and exclaim over its beauties, its power, and its significance from any standard preconception of what his art is all about.

Goya's life was split in two near its midpoint by an illness that very nearly killed him when he was forty-six years old. If he had died, he would have left a large body of work establishing him as one of Spain's finest artists and its only great representative of the eighteenth-century style. But he lived, and the traumatic experience released powers never before fully expressed. During the latter half of his life, Goya became the genius we think of him as having been from the first. In this late blooming he is exceptional among painters, whose mature work is usually prefigured in their early paintings.

Francisco José de Goya y Lucientes was born in Fuendetodos, near Saragossa, in 1746, the son of a gilder. By the time he was fourteen he was apprenticed to a painter named José Luzán, who followed the Neapolitan baroque formulas. Luzán was not much of a painter, and it would probably be forcing a point to believe he had much lasting influence on Goya, though the black-shadowed Neapolitan manner can be traced as a persistent and eventually triumphant factor in Goya's stylistic development.

In his teens Goya was probably executing small commissions in the churches of Saragossa. Legend has created a sympathetic picture of the young Goya as a fine, vigorous, free-loving, joyfully battling son of the Spanish soil, untainted by the degeneracy of the aristocracy. His letters show that he loved bullfights and street festivals. But an occasional biographer rejects the honest-and-earthy ideal picture for one that shows a quarrelsome, undisciplined, and uneducated youth at the mercy of his emotions. His reason for leaving town for Madrid in 1763 may or may not have had to do with certain complications, including knifings, that resulted from amorous adventures. Ambition would have supplied just as reasonable a stimulus for his departure, since Goya

Goya, in a melancholy self-portrait painted in 1815 when he was sixty-nine years old.

By JOHN CANADAY

FAMILY AND FRIENDS

The unrivaled Spanish portraitist of his time, Goya was known chiefly for his official paintings of the royal family and their court—whom he viewed with an aloof, businesslike, and often disapproving eye. But his portraits of his own family and friends reveal a more affectionate side. A few are grouped here: a demure young lady who is thought to be his wife; his brother-in-law, Francisco Bayeu, the academic painter who secured him his first important commission, in 1774; an architect acquaintance of later years; his only surviving child, Xavier, and his grandson, Mariano, heir to Goya's villa, "Deaf Man's House."

Goya's wife, Josefa Bayeu

Josefa's brother, Francisco

had a fantastic capacity for work—a really compulsive need to keep at it—and a great respect for money.

In Madrid Goya, not quite eighteen, competed for a scholarship to the Royal Academy, which he failed to win. He entered the studio of Francisco Bayeu, tried for the scholarship and failed again, and then went to Italy, visiting Rome and submitting a painting (now lost, but praised at the time) to the Parma Academy. He is said to have covered part of his expenses by traveling with a company of bullfighters.

Probably discouraged by his reception in Madrid, he returned to Saragossa. Records of his commissions show that he did quite well there, but he could not have helped feeling restless and cramped. He remedied this. In 1773, when he was twenty-seven years old, he made a trip to Madrid to marry Bayeu's sister, Josefa, and in short order was back in the capital to stay. Bayeu recommended him to the Royal Tapestry Factory of Santa Barbara as a designer. Goya and Josefa began their life in Madrid in Bayeu's house, and their first son was born there in 1775. In thirty-nine years she bore at least five—and perhaps as many as twenty—children, only one of whom is known to have survived.

For ten years or so, Goya's cartoons —the completed paintings on which the tapestries were based—were his major work, although he also did some engraving and began his career as a portraitist. There had not been a Spanish painter of consequence for the hundred years since Velázquez, and hardly even a first-rate follower of the foreign artists, mostly French, who were imported by the Spanish court.

But there had been one sparkling exception: the great Tiepolo had come to Spain in 1762 and had worked at court for the last eight years of his life. His tradition was carried on, though reduced in force, by his son Lorenzo and was Goya's point of departure for the tapestries.

It was the late rococo tradition of lightness and gaiety but without the allegorical pegs that ordinarily supported rococo fancies. Goya brought to it a new emphasis on the informal, even the bohemian, life of Madrid, a life that had a literary counterpart in popular farces and satires and had a precedent, for that matter, in Bayeu's tapestry designs, which show an interest in genre subjects. But Goya intruded a sinister note now and then: a cloaked figure, easily linked to the maskers at play in the work of Tiepolo and other Venetians, changes character inexplicably and becomes a threatening presence at the revel or the picnic.

During this period Goya quarreled with his brother-in-law over a division of authority in a dual commission in the Saragossa cathedral, and lost the argument. Leaving some work unfinished, he went back to Madrid, his professional and personal relationship with Bayeu violently ruptured. But in the meantime Goya had found a new teacher. Having access to the royal collections, he had discovered Velázquez, who became, in effect, his first master in portraiture.

The quarrel with Bayeu was patched up a few years later, but Goya, who was by now beginning to outdistance his first sponsor, was probably relieved to be rid of him for a while. Goya was in good favor at court and was doing well at countering the intrigues that, naturally, began to be perpetrated against him. So much is made of Goya's humanity, his liberal aesthetic and social conscience, his independence and his fearlessness, that we forget how many years he had to spend in winning a position that enabled him to indulge in these virtues.

He was nagged by an insecurity left over from his early poverty, and he could be irascible, envious, and merciless with an opponent over a

Tiburcio Perez, an architect

Goya's son, Xavier

Goya's grandson, Mariano

small point. Impatient by nature, often rude by impulse, he worked hard at curbing his temper before influential patrons whom he despised. Little by little, Madrid fell to him. In 1780 he was elected to the Royal Academy. In 1785 he was given the position, though an unimportant one, of Deputy Director of Painting at the academy. The next year he was named Painter to the King—of which there were a generous number—and then in 1789 he became Painter of the Household to Charles IV. There were other honors to be won, but it was already apparent that Goya was the leading Spanish painter, no matter how many functionaries among his colleagues might nominally outrank him. And as an unrivaled portraitist he was making money.

This was the situation in 1792 when an illness that has never been satisfactorily identified struck him. For more than a year he could not paint. He was left stone deaf, but this isolating misfortune apparently crystallized and released the genius that had been checked by a fuller contact with the world. A new Goya emerged—Goya the humane and bitter social observer, the scourging and despairing delineator of vice and cruelty, the fantasist whose pictured nightmares explored the most desperate realities.

At the Spanish court Goya was advantageously placed to observe vicious frailties at their most extreme. At the time that he became Painter of the Household, Charles IV had just succeeded to the throne in place of his imbecile elder brother. Charles himself, if not an imbecile, was a simpleton. His queen was the monstrous Maria Luisa of Parma, a dissolute and unsightly woman whose bed was occasionally shared by well-muscled stable boys but whose official lover was an ambitious army officer, five years her junior, named Manuel de Godoy. He was well paid for his services: Charles relinquished not only his wife but virtual control of the government to Godoy, appointing him Prime Minister in 1792. Between them, combining stupidity with corruption, Maria Luisa and Godoy managed to involve Spain in a series of debacles that ultimately led to the Franco-Spanish defeat at Trafalgar.

Goya observed these repellent creatures as individual beings rather than as the disastrous social and political powers that they were; his portraits of them so reveal their grotesqueness that it is hard to see how the subjects could have tolerated them. Blinded by vanity, these freaks were probably flattered by Goya's accurate reflection of the images they knew in the mirror.

But if he saw vice, corruption, and foolishness in high places, Goya, unlike many of his contemporaries in France and England, did not discover a compensatory nobility in the common man. His first great etchings, the set of eighty called *Los Caprichos* (*Caprices*), are fantastic visions of universal greed, vanity, superstition, and cruelty—personifications of stupidity that were the Four Horsemen of Goya's own apocalypse. His friends in Madrid were the intellectuals who represented the Enlightenment, the triumph of reason. But he seldom shows reason or truth as anything but hard-pressed. Vice and folly are the victors in a war that they do not even bother to wage, so negligible are the positive forces in human nature pitted against them.

In *Los Caprichos* Goya continued to find inspiration in the foibles of city life, but the sinister hints that he had introduced earlier in such subjects now became the main theme. His nightmares anticipate a concept of society familiar to our own times: that of a precarious structure held together by a thin skin of conventions that the irrational pressures motivating all of us may cause to burst at any moment.

This was a very great extension of the first, tentative suggestion—made by such eighteenth-century occultists as Swedenborg, Martínez Pasqualis, Mesmer, and others—that the world of dreams can reveal truths that we have concealed from ourselves.

The *Caprichos*, among the first etchings to be done with aquatint, were completed between 1796 and 1798 and were put on sale as a book the following year. They had begun to take shape in the form of sketchbooks, particularly one called the *Madrid Sketchbook*, soon after Goya's recovery from his illness. In the silent, isolated world that the artist now inhabited, his observations of city life shifted from genre, satire, or burlesque into a bitter depiction of the nature of society. This new mood must have puzzled, even if it did not shock, a public that had never seen anything like the *Caprichos* before.

Only twenty-seven sets were sold in fifteen days, and the prints were withdrawn from the market. Their poor public reception may not have been the only reason. The Inquisition perhaps insisted on the withdrawal, or it may have been done as a matter of precaution in anticipation of such a demand. The *Caprichos* included monks and priests among the devilish and folly-ridden assembly, and Goya was denounced by the authorities of the church. But with his talent for skirting disaster, he managed to turn the incident to his advantage. He made a gift of the plates to the king—who returned the favor by granting a yearly pension to Goya's son, Francisco Xavier.

At about the time that he began work on the *Caprichos* Goya also began his famous but always somewhat ambiguous affair with the Duchess of Alba, probably the most vivid figure that her society produced. In 1795 (Goya was just a year short of that sobering birthday, his fiftieth) she visited his studio, as we know from a coarse reference he made to the incident in a letter. The duke died the following year, and whether or not the affair had begun during her husband's lifetime, it continued until the duchess's death in 1802.

The Duchess of Alba was a spirited and capricious beauty, and her liaison with Goya opens the door to all manner of romantic speculation. A sophisticate who had every handsome young buck in Madrid at her feet, she chose as her lover a stocky, coarse-featured commoner—in his middle age and stone deaf. In spite of his association with aristocrats and intellectuals, Goya had never taken on much polish. His letters are crudely written. His manner of expression, while cogent, remained that of a countryman. He seems to have had no elegance. But he had force. Whatever the details and the satisfactions of their relationship, Goya and the duchess were lovers, and when they could they left Madrid for her estate in Andalusia.

Goya left an ambiguous comment on the affair in the form of a portrait of the duchess (see cover painting) wearing two large rings, one of them bearing Goya's name and the other her husband's. While looking the observer straight in the face, she points at an inscription scratched in the earth at her feet (see detail below). "*Solo Goya*," it says—"Goya only"—presumably referring to the death of the duke. The inscription was revealed by a recent cleaning, and there are questions as to whether it was part of the original scheme and when and why it was painted out. In odd ways Goya and his duchess have maintained for posterity a remarkable privacy concerning their liaison. We know hardly anything more about it than that, in one form or another, it existed.

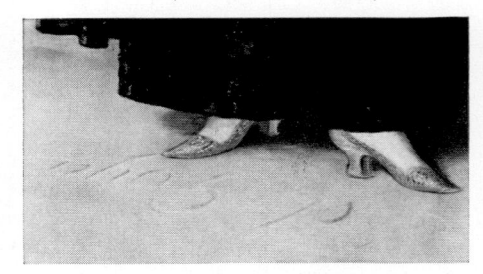

As he entered his sixties, Goya's isolation from the world in which he still seemed to move so freely was increased by factors other than his deafness. In the final stage of its dissolution as a great power, Spain was in a state of political and social chaos. The libertarian idealists made temporarily effective forays against the regime—and were repeatedly and mercilessly repressed. Some of Goya's friends were imprisoned or exiled. Goya had not yet made any overt political statements in his art and was in an equivocal position. As the first artist of the court, working primarily as a portraitist, he was perfectly safe because his position did not require him to turn his art to political or propagandistic ends. But as a draftsman and print maker, observing society from a libertarian point of view, he could comment only in opposition to the ideals of his royal patrons. The result was that Goya began to work for himself and his friends alone.

The Napoleonic invasion of Spain in 1808, with its guerrilla excesses, supplied Goya with the most appallingly direct evidence of man's capacity to degrade himself through violence. Between the year of the invasion and about 1814 he created a second series of etchings with aquatint, *The Disasters of War*, scenes of sickening butchery punctuated occasionally with political allegories. Their publication during French occupation or Spanish alliance with the French was of course impossible; the plates were not printed until 1863. Except for the photographs by Matthew Brady of the American Civil War,

Goya left his monument to the witless corruption of the Spanish throne in this painting of Charles IV and his family; the royal cuckold and the rapacious Maria Luisa are shown with two of their offspring in a detail from a group portrait of 1800. Behind the king are his brother, Prince Don Antonio, and an older daughter. The painting led the French novelist Theophile Gautier to remark that the couple looked like "the corner baker and his wife after they won the lottery."

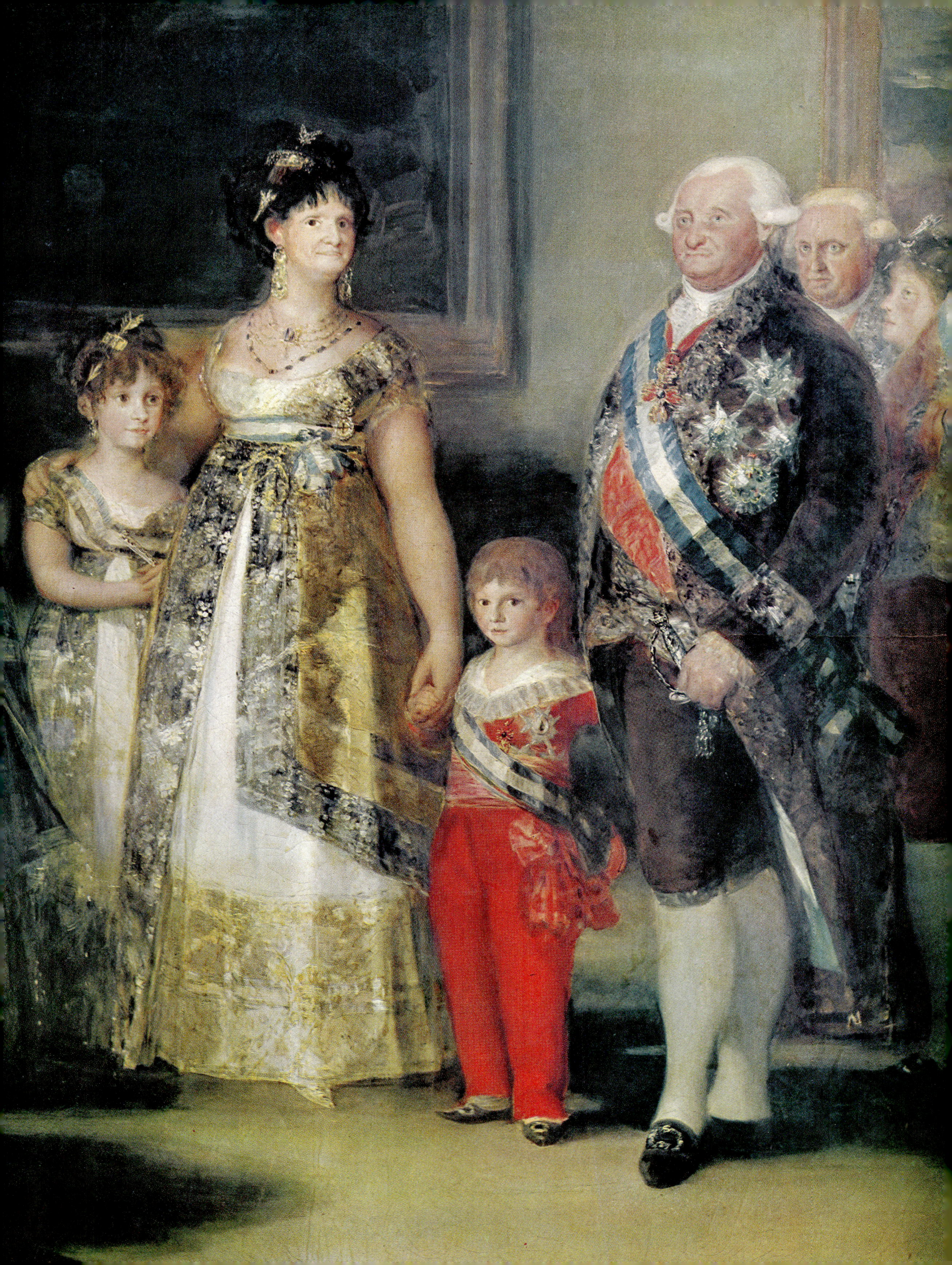

which were just then appearing, they had no equal in their treatment of war for what it is, without overtones of the picturesque or the ideally heroic.

Goya's single direct declaration of his political sympathies was made in two paintings done during the short-lived liberal Regency of 1814, only a matter of weeks before it fell to the reactionary Ferdinand VII. In *The Second of May, 1808*, Goya commemorated an uprising in the streets of Madrid, when citizens armed only with sticks, stones, and knives attacked the Egyptian cavalry that Napoleon had sent to support his brother Joseph's puppet throne. The picture is a melee of forms and colors devoid of any hint of the classical tradition of history painting, a romantic fanfare more immediately apparent as an exciting battle scene than as a patriotic tribute. But the companion picture, *The Third of May, 1808*, is another matter.

The uprising of May 2 had been immediately quelled, and on the following day batches of suspects were rounded up more or less indiscriminately, taken to the outskirts of the city, and shot. Goya shows half a dozen victims kneeling in a group among the bloody corpses of their fellows, while other citizens, waiting in a file to die, cast down their eyes in horror. We are at the moment of firing. One of the condemned men hides his face; another, a monk, prays; two others overcome their terror to glare at the riflemen. The group—and the picture—comes to its climax in the figure of a young man flinging both arms upward in defiance. A man may be easy to kill, his gesture says, but the human spirit is unquenchable.

Like all great historical and philosophical themes, this one is extremely vulnerable to trite interpretation. The originality of Goya's treatment is in his depiction of the executioners. Where they might expectably have been represented as villains or fiends, they are mere robots—anonymous, inhuman forms; thus, by contrast, the men who in a moment will fall to their bullets are endowed with eternal life. Just how the reactionary authorities rationalized these pictures is hard to understand. Most likely, Goya's eminence and his tactful reversion to political reticence accounted for the fact that he remained unmolested.

Between 1815 and 1816 he completed his third series of etchings, the *Tauromachia*, which related the history of the sport of bullfighting. But he had also been at work since 1813 on a fourth series, which extended the nightmares of *Los Caprichos*. By 1823–24 he had completed the twenty-two plates now known, plus probably some that are lost. He called them the *Disparates*, or *Follies*, though they are usually given the name *Proverbios*. The exact subjects are seldom identifiable; some seem, indeed, to be illustrations of Spanish proverbs, but there are others that can only be interpreted as personal visions of evil as the indomitable source of universal energy.

As black as this concept may be, it is not exactly despairing. While Goya offers no hope for the triumph of good, and while he refuses to recognize evil as anything but evil, he pictures it not with futility but with unrelenting vigor and passion. He is never admiring of witches and devils, but he is always fascinated. He never consents as a partner, yet he never rebels as a victim. The question is why do we not find in this ambivalent attitude a symptom of moral flaccidity?

CONTINUED ON PAGE 105

A GOYA PORTFOLIO

A preoccupation with mystery, violence, and the irrational was always present in Goya's art; as the years passed, casual observations of the foibles and horrors of the world were transfigured into a vision of life that came to dominate his work. On the following eight pages HORIZON reproduces a selection of paintings tracing the development of what was barely a murmur in his early works but a bloodcurdling scream in the end.

The first signs of Goya's interest in the fantastic appear in cartoons for tapestries, such as *Maja and Cloaked Majos* of 1778 (1). In a colorful genre scene set in an Andalusian wood a "woman of the people" dressed in her festive best promenades with her escort. But what do the threatening glances of the onlookers signify? Goya does not tell us. By 1793 he was painting macabre pictures like *Burial of the Sardine*—or as it is sometimes known, *Ash Wednesday* (2), a view of a Madrid carnival reaching its frenzied climax in a mock funeral procession. In *Witches' Sabbath* (3), five years later, the mood of menace has become more intense, the meaning more obscure: beneath a swarm of bats and a quarter moon, crones offer their dead or dying children to a monstrous goat (the pagan god Pan?).

About 1820, ill and deaf and a recluse, Goya unleashed the full power of his imagination in fourteen murals for his small country villa. These so-called "black paintings," done in his mid-seventies, are by all odds his most puzzling works. What is the meaning of the linked figures floating in mid-air in *Fantastic Vision* (4)? Are the soldiers, bottom right, aiming their guns at them or at the cavalry skirmish in the background? And what of the rock swelling like a tumor in the landscape? A pilgrimage to a miraculous fountain is the subject of *Festival of San Isidro* (5, a detail), but in Goya's depiction of the crowd raising fanatic voices in song the line between religious ecstasy and nightmare is blurred indeed. *Saturn Devouring One of His Children* (6) must stand as Goya's ultimate vision of ravening evil: time itself. For Saturn, or Cronus, the god of time, ultimately consumes all creatures. The painting was done on a wall in Goya's dining room.

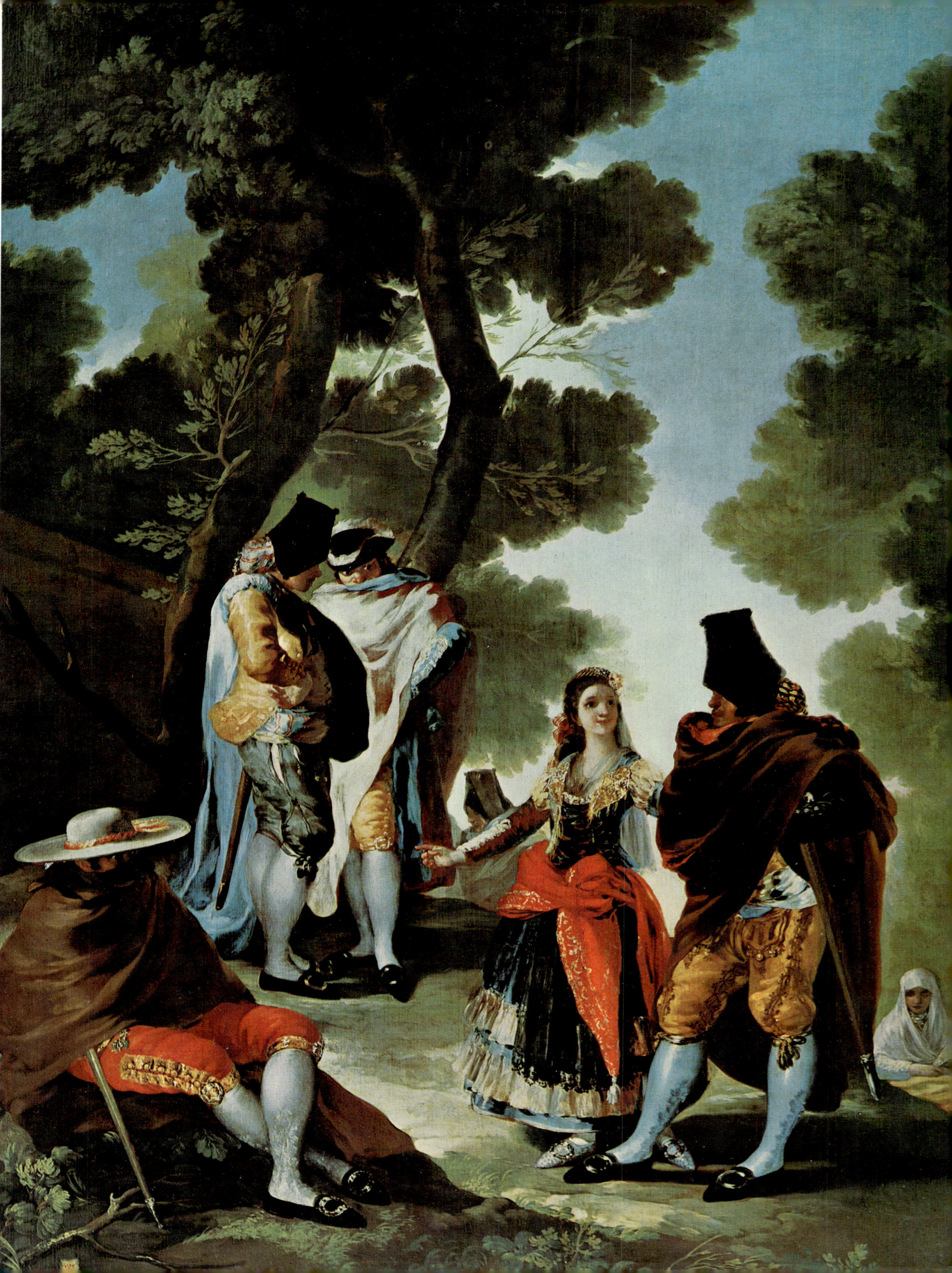

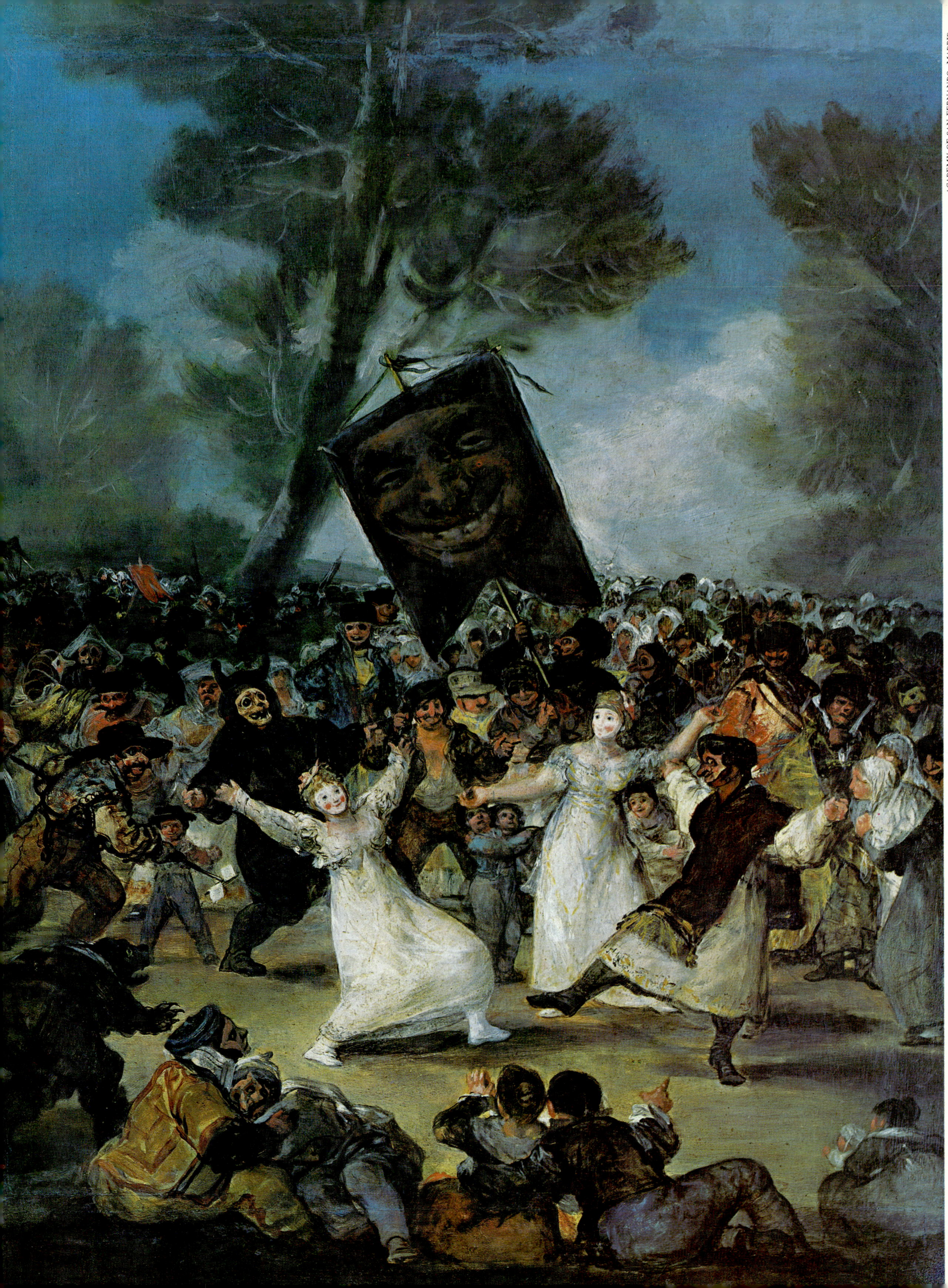
ACADEMY OF SAN FERNANDO, MADRID

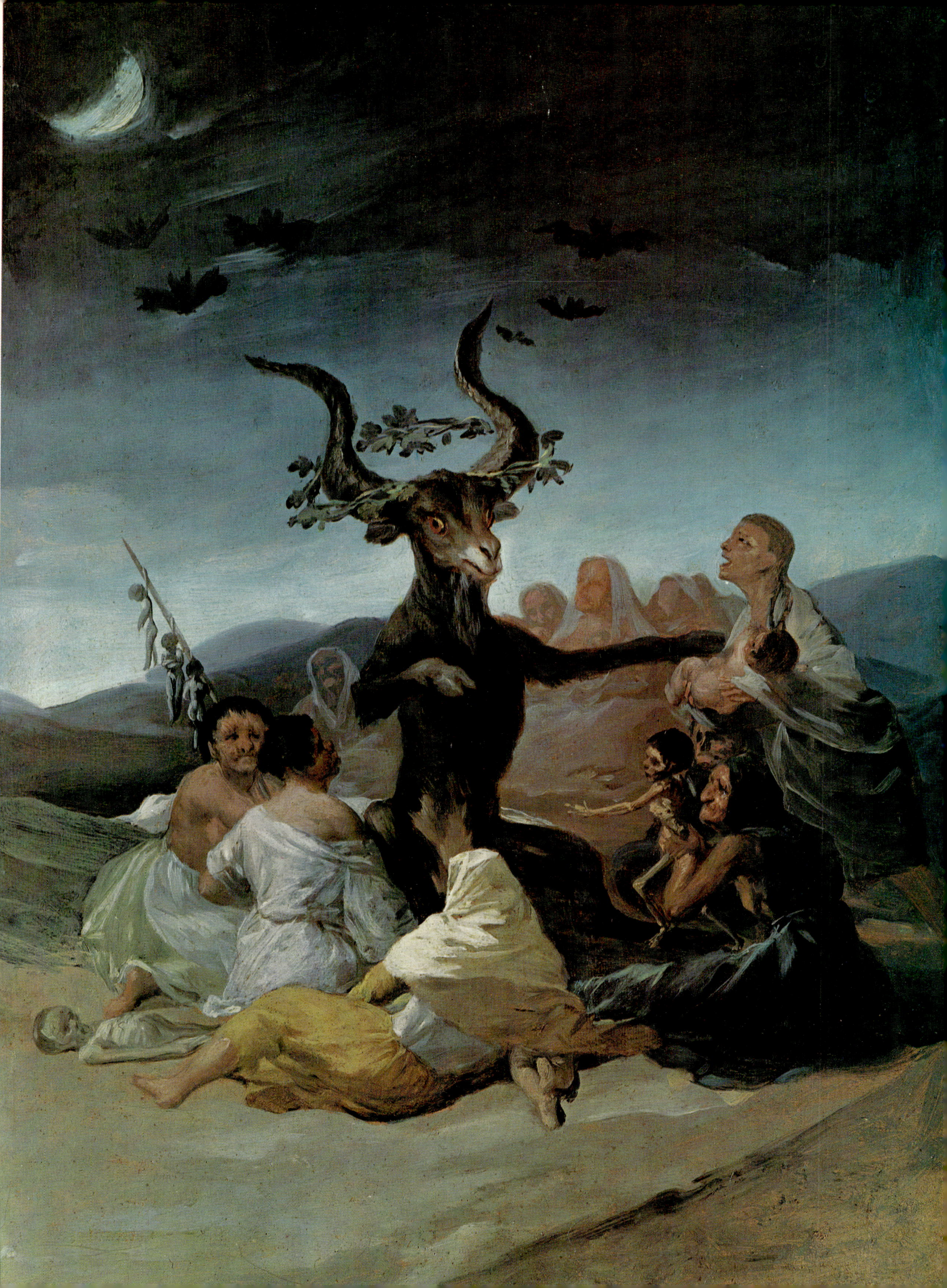

LAZARO GALDIANO MUSEUM, MADRID

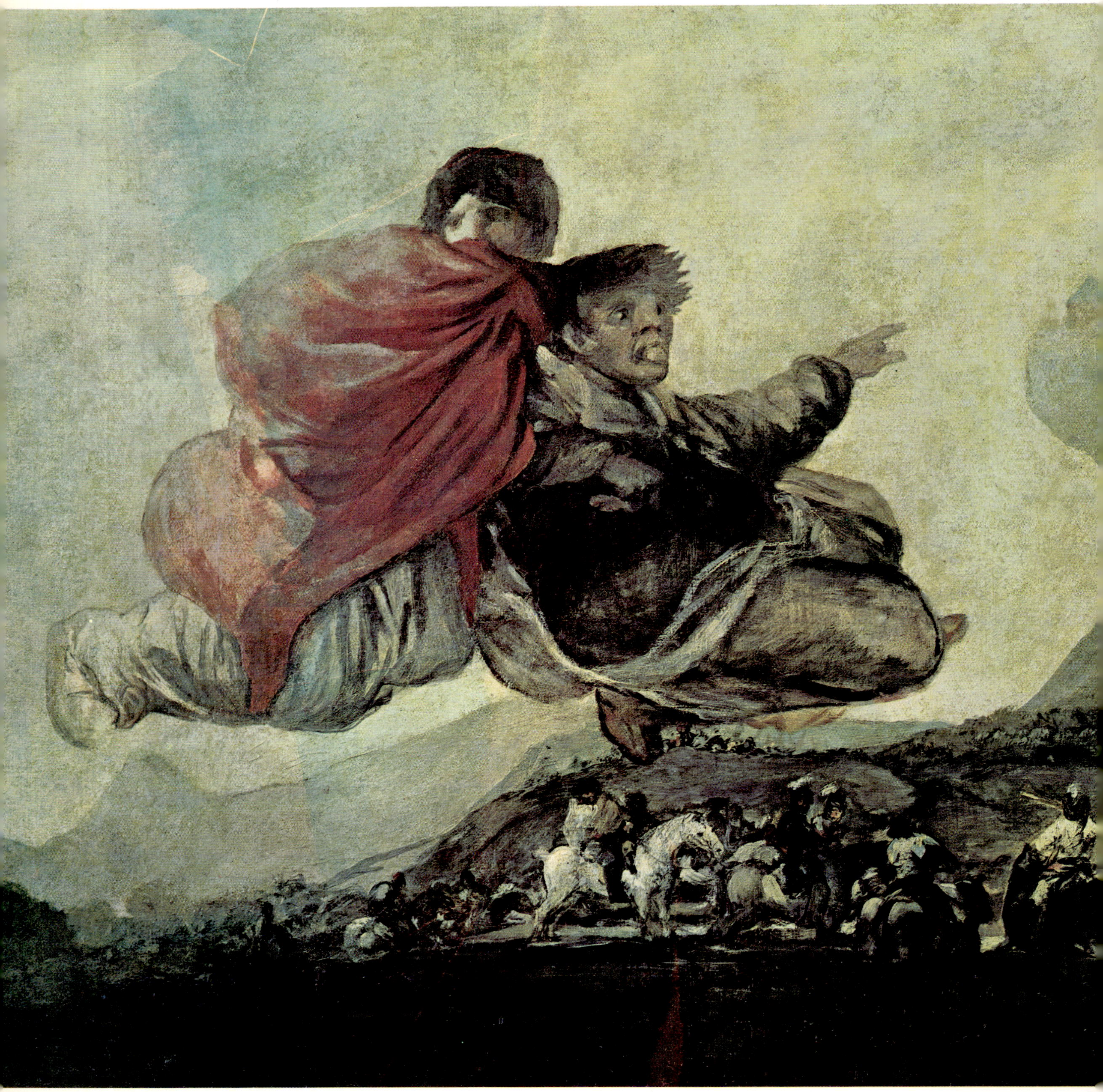

PRADO, MADRID; OVERLEAF: SAME

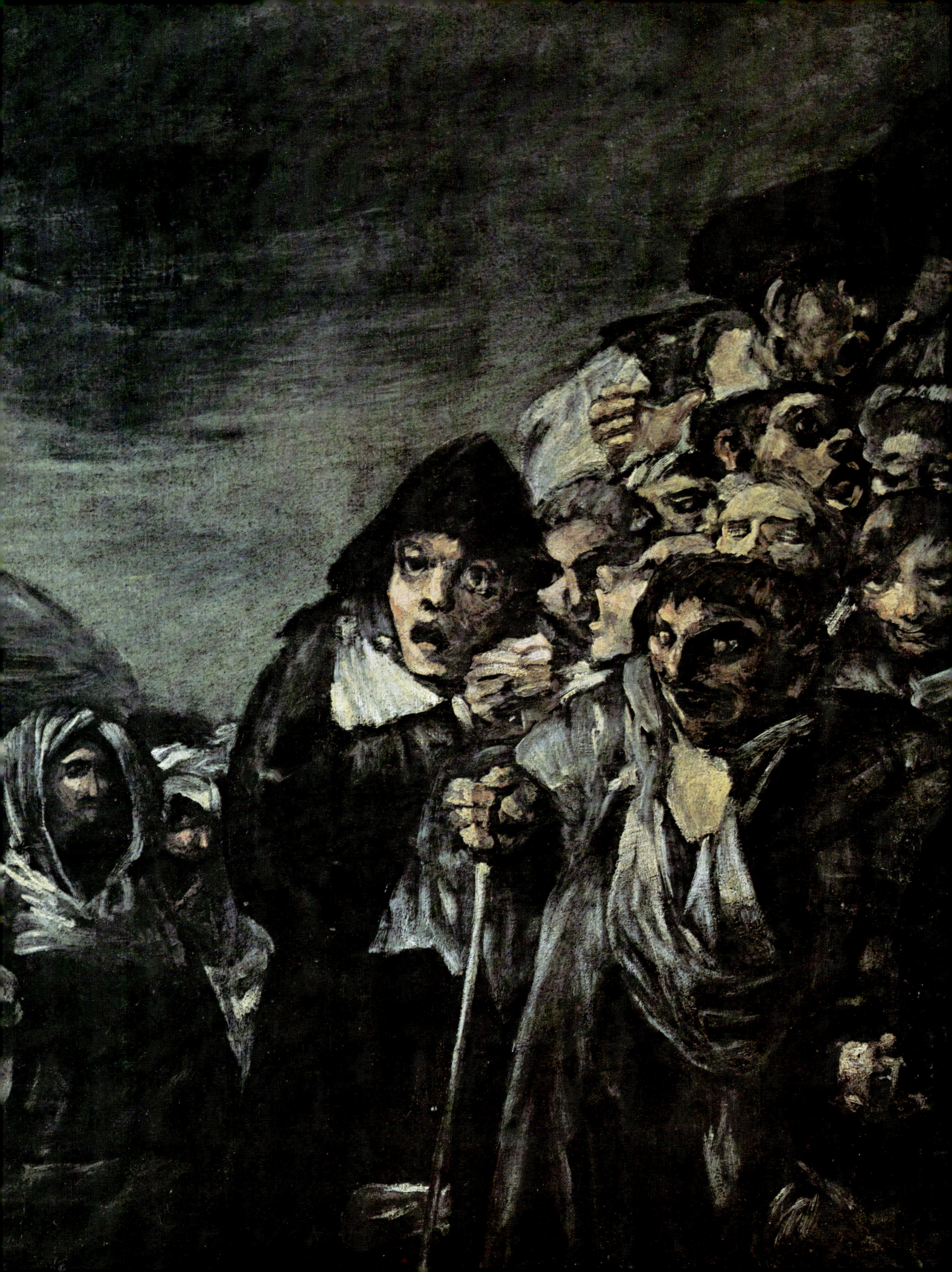

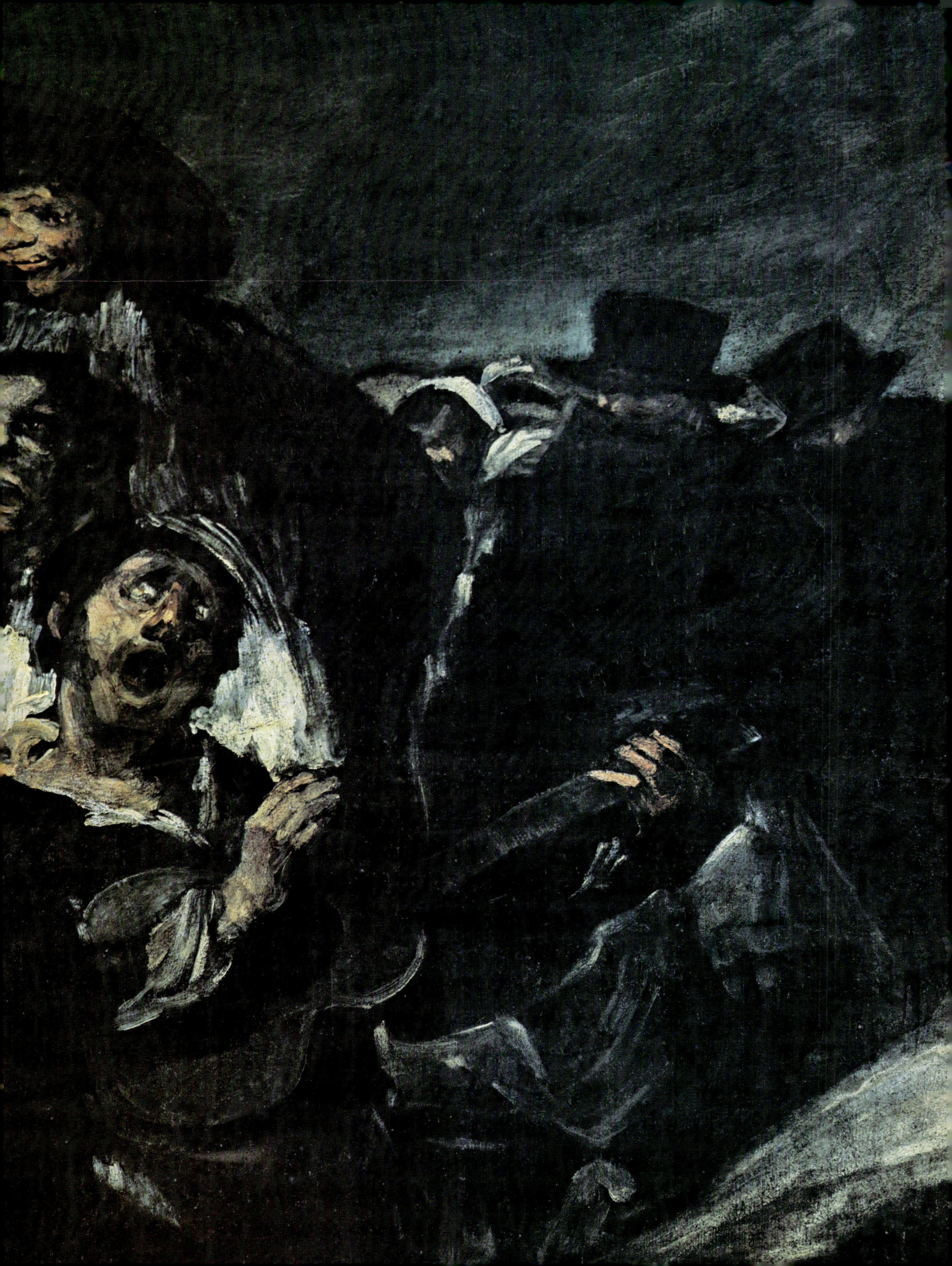

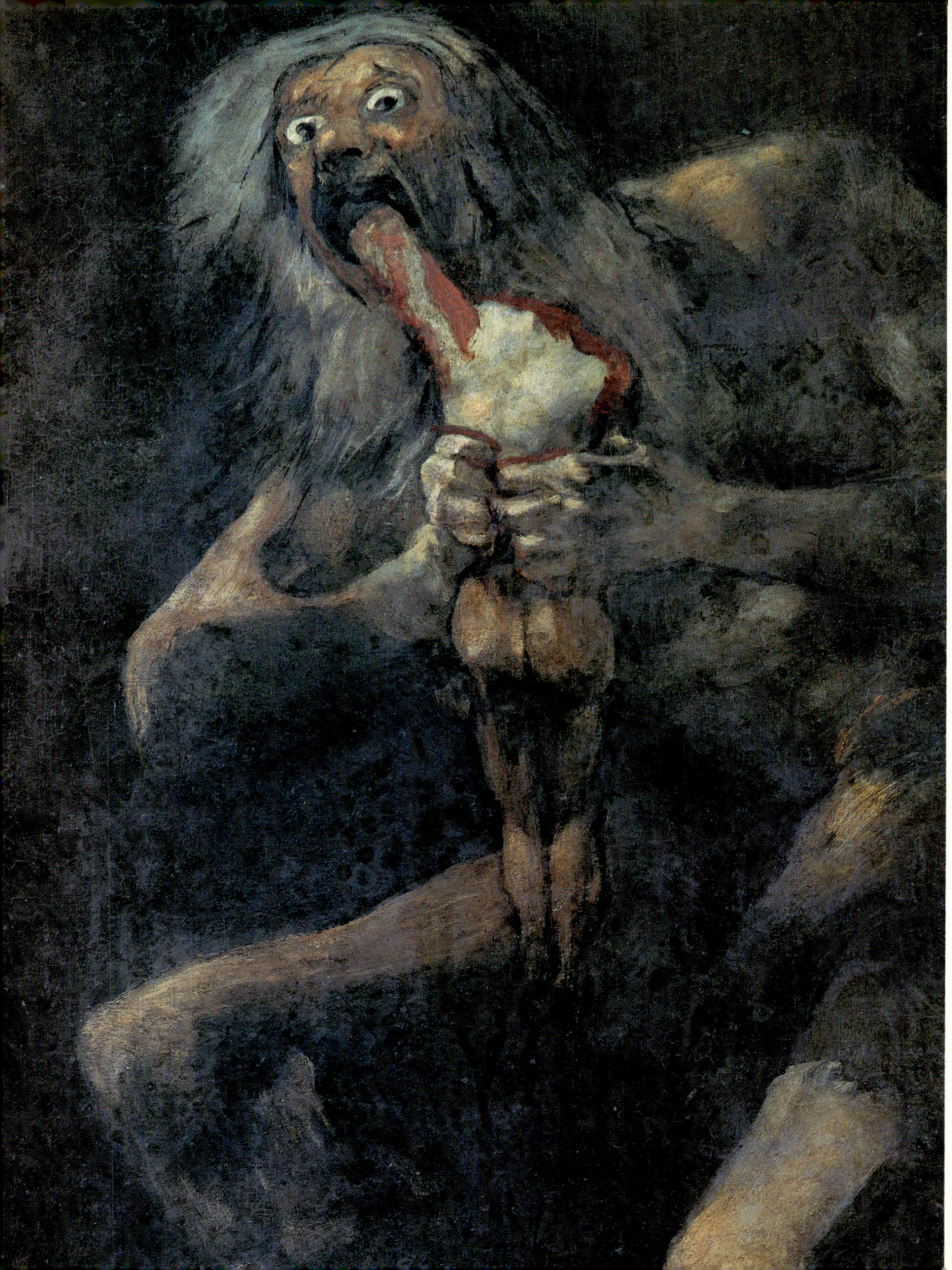

CONTINUED FROM PAGE 96

Somehow we never ask why a man whose friends in maturity were among the most enlightened thinkers and the most devoted moralists of the age of reason—a man who, we keep telling ourselves, shared their convictions—gives so little indication in his powerful art that reasonable convictions can be translated into effective action or even that there is a moral obligation to make an effort in that direction.

The answer to the contradiction may be inherent in some of Goya's last, perhaps greatest, and certainly most personal paintings—the murals in his villa near Madrid, the *Quinta del Sordo* (Deaf Man's House). He bought the villa in 1819, when he was seventy-two years old, and during the next three years covered its walls with his famous "black paintings." (They were detached in 1873 and are now in the Prado.) Black in tone, relieved only by lurid shades of raw color, and black in spirit without relief of any kind, the murals represent a congress of witches, skeletons, crones, violent gods, hysterics, monsters, and lunatics —howling, struggling, dancing, and feasting on one another in their final triumph, a combination of primeval genesis and the consummation of the power of darkness.

These demons were the old man's chosen companions during his last years in Spain. They had also been, if not the companions, at least the ever-present spirits of his childhood. That he continued to believe in them despite his association with humanistic intellectuals seems farfetched; yet one can still respond emotionally to nonsense or fantasies or superstitions even when, intellectually, one has put them aside. Goya painted his evil spirits with total conviction. In effect he did believe in them. Nothing could rout the idea that whatever is good in the world exists only by the sufferance of evil.

Goya lived in his *Quinta del Sordo* a scant four years. In 1823—he was seventy-seven—he gave the house to his grandson and the next year received permission to leave Spain for France. He still held his position as first painter to the court, but even so, with the final triumph of Ferdinand, he had gone into seclusion.

Goya saw Spain once more, during a brief visit in 1826, but he completed his life as a voluntary exile in the Spanish colony of Bordeaux. In these last years he mellowed a bit. He had been experimenting with the newly invented medium of lithography and employed it in 1825 to create a series of five bullfight scenes full of orgiastic vitality, *The Bulls of Bordeaux*. His painting was as fresh, as sparkling, as the happiest work of his youth, and as rich as the best work of his maturity. He visited Paris, and legend says that he was glimpsed in his round of the studios by the young Delacroix.

Delacroix became his first true heir. Goya found no followers during his lifetime, but by the middle of the nineteenth century he had become a god of the romantics—not only the painters, but such literary figures as Victor Hugo. And he has been adopted on one ground or another as the natural father of successive generations of innovational painters. But, all historical considerations aside, the ultimate question in the case of Goya is an uneasy one: what has he told us about ourselves?

He has told us that we are vain, cruel, superstitious, and easily deluded; that at our best, when we rise to affirm our noble potential, we are most likely to be annihilated as individuals. But he believed in one thing, and his work says it again and again: in spite of everything, to have been alive has been worthwhile. He knew that life is as wonderful as it is terrible, and that the only thing more terrible than life is its alternative—nothingness.

He died in 1828 shortly after his eighty-second birthday, in Bordeaux.

This twelfth in a series by John Canaday, art critic of The New York Times, *is adapted from his book* The Lives of the Painters, *to be published this fall by W. W. Norton & Co., Inc.*

AT LEAST THEY HAVE CHAIRS

AND THEY ARE FIERCE

RECENT UNHAPPY EVENTS IN MADRID . . .

"SIMPLE SIMON"

Themes of violence and fantasy are plentiful also in Goya's etchings. Above, from top, are a bitter comment on the poor, from the Caprichos *(1796–98); a scene from* Disasters of War *(1808–14); a bullfight disaster, from the* Tauromachia *(1815–16); and a depiction of the proverbial fool, from the* Disparates *(1820–24).*

105

High-Seas Society

By TIMOTHY S. GREEN

> "What palace, what Triumphal Way,
> what memorial have we built to perpetuate
> our civilization, as the cathedrals
> perpetuate that of the Middle Ages, the castles
> of the Loire that of the Renaissance,
> and Versailles that of the age of Louis XIV?"
> —A Frenchman on board the *Normandie*, 1935

Whenever that prince of art dealers, Lord Duveen of Milbank, boarded an Atlantic liner on his yearly pilgrimage to and from Europe (in keeping with his irrefutable observation that Europe had plenty of art and America plenty of money), his first task invariably was to scan the passenger list. Having picked out a wealthy passenger who might well be persuaded to invest at least a part of his fortune in works of art, Duveen would go in search of a friendly deck steward, hand him a one-hundred-dollar bill, and ask him to be so kind as to place his deck chair next to that of his potential client. Then, as the two men, snugly wrapped around in steamer rugs, sipped their morning bouillon in mid-ocean, Duveen would casually strike up a conversation, and it was never long before he turned it to his favorite topic—art. In more than fifty years of Atlantic travel, right up to his death in 1939, Duveen became, understandably, a popular man with deck stewards. But his investment in them was handsomely rewarded. On one occasion an obliging steward placed the art dealer's deck chair next to that of Alexander Smith Cochran, the millionaire carpetmaker from Yonkers. The acquaintance thus begun resulted in Cochran's buying more than five million dollars worth of art objects from him over the years.

It was a rare voyage when Duveen could not find some distinguished patron—or potential patron—of art among the galaxy of tycoons, politicians, writers, and actresses who crowded the luxurious first-class accommodations of the Atlantic liners before World War II. Indeed he found that the unique atmosphere aboard the liners helped to soften his clients' resistance to the extraordinarily high prices he invariably charged. The fifty years of Duveen's voyaging coincided, happily for him, with the high-water mark of Atlantic sea travel, when the watchword was "the best of everything"—whether the champagne and caviar, the marble baths in the staterooms, or the Persian carpets in the lounges. Coupled with this opulence were snobbery and social pressures quite as potent as any on dry land.

The Atlantic ferry—or "ocean railway," as Samuel Cunard, whose *Britannia* pioneered a scheduled Atlantic passenger service in 1840, liked to call it—developed in time a mystique and tradition all its own. The splendor of the ships became a matter not just of commercial pride but of national pres-

106 THE SKETCHES ILLUSTRATING THIS ARTICLE ARE FROM A BROCHURE PUBLISHED BY CUNARD IN THE 1920'S

tige among the British, the Americans, the Germans, the French, the Italians, and the Dutch. Governments were frequently persuaded to subsidize luxury liners far beyond their economic value. As a result no other shipping route in the world has ever spawned such extravagances or such follies. Where else have ships had Byzantine chapels and Pompeian swimming pools, dining rooms styled like the palace of Versailles, lounges decorated in mock Inigo Jones, and Turkish baths like eastern harems?

The rivalry between these colossi was so intense that one Frenchman, writing at the time of the maiden voyage of the *Normandie* in 1935, speculated: "What palace, what Triumphal Way, what memorial have we built to perpetuate our civilization, as the cathedrals perpetuate that of the Middle Ages, the castles of the Loire that of the Renaissance, and Versailles that of the age of Louis XIV?" His answer was, of course, the *Normandie*.

The special snobbery that blossomed aboard the ships often made it easier for captains to pilot their way around the drifting icebergs off the Grand Bank than to chart a course through the social shoals of choosing guests for the six or eight places at the captain's table. One captain recalled in his memoirs that his sole bedside reading during his first three years in command was the British and American *Who's Who*, so that he could whittle out from the passenger list the right half-dozen to join his table.

The beginnings of the liners, of course, were much more humble. The *Britannia*, the wooden paddle-steamer that sailed from Liverpool for Boston with sixty-three passengers on July 4, 1840, inaugurating Samuel Cunard's "ocean railway," was a mere two hundred and seven feet long. She would have fitted snugly on the foredeck of either of the *Queens*. The real achievement of the voyage, which took fourteen days, was the comforting knowledge that because the *Britannia* and her three sister ships in Cunard's infant fleet were steam-driven, they would arrive at their destination close to schedule. This was true luxury after the days of occasional sailing packets when an Atlantic voyage might take anywhere from thirty to one hundred days, with passengers supplying their own food.

Charles Dickens, who made a crossing on the *Britannia* in the winter of 1842, was hardly impressed by the opulence of the accommodations. The stateroom of "'Charles Dickens, Esquire, and Lady,'" he recalled in his *American Notes*, was an "utterly impracticable, thoroughly hopeless, and profoundly preposterous box." As for his bunk: "nothing smaller for sleeping in was ever made except coffins."

Once Dickens had recovered from the worst throes of seasickness, he managed to sample the minimal charms of the saloon of an Atlantic passenger ship of the 1840's. "At one, a bell rings, and the stewardess comes down with a steaming dish of baked potatoes, and another of roasted apples; and plates of pig's face, cold ham, salt beef; or perhaps a smoking mess of rare hot collops. We fall-to upon these dainties; eat as much as we can (we have great appetites now); and are as long as possible about it. If the fire will burn (it *will* sometimes) we are pretty cheerful. If it won't, we all remark to each other that it's very cold, rub our hands, cover ourselves with coats and cloaks, and lie down again to doze, talk, and read . . . until dinner-time."

Sailing the stormy Atlantic was still high adventure, and William Makepeace Thackeray, on his voyage across the Atlantic on the *Canada* in 1852, was almost overcome with admiration for captain and crew. He says in *Roundabout Papers*: "We trust our lives to these seamen, and how nobly they fulfill their trust! . . . Whilst we sleep, their untiring watchfulness keeps guard over us." Mark Twain declared that those "practical, hard-headed, unromantic Cunard people would not take Noah himself as first mate till they had worked him up through all the lower grades and tried him ten years. . . ."

The immediate success of the Cunard fleet did not go long unchallenged. In 1849 the New York shipowner E. K. Collins announced he was building a steamer fleet "to sweep the Cunarders off the Atlantic." The United States government was persuaded to forget its traditional hostility to subsidies and grant the Collins Line nearly twenty thousand dollars per voyage for mail carrying. The ships were to be faster and more luxurious than the Cunarders, with steam heat in the staterooms and electric bells for summoning the stewards.

Tea-time port side

The Collins challenge ended, however, in tragedy. In 1854 the line's *Arctic* sank after a collision in fog with a French ship; more than three hundred lives were lost. Less than two years later the Collins's *Pacific* sailed out of Liverpool with one hundred and fifty-nine passengers and crew and was never seen again. Not surprisingly, the United States government now began to fight shy of maintaining the mail subsidy, and in 1858 the Collins Line collapsed.

But the spirit of transatlantic competition continued to thrive. The commercial and national rivalries that were to blossom into such extravagance at the end of the century had already been born. The Germans had entered the fray with the Hamburg-American Line in 1848 and the North German Lloyd Line in 1857; the Compagnie

Générale Transatlantique (French Line) started operations in 1861; the Holland-America Line began as a private Dutch company in 1872. In Britain itself the White Star Line, the Inman Line, and the Guion Line were all attempting to woo passengers away from Cunard ships.

When Dickens traveled on the *Britannia*, there had been a cow on deck in a padded stall to supply fresh milk for the voyage. By the early 1870's the breakfast menu alone offered beefsteaks, mutton chops, pork chops, veal cutlets, smoked salmon, broiled chickens, eggs, and mushrooms. The wine and spirits bar was open from 6 A.M. to 11 P.M., selling first-quality claret at six shillings per quart and brandy at three shillings a pint. There were still some regulations, however, that would have been entirely alien to the next generation of transatlantic passengers. Lights were put out in the saloons at 11:30 and had to be out in staterooms by midnight. Little notices reminded passengers: "As the labor of the servants must be very great, and the space required for a larger number absolutely prevents an increase, the passengers are requested to spare them as much as possible between the Meal Hours, and particularly preceding dinner."

But comforts were slowly creeping in. Private bathrooms were first introduced in the *Abyssinnia* and the *Algeria* in 1870, while the *Gallia*, launched in 1879, gave the first hint of the opulence of later years. Her saloon was decorated "in Japanese style, the walls being in panels of jasper red lacquer, with delicate Japanese designs in gold and soft colors portraying birds and flowers." There was even a fountain spouting in the center of the smoking room. Pianos were now installed in the saloons, and concerts took place. The *Aurania News* recorded in 1888 that on one voyage "Lord Henry Grosvenor took the chair at the concert. Lady Henry Grosvenor sang 'The Brook,' a duet called 'Oh, wert thou in the cauld blast,' and 'Home Sweet Home.' " It was a perfect replica of a genteel musical soiree at an English country house.

The real heyday of Atlantic travel came, however, only after considerable engineering and other technical advances. Even in the 1870's and 1880's the real triumph of Atlantic travel was still the sheer feat of getting across the ocean safely on time. Only with the advent of steel ships, of twin and then quadruple screws driven by turbines, of electric lights and refrigeration, could real luxury be offered.

Lillie Langtry, the actress, found how trying an Atlantic voyage could still be when she first crossed from Liverpool to New York on the *Arizona*. "There were rats on the *Arizona*, long-coated and tame," she wrote in her autobiography, *The Days I Knew*. "Poor Mrs. Labouchère [her traveling companion], who was a victim to *mal de mer*, remained in bed nearly the whole of the voyage, and one morning, on opening her eyes, she was horrified to find a fat, genial rodent sitting on her chest. Alas, I knew that fellow! He used to sit and listen while I read to the invalid, and, with unwelcome familiarity, would indicate his need of water by rattling the chain in the washbasin."

John Burgess, the historian who crossed from Boston to Liverpool in 1871, wrote: "There were no napkins at the table, and when our passengers made a sort of protest to the company in regard to what we considered our hardships, on our arrival at Liverpool . . . old Mr. McIver [one of the early Cunard partners] replied that going to sea was a hardship, that the Cunard Company did not undertake to make anything else of it . . ." Vastly different sentiments were expressed in a Cunard "logbook" that was handed to each passenger in 1902. "From the moment of booking a berth the passenger's welfare is studied with the solicitude and aptitude born of long experience in conveying passengers between the Old World and the New. He is gently encouraged to do all that will add to his comfort and convenience but guarded against falling into the many little errors to which the untraveled are prone, with a nicety which is quite an art." As for the ships—they were now what Cunard liked to call "a silent sermon in good taste."

In the space of thirty years a revolution had taken place in Atlantic travel. In 1876 the White Star Line's *Britannic*, holder of the Blue Riband for the fastest crossing, was a mere five thousand tons. The *Mauretania*, launched in 1907, displaced thirty-two thousand tons, while the giant *Bismarck*, launched at Hamburg in 1912, was more than fifty-six thousand tons. The liner, in the sense that we understand it today, had arrived. There was now space enough not only to carry ample crew to minister the travelers' every whim but to install gymnasiums, swimming

The swimming pool of the Berengaria

pools, public rooms, and luxurious private suites. The first of the new generation were Cunard's *Lucania* and *Campania*, which the company labeled "the aristocrats of the Atlantic."

Actresses, opera singers, authors like Oscar Wilde, now found pleasure in crossing the Atlantic in comfort on their way to theatres or lecture tours in the United States. In 1893 alone, Cunard carried 18,500 first-class passengers across the Atlantic—far more than any of its rivals.

"Lily Langtry was installed in Twenty-third Street, New York," wrote F. Lawrence Babcock in his book *Spanning the Atlantic*; "Sarah Bernhardt, Yvette Guilbert, Eleanora Duse, Emmy Destinn, Ellen Terry, and dozens of other beautiful and talented women had crossed the ocean to find the metropolitan portions of American youth ready to fall at their feet. Hardly a Cunarder arrived but there was a throng of 'stage-door Johnnies' of the best quality waiting at the pier to greet some celebrity."

The traffic was not one way. Now that the Atlantic crossing was no longer an ordeal, it became fashionable for young American men to be seen sipping a glass of wine in Montmartre cellars or for daughters of rich New Yorkers to be allowed a year in Paris to round out their education. This was the age of tourism on a grand scale.

For the less well off, enterprising American travel agents advertised European cycling tours at one hundred dollars for the round trip. "Try steerage," one advertisement suggested. "As Hazlitt said of the 'Fairy Queen,' it won't bite you." Indeed steerage class was at last beginning to enjoy some of the benefits already accorded to the upper decks. The majority of the millions of emigrants who crossed the Atlantic in the last half of the nineteenth century had traveled in steerage. They were crammed into the bowels of the ship, bedded down on straw mattresses that were thrown overboard before it arrived at New York. They were fed from iron buckets. Some steamship companies even carried cattle in the steerage accommodations on the return voyage from New York to Europe.

Now, as the first-class passengers tucked into their champagne and caviar, steerage passengers were at least getting three meals a day served properly by stewards and even had a piano in their lounge. They no longer had to bring their own towels, and after 1900 the very term "steerage" was often replaced by "tourist" class.

Meanwhile, up on the first-class decks the splendors of the Edwardian era ashore were being emulated at sea. Orchestras, which became a regular feature of the liners after 1905, played the melodies of Lionel Monkton or the operettas of Gilbert and Sullivan far into the night. The steamer trunks were now crammed with white tie and tails for the men and a constant change of gowns for the ladies. "Remember . . . the one essential garment for a man aboard ship is a dinner-jacket," wrote Basil Woon in *The Frantic Atlantic*, a guide to Atlantic social etiquette. "He can (and frequently many of us do) dispense with all else, but the dinner-jacket is as necessary to an ocean traveler as a tailcoat is to a waiter. Without it you may not, except on the first and last nights out, come down to dinner. Without it you will have to sneak out of the smoking-room at eight P.M.

"Without it you will have no dances and no Great Moments with the young thing in crêpe-marocain on the lee of the starboard ventilator."

The pursuit of excellence aboard fomented national rivalries to build larger, faster, and more de luxe ships; and safety, as the *Titanic* was to demonstrate so tragically, was sometimes sacrificed for high living afloat. Together with the *Titanic*, the White Star Line's *Olympic* and the German trio *Imperator*, *Vaterland*, and *Bismarck* were all giants of more than forty thousand tons. All were decorated in a potpourri of styles.

The final glory was Cunard's *Aquitania*, which made her maiden voyage on the eve of World War I. The main drawing room was based on Robert Adam's plans for Lansdowne House in Berkeley Square, London. It had a high dome with lunettes in the center and a perfect Adam fireplace. There were large bay windows (not a porthole in sight). Over the chimney piece of carved statuary-marble was a copy of a painting by Giovanni Cipriani. The walls were decorated with classical fluted pilasters supporting an Adam frieze of scroll foliage surmounted by a cornice, and were hung with copies of paintings by Copley and Reynolds of the Duchess of Devonshire, the Marchioness of Hertford, and the

Dressing for dinner

daughters of George III.

The first-class dining room, complete with minstrel gallery, was supposed to convey to the passengers the sense that they were eating in the palace of the Sun King at Versailles. Over a marble buffet was a view of the park of the Grand Trianon; in the center of the ceiling was a massive oval painting, *The Triumph of Flora*, described as "after Jean Jacques Lagrenée" (a minor, late-eighteenth-century French painter). In the midst of the clouds floating across the sunlit sky the Goddess of Flowers welcomed other divinities who had come to pay her court.

The *Aquitania* boasted eight luxury suites named after famous painters—Holbein, Velázquez, Vandyke, Rembrandt, Reynolds, Gainsborough, Romney, and Raeburn. Copies of their paintings adorned the walls of each suite. This exotic decoration was responsible for inspiring perhaps the most notable of Lord Duveen's mid-Atlantic art coups. The astutely positioned deck chair was only a part of the art dealer's seagoing campaign to wear down his clients' resistance to his high prices. He made sure, too, that his suite was strategically placed near that of a potential client.

Thus on one memorable *Aquitania* voyage Duveen was installed next door to the California railroad magnate H. E. Huntington and his wife Arabella, who had booked the Gainsborough Suite. Huntington was a regular client of Duveen's, and naturally the art dealer was invited to dinner in the Gainsborough suite. Pride of the place in the private dining room went to a reproduction of *The Blue Boy*. During dinner, conversation turned to the picture. In his biography of Duveen, S. N. Behrman faithfully reports the exchange:

"'Joe,' said H. E., with the confidence of one who knows that he can get the answer to anything, 'who's the boy in the blue suit?'

"Duveen said, 'That is a reproduction of the famous "Blue Boy." It is Gainsborough's finest and most famous painting.'

"'Where's the original?' Huntington went on, with even more confidence. Duveen did not let his inquirer down. 'It belongs to the Duke of Westminster and hangs in his collection at Grosvenor House, in London.'

"'How much is it?' asked H. E.

"Duveen was discouraging. 'It can probably not be had at any price,' he said."

Huntington, however, was not a man to be thwarted so easily. He pressed Duveen for a price, and finally the dealer said it might be six hundred thousand dollars—which was far more than the millionaire had ever paid for a painting.

"I might see my way clear to paying that much," Huntington said.

The Huntingtons disembarked at Cherbourg, but Duveen went on to Southampton. When the boat train deposited him in London, he hastened to call on the Duke of Westminster at Grosvenor House. He found the duke, whom he knew to be rather in need of some ready cash, quite happy to sell *The Blue Boy* and anything else in his collection that Duveen fancied. Duveen settled for *The Blue Boy*, together with Reynolds's *Sarah Siddons as the Tragic Muse* and Gainsborough's *The Cottage Door*. He paid about six hundred thousand dollars for all three, then hurried off to Paris to deliver *The Blue Boy* to the Huntingtons, whom he charged six hundred and twenty thousand dollars for the one picture. They were delighted at the coup; their sole complaint was that the original *Blue Boy* was not as blue as the reproduction in their *Aquitania* suite. But Duveen assured them that was no problem; he would have the painting cleaned and thus restored to the fresh blue that had first entranced them in their suite in mid-Atlantic.

Many other Duveen clients—An-

The Captain's table

drew Carnegie, Henry Clay Frick, and J. Pierpont Morgan—were regular Atlantic voyagers. They were treated with reverence by the shipping lines. Morgan was even shown the plans for the *Titanic* before she was built so that he could choose where he would like his suite to be. Whenever Morgan was returning to New York, his private yacht *Corsair* put out from the harbor with pennants flying to greet the incoming liner. Morgan would stand at the rail and wave his handkerchief enthusiastically as the ship came into berth. Then, the moment the lines were made fast to the dock, the *Corsair* would come alongside, and Morgan would step aboard her and steam off direct to his home. Once, when his wife was arriving alone on the *Oceanic*, Morgan took the *Corsair* out of the harbor to meet her and had his crew skillfully bring the yacht alongside the liner at sea. He grabbed for a perpendicular steel ladder running down the ship's side and began the long climb of sixty feet up to the deck with a cigar between his teeth and a straw hat on his head. He was then sixty-two years old and hardly a fit man. But, as passengers on the *Oceanic* placed bets on whether or not he would make it, he clambered over the rail, his face dripping with perspiration, and hurried off toward his wife's suite.

Not surprisingly, the close confines of these liners heightened all the social snobbery of dry land. Before the voyage the captain and the purser spent as much time scrutinizing the list of perhaps one hundred and fifty passengers whom the head office had pointed out as being particularly important as they did debating fuel supplies or studying advance weather reports. It was not simply a question of a person's social, political, or business importance—the captain had to be the perfect diplomat in not, quite unwittingly, selecting violent adversaries to sit side by side at his table for five days.

The guest list for cocktail parties caused equal agonies of mind; some people clearly rated an invitation from the captain, others were equal only to the purser. One liner captain recalled tentatively suggesting a particular couple at his early morning social strategy session with his purser. "Oh no, sir," replied the purser, appalled, "*they* are not for *you*. Leave them to me."

The passengers, in turn, waited anxiously for the printed white cards inviting them to this table or that party. A lavish 1920's promotion booklet, in the form of an ecstatic diary of an *Aquitania* voyage, notes: "Tuesday—Tonight I had the honor of being invited to the captain's room for cocktails before dinner. I enjoyed the little party tremendously. The captain of such a famous ship must always be a great seaman but I was not prepared for so much wit and charm—and knowledge to boot—and I do not wonder that his invitation is the most coveted honor on board ship."

The old lady who, on being invited to sit at the captain's table, snapped back to the purser, "young man, I haven't paid all this money to eat with the crew" was indeed a rarity. And half of the pleasure of an Atlantic voyage was the intimate shoulder-rubbing with the great.

Over the years passengers developed special devotions to captains, to officers, to particular tables or cabins or even stewards. The true art of being an Atlantic purser was to know exactly which cabin this judge or that colonel liked; the art of the restaurant manager was not just to conjure up food but to know every whim of a whole generation of Atlantic travelers. For example, Henry Ford, Jr., met his first wife in the Verandah Grill aboard the *Queen Mary*; for many years afterward the same table at which he had first been introduced to her was always reserved for him on subsequent voyages. Even in the lounge or smoking room the stewards stayed on for decades, and on the first night a regular passenger would be greeted automatically with "Good evening sir, your usual table is waiting."

They were, of course, well rewarded. Tips on the Atlantic have always been nearly three times as high as on the other main sea routes of the world. Captains and pursers often received handsome boxes of Havana Havanas from grateful passengers. One American lady even went so far as to bequeath almost her entire fortune to the officers and crew of the *Lucania*, with a special fifty thousand dollars set aside for her commander, Captain McKay.

The First World War did nothing to dim the enthusiasms or the prejudices of the Atlantic traveler. Indeed the 1920's ushered in the final fling of the giant liner. The competition to begin with was a little one-sided, for the three German liners *Imperator*, *Vaterland*, and *Bismarck* had all been taken over as part of Germany's reparation payments. They now became the *Berengaria* of the Cunard fleet, the *Leviathan* of United States Lines, and the *Majestic* of the White Star Line.

The social whirl continued undisturbed—although the *Berengaria* had a stock exchange aboard so that anxious investors could keep an eye on Wall Street and the City in London in between Turkish baths and before-lunch drinks in a smoking room that looked like a baronial mansion. One English baronet was so entranced with the ship

Greeting an old friend

that he used to fly around the world to pick up the *Berengaria* in New York or another port when she was cruising, solely to challenge her chef to culinary contests.

"Everybody on the Berengaria, even the dogs, were 'socially prominent,'" wrote one Cunard captain. "There was Gertrude Lawrence's dog, which she liked to exercise on deck each morning in defiance of regulations, and the melancholy incident when I caught her doing so and escorted her in grim silence back to the kennels. She sobbed all the way, bitterly and magnificently . . . [the *Berengaria*] was principally a gleaming and bejewelled ferry boat for the rich and titled: for the Sultan of Johore, Lord Duveen, the Earl of Warwick and many Cortlandts, Vanderbilts and Swopes." There was so much wealth aboard that a junior purser would regularly walk through the smoking room announcing "Ladies and gentlemen, we have reason to believe there are cardsharpers on board" just so no one could claim they had not been warned.

The liners were a happy hunting ground for a small army of swindlers and cardsharps who sometimes cleaned up with a five-thousand-dollar profit in one evening. Charles T. Spedding, *Aquitania* purser in the early twenties, wrote in his memoirs, "there was practically not a voyage but at least one gang was on board." Although one cardsharp threatened to shoot a purser when he was unmasked, most of them behaved outwardly with as much decorum as their fellow passengers. Indeed one, whom Spedding called "a perfect gentleman," made a fortune from traveling on Cunard and White Star Line ships and finally retired to write a book on the iniquity of gambling. By the end of his career he was so well known aboard the ships that he could no longer cheat, but he enjoyed such a colorful reputation that many passengers asked to play with him just to be able to impress their friends ashore with tales of gambling at sea.

Not all mid-Atlantic gambling ended so peacefully. One young German was swindled into thinking he was playing for a shilling a hundred instead of a shilling a point, then had to settle his debts out of his firm's money. He committed suicide a few weeks later.

Confidence tricksters worked a multitude of schemes. The simplest and most profitable was for a "lady" to strike up a conversation with her victim in the bar before dinner. After a couple of drinks she would suggest they adjourn to her stateroom, confiding that her "husband" was off having cocktails with the captain. Then, at the crucial moment, the "husband" would burst in. The compromised passenger almost invariably reached for his checkbook; many parted with a thousand dollars to avoid a scandal.

Passengers' wealth was also tapped, perfectly legally of course, for seamen's charities at the daily tote on the ship's run and at concerts. It became a tradition for actors, actresses, or opera singers crossing the Atlantic to give their services at these concerts. Nellie Melba sang arias, P. G. Wodehouse read Jeeves stories, and an entire revue starring Gertrude Lawrence and Beatrice Lillie was staged in mid-ocean when the show was transferring from London to New York. The collections after the concerts occasionally raised as much as ten thousand dollars.

Charlie Chaplin, returning to Europe in the early 1920's for the first time since he had become an international star, reveled in the peace and elegance of first class on the White Star Line's *Olympic*. In *My Autobiography* he remembers: "At last I was alone in my cabin, which was stocked with flowers and baskets of fruit from my friends. It had been ten years since I had left England, and on this very ship, with the Karno Company; then we had

A bridge hand in the lounge

The dogs' promenade

Luncheon on a private verandah

The cocktail bar

traveled second class. I remember the steward taking us on a hurried tour through the first class, to give us a glimpse of how the other half lived. He had talked of the luxury of the private suites and their prohibitive price, and now I was occupying one of them.... A few hours out and the atmosphere was already English. Each night Eddie Knoblock and I would dine in the Ritz restaurant instead of the main dining-room. The Ritz was à la carte, with champagne, caviar, duck *à la presse*, grouse and pheasant, wines, sauces, and crepes suzette. With time on my hands I enjoyed the nonsense of dressing each evening in black tie. Such luxury and indulgence brought home to me the delights of money."

Even princes found that in the heady atmosphere of an Atlantic liner they could relax more easily than ashore. The Duke of Windsor, when he was Prince of Wales, once hired the *Berengaria*'s orchestra to stay aboard the ship late at night after she was docked at Southampton so that he could conduct his own private concert. Before a tiny audience of startled ship's officers, the prince took the stand, Lord Louis Mountbatten took over the drums, and they whipped through a serenade of popular music that went on into the night. The prince explained afterward to the officers that this was the one place he could think of where he could escape the stiff formalities that inhibited him ashore.

Prohibition in the United States gave an added stimulant to the hilarity of Atlantic crossings. The moment the ship left her berth on the New York waterfront, a thirsty crowd of passengers gathered outside the bars, waiting for them to open the moment the magic three-mile limit was crossed. Then they drank as if they expected the ship to run dry at any second. On the return voyage there was even greater determination to knock back that final extra drink before the Ambrose lightship hove into view and the bar shutters snapped shut.

By the late 1920's national rivalries on the Atlantic were reasserting themselves as the North German Lloyd's *Bremen* won the Blue Riband that the Cunard liner *Mauretania* had held since 1907. The Italians with the *Rex*, the Germans with the *Europa*, and the French with the *Normandie* were all fighting for the prestige of having the newest and fastest ship on the run to New York. Cunard responded with the *Queen Mary* and later the *Queen Elizabeth* (which was completed only on the eve of war and did not make her proper maiden voyage until 1946).

Yet by the time most of these ships were in service, the grand era of the Atlantic ferry was almost over. The onset of the Depression had halved in one year the number of passengers crossing the Atlantic. Only for a few years immediately after World War II —when there were too many passengers chasing too few berths in the handful of remaining luxury liners— did the Atlantic trade return to anything like its former glory. But it was a short-lived finale. Already the character of the ocean liner business was changing. Shipping companies had to admit—and it took some of them a long time to do it—that they could not compete with air transport. The arrival of long-haul jets finally drove home the point to any shipowners who still dreamed nostalgically of the old days. On the liners that remain today there is a spirit of democracy that would have caused a mid-ocean crisis a generation ago. Instead of issuing that treasured handful of invitations to the captain's cocktail party, most captains now give a cocktail party for *all* their passengers, including those in tourist class. Cunard's new *Queen Elizabeth II* is essentially a one-class ship.

While the recent sales of the *Queen Mary* and the *Queen Elizabeth* have marked the final eclipse of Samuel Cunard's ocean railroad, many connoisseurs of the art of Atlantic travel saw the true end to the great era in 1950 when the thirty-six-year-old *Aquitania* steamed off on her final voyage to the breaker's yard. The *Aquitania* even more than the *Queen Mary* was a symbol of a unique period of ocean travel. "She was," as the British newspaper proprietor Lord Northcliffe once wrote, "a country house at sea with just the right number of people in it and plenty of room for them all."

Timothy S. Green, English journalist and former HORIZON *London correspondent, is the author of* The World of Gold, *about man's most fascinating commodity.*

Arriving at Southampton

SEX AND THE KING OF FRANCE

No monarch's love life was ever quite so carefully watched
and recorded as that of young Louis XIII.
In panic he fled his queen and court to build a woman-free
hunting lodge—the palace of Versailles

By JOSEPH BARRY

By whatever avenue you arrive you are led ineluctably to it. All three avenues of Versailles converge on the Royal Grill of the great palace—the medial Avenue de Paris like a three-hundred-foot-wide shaft of a giant arrow—and they point across the courtyard, not to the Royal Chapel, but to the royal bedchamber.

That the Sun King should install his bedroom at the very center of his palace, then the center of Europe and thus of Western civilization, is piquant enough. More to the point, he had installed it in the little château, the hunting retreat, of his father, Louis XIII. The château—the touching, visible heart of the great palace of Versailles—can be seen clearly by climbing the vast cobbled courtyard of the entrance: a little castle of fairylike beauty with walls of faded brick and white stone, poised above its own tiny courtyard of marble and surrounded on three sides by the monumental wings and façades of Le Vau and Mansart.

That "little castle of cards" was the beginning, for Versailles was born not of Louis XIV but of Louis XIII; not out of love for, but a most un-Bourbon fear of, women.

Louis XIII's mother, Marie de Médicis felt the first labor pains of Versailles's future begetter at Fontainebleau. Feverishly—he was many times a father, but this was the first legitimate offspring—Henry IV sent for the midwife. He also sent for his cousins, the princes of the blood, to witness the birth. It was a custom and precaution that did not originate with the Bourbons. Questions of legitimacy could instigate civil war. In the case of Henry IV it was a particularly wise precaution. As a rollicking folk song of the period expressed it: he could drink, he could fight, and he could make love.

The royal bed in the queen's oval chamber was covered in crimson velvet; so was the smaller bed next to it, in which she labored, and the chair next to that, in which she gave birth. The midwife sat on a smaller chair before her and received the child. The king beckoned the three princes closer. They bent and looked. The cord was cut, the baby put into its crib. It moved feebly. The midwife called for wine. Her hands were full; the king held the wine bottle to her lips. She filled her mouth, then filled the child's from hers. It stirred more strongly.

"*E maschio*?" the queen asked twice, and rose to her feet to look. Across the room the midwife uncovered the child for the king. "We have a beautiful son!" he cried, thanked God, and let the tears fall. The queen, too, cried and fainted. The king threw open the doors to the antechamber. Two hundred of the court pressed in. The midwife protested. "This child," the king replied, "belongs to everybody."

As the newborn dauphin's governess, he named Madame de Montglat, a tall, thin, and domineering woman, "her character as sharp as her elbows." As the dauphin's personal physician, the king appointed the remarkable Jean Héroard, whose meticulous journal of Louis XIII's life, beginning with the day of his birth in September, 1601, and ending with Héroard's own death some twenty-six years later, fills six folio volumes. It may be the most faithful case history of any king of any time, recording everything from food to evacuations, temper to temperature, conversations to love life, or rather, in Louis's instance, its relative absence.

For the first few days, Héroard notes, the dauphin had difficulty taking his milk, until an encumbering membrane was cut under his tongue. Then he needed two nurses (his father had sucked a legendary eight dry), but he was left the rest of his life with a speech defect. Within weeks he was taken on tour for another public exposure—from Fontainebleau to Melun, Villeneuve-Saint-Georges to Paris. Finally, after a stop at the Louvre and the Tuileries, the procession ended at the grim, gray-stone château of Saint-Germain en Laye, eleven miles west of Paris, which had been chosen by Henry IV as the dauphin's residence.

Throughout Louis's infancy affection came from his father, but it was not undivided. The king continued to distribute his energy among his affairs of state, his second wife (he had divorced Marguerite de Valois), his many mistresses (particularly Henriette d'Entragues), and his dozen or so other children. At one time there were nine children by five different mothers living at Saint-Germain; they were familiarly referred to throughout the land as *le troupeau* (the flock). Henry would come to the dauphin's room with the queen and then return shortly afterward with Henriette. Louis, it might be noted, liked neither lady, and with reason. Marie de Médicis may have been many things, but she was not a good mother. The little dauphin also took a pained view of mistresses. When he was seven, the king had taken him for a walk in the gardens of Fontainebleau, pointed to the Comtesse de Moret, and said, "My son, I have given this beautiful lady a child. He will be your brother." The dauphin had blushed and stammered "He is no brother of mine." And he turned his own "affection" to birds with such a ferocity that he became perhaps the greatest killer of winged game in the history of that royal sport.

As a child Louis was very neat, tidying up Héroard's room, to which he often crept, when he found it in disorder. And, yet a child, he was whipped by the king when he crushed the head of a live sparrow. He was frequently whipped by Madame de Montglat, who would sternly command, "You, sir, bare your arse!" ("Whip him," the king had advised her. "There is nothing better.") Her language was famously coarse and repeatedly shocked Louis.

Before he was one year old, according to Héroard, it was decided that the Spanish infanta would be his wife. At two he was asked if he would be as

---

Joseph Barry is a regular contributor to Horizon; *he wrote "The Twilight Princess and the Sun King," about Louis XIV and Marie Adélaïde, for Spring, 1967.*

ribald as his father. No, he said, "coldly." Not yet four, he tried to strike his younger sister. "I am afraid of her," he explained. Why? he was asked. "Because she is a girl." At seven he was teasingly asked if he were in love. "I flee from love," he answered solemnly. "And from the infanta, Monsieur?" asked Héroard. "No," he said; then: "Ha, yes. Yes!" (He knew Héroard was noting his remarks and would sometimes shout after one, "Write that down!")

When he was still only six, the dauphin found himself at the château of Noisy-le-Roi one day and was seized with a sudden desire. "Tétay," he cried to his steward, Ventelet, "prepare the carriage and the birds. I want to go hunting!" That evening he returned with a small hare run to earth by his hounds, and five or six quail and a brace of partridge taken by his hawks. At supper he talked of little else. It was his first hunt in his father's favorite woods, the woods of Versailles.

Louis was past seven when he was switched from the hard but feminine hands of his governess into those of a tutor, put into a ruff, and taught to shoot. He was not yet nine when he had dinner with the king on May 12, 1610. It hadn't happened often; it didn't happen again.

Two days afterward, before a shop with the sign of a crowned heart pierced by an arrow, Henry IV was stabbed to death by François Ravaillac. Hurriedly he was brought back to the Louvre, carried to his bedroom on the second floor, and laid out on the bed. The dauphin, riding elsewhere in Paris, was also hurriedly brought to the Louvre and taken to his father. "The king is dead," he heard from the queen. "Your Majesty must excuse me," he heard the chancellor tell her, "but kings never die in France. *Voilà*," he pointed to the eight-year-old Louis, "the living king!"

And the king cried like a baby.

Later that day Louis was again facing his public—the crowd that filed through the Louvre to stare at its new sovereign. Finally, exhausted, he went to bed, but he could not sleep. He rose, went to his tutor, said pathetically, "I am afraid of dreaming," and lay down beside him until almost midnight, when he was carried back to his own bed. There he slept with his half brother, Henriette's son, fetched by order of the queen.

Never was a king mourned more widely in France than Henry IV. "The village poor," said an eyewitness, "massed on the highways, stunned, haggard, arms crossed, telling people passing of the disastrous news . . . finally disbanding like sheep without a shepherd." Louis's inheritance, in short, was the crushing legacy of a great father. "If only," he sighed to his nurse, "my father the king had lived another twenty years!"

A few days later the new king of France was spanked for obstinately refusing to say his prayers. "At least," he said to his tutor, "don't strike too hard." Afterward he went to see the queen, now regent, who had ordered the whipping. She rose to make him the curtsy due him as king. "I would rather," he said wistfully, "not have so many curtsies and honors, and not be whipped." On September 17, 1610, Louis XIII was again spanked; on September 21, he signed a military alliance with England.

At ten Louis was writing verses and slaughtering game. And from that age on he was taming falcons; ultimately, he reached the height of taming the great eagle. He was to hunt wild duck with falcons, quail with merlins, partridge with goshawks, hares with sakers, and to train teams of birds as if they were commandos. And he was to find his father figure in the form of an ambitious falconer, Charles d'Albert, Duc de Luynes, twenty-three years his senior. Rapidly Luynes rose in power, becoming Louis's favorite, and his bedroom Louis's refuge Thus Louis flew his birds, painted, danced, and composed, dreamed of—and wrote verses to—Luynes, cooked poached eggs, played the lute, and at the age of fourteen married the Spanish infanta, who was five days older than the king. She was blonde and might have been pretty had it not been for her long Habsburg nose. Indeed, Anne of Austria (her mother was Margaret of Austria) looked remarkably like Louis, which in view of their Habsburg consanguinity was no coincidence.

They were married in Bordeaux on November 25, 1615. After the ceremony they each went to separate chambers in the archbishop's palace and supped. Tired, the little king ate in bed while Messieurs de Guise and de Grammont and other cavaliers, according to Héroard, "regaled" him with coarse stories that were aimed at giving him "confidence." Toward eight o'clock that evening, the queen mother came to his chamber.

"It is not enough, my son," she told him, "to be married. You must go to the queen, your wife, who is awaiting you."

"Madame," said Louis, "I was but

A king at eight, Louis stands beside his widowed mother, Marie de Médicis, the queen regent. She was, said the diarist Saint-Simon, "imperious, jealous, stupid to a degree and ruled . . . by the dregs of the court."
BIBLIOTHEQUE NATIONALE; PAGE 114: SAME

waiting your command. If it pleases you, I will go to her with you."

He was handed his bathrobe and small, furred boots, and he went down the passage with the queen mother, his and the little queen's nurses, Messieurs de Souvré (his tutor) and Héroard, the Marquis de Rambouillet (master of the wardrobe), and Monsieur de Beringhen (first *valet de chambre*), who lighted the way with a candle.

"My daughter," said the queen mother to the queen, "I bring you your husband. Receive him well, I pray you."

Anne replied in Spanish that she had no intention other than to obey and please him, and Louis was put into bed beside her. Marie de Médicis whispered something to them in a low voice, then ordered all but the two nurses to leave.

Two hours later Louis called for his bathrobe and furred boots and returned to his bedroom. France was in the midst of civil war. But the rebellious nobility opposed to the marriage would now find it all but irrevocable. As for Louis he was to recall that night with revulsion the rest of his life. It was three years before he could be brought to bed again with Anne; it was another twenty years before he became a father. But before either event could take place, there was Luynes to be removed as an inhibiting factor.

With this in mind, Marie de Médicis and the entire court connived to marry Luynes off to the pretty, charming, highborn, and rich Marie de Rohan. They were successful; the marriage was successful, but subsequent approaches to Louis were not. Pressed by the Spanish ambassador and the papal nuncio to give France an heir, Louis resisted, pleading, "I am too young. It would be bad for my health." Then his half sister, Mademoiselle de Vendôme, daughter of Gabrielle d'Estrées, was married to the Duc d'Elbeuf, and efforts were redoubled.

"Sire," said the papal nuncio to Louis, now seventeen, "I do not believe you would want the shame of your sister having a son before Your

Majesty had a dauphin." Embarrassed, Louis allowed that he would not.

By no accident, he was invited to the wedding chamber and encouraged to stay on as a spectator, the bride and groom lending themselves for a royal lesson. "Their act," the Venetian ambassador was to report, "was repeated more than once, to the great applause and particular pleasure of His Majesty. It is thought that this example has excited the king to do the same. It is also said that his half sister encouraged him, saying, 'Sire, you do the same with the queen, and you will be the better for it.'"

The king's pleasure and applause seem to have been greatly exaggerated. Five days later, at eleven at night, Luynes himself had to go to Louis to coax him to the queen's bed. Louis resisted. Luynes insisted. Annoyed, then anguished, Louis was carried weeping in Luynes's arms down the corridor to Anne's chamber. And once again Monsieur de Beringhen lighted the way with a candle. The two adolescents were left alone together, except for Madame de Bellière, the queen's first *femme de chambre*. It was presumably she who provided Héroard with the matter of the day. The king, he noted, "*s'efforce deux fois, comme l'on dit*" (did his best twice, it is said). Louis returned to his bedroom at two and slept unusually long, until nine o'clock.

The public concern for so private an affair reached such a peak that not only the pope (to whom the nuncio wrote on April 14, 1618, that the Huguenots were using Louis's chastity for their own purposes) and the king of Spain (father of Queen Anne) felt legitimately involved but the Duke of Savoy as well. An enemy of Spain, he was told by *his* man at court that the farther the king could be kept from the bed of the queen, the closer he would be to the house of Savoy. In a dispatch dated February 16, 1618, the Savoyard ambassador related his own efforts to persuade the Duc de Luynes to prevent the consummation.

"What wouldn't the Spanish do," he quoted himself saying to Luynes, "of what would they not be capable, once *their little queen* had the person of the young king in her arms every night?"

The day following Louis's noble efforts Anne joyfully sent her Master of Ceremonies to the papal nuncio and the Spanish envoy to tell them of it, and couriers were booted for the ride to the capitals of Europe. On January 30, 1619, the nuncio wrote Pope Paul V: "The king finally decided *conjiungersi colla Regina* . . . Since the first night, except for one, their majesties continue to come together . . . but for the sake of the king's health, it will be seen to that His Majesty goes to the queen at properly spaced intervals." An interval of two weeks was recommended by the court doctors as more likely to result in a dauphin.

Louis continued to have but one friend—the Duc de Luynes—and he died in 1621. Moreover, France was again in fratricidal war. At this mo-

---

This print commemorates dual dynastic marriages. Louis, aged fourteen, is wed to Anne of Austria, a Habsburg princess (foreground), while his sister is wed to Anne's ten-year-old brother, Philip, the future king of Spain.
BIBLIOTHEQUE NATIONALE

ment Armand Jean du Plessis de Richelieu reached the foot of the throne and eventually became the iron-willed ruler of Louis's reign. A kind of equilibrium was established. If it was not quite the glamorous time of Dumas's *Three Musketeers*, in which the dashing Duke of Buckingham publicly pleaded his love to the neglected queen, Anne of Austria, life was gay enough, it seems, for all but the frustrated king. He had lost Luynes. He had Richelieu but no intimate.

He had only Versailles.

Increasingly, Louis escaped to the woods near the little village of Versailles au Val de Galie, a cluster of huts with four or five hundred inhabitants. It had a rude inn or two, a windmill and twelfth-century church on the butte, the half-ruined château of the Gondi, and a little nearby stream, the Galie. It was a rendezvous for hunters, not a place to spend the night. It was a halt for carters and wagoners, their vehicles heavy with beef from Normandy for the markets of Paris.

But there were the sweet woods of the Ile de France, full of game and grace. They were worth the long ride back after dark to Saint-Germain, eight miles distant. But why the ride back?

Modestly Louis planned a small château, no larger than a hunting lodge. Guardedly he budgeted it under *menus plaisirs*—we might call it light entertainment—rather than *bâtiments*, or buildings. Discreetly he had it constructed, pausing during his hunting to watch its progress, as he did on August 2, 1624, when he saw the battery of kitchen utensils installed.

This very first Versailles structure was of brick and stone, in the style we now know as "Louis XIII." It was about eighty feet in all along the façade facing the small park, and only nineteen feet in depth. It was, in the words of Bassompierre, "but a *chetif château* [paltry country house] which any ordinary gentleman wouldn't boast having built." There were three or four rooms for the king and a dozen or so for his suite,

117

Charles d'Albert, Duc de Luynes

but none for the queen, the queen mother, or any of the ladies of the court. They might be invited for a fete, but they had no overnight privileges. This Versailles was a male paradise. But it need not hold us for long, for it was soon to be replaced, after the famous Day of Dupes.

Leagued against Richelieu—to whom Louis relegated full power, if only to assure himself repose—were the king's only legitimate brother and his wife and mother, the two queens of the "Spanish party," who were not above conspiring with their relatives among the enemy (Anne of Austria's brother was now Philip IV of Spain). And this struggle against the cardinal was to reach its climax at Versailles.

Convalescing from an almost fatal illness, harassed by Marie de Médicis, Louis seemed about to acquiesce in the dismissal of his minister. The critical conversation took place on November 10, 1630, in the queen mother's Luxembourg palace. Unexpectedly, as it was ending, Richelieu appeared. Outraged, Marie de Médicis denounced and insulted him in a flowing mixture of Italian and French. He fell to his knees. He wept: out of office could have meant out of life. He begged pardon. He promised to do whatever Marie demanded. Louis paled and tried to interrupt. Haughtily Marie asked him whether he preferred "a valet to his mother." Louis then ordered Richelieu to rise and leave the room. He himself soon took leave of Marie. It was late, and he had to reach Versailles before it was too dark. In the courtyard Richelieu desolately watched as Louis departed without a look or sign. Inside the palace the cardinal's many enemies celebrated with Marie de Médicis. Richelieu returned to his own palace, the Petit Luxembourg, ordered his silver and his papers packed, and prepared for flight. Then word arrived from the king: Richelieu was to join him immediately at Versailles.

Away from Paris, the court, and his mother, Louis recovered his composure in the late-autumn serenity of Versailles. He went up to his cabinet and waited. Soon the cardinal came to him, fell at his feet, wept, offered his resignation—and allowed himself a refusal. He stayed that night directly below the king. The next morning those who had gone to sleep in victory awoke in defeat. Richelieu had triumphed.

Following that Day of Dupes, when Versailles first entered history, Marie de Médicis was banished, eventually to die in exile in The Netherlands. The Maréchal de Marillac, who had aspired to Richelieu's office, was tortured and put to death; the Duc de Montmorency, a childhood playmate of Louis's, was beheaded. (Refusing to give clemency, Louis remarked, "I should not be king, if I had the sentiments of private persons.") And parcel by parcel, in a series of forty-six separate purchases, the royal domain of Versailles was doubled. Land and rights were bought from Jean-François de Gondi, Archbishop of Paris, and Louis's modest little hunting lodge was completely remodeled.

To begin with, it was enlarged—under the direction of the architect Philibert Le Roy—but not enough to include rooms for the ladies. Femininity was reserved, one might say, for the building itself, for the brightness of its color, the gaiety of its architecture. It was blue, white, and red: roofs of blue-black slate, walls of red brick "chained" by white stone. It was gay with balconies of wrought iron, gilded terminals, tall white pinnacles, chimneys with decorative blue ornaments. The moat, too, was more decorative than defensive, its stone balustrade out of a fairy tale. And at each corner of the château, symmetrically placed, was a free-standing pavilion.

It was this "little castle of cards," as Saint-Simon called it, that the Sun King, not yet born, was to discover in his adolescence and preserve in his maturity as the center of his own great palace, court, and power. But it was here that Louis XIII went to escape his court and the cares of power, the intrigues of courtiers and their plots. Here in Versailles Louis felt secure, free of women, less spied upon. When smallpox threatened Saint Germain, he sent the queen to Noisy, not to Versailles. "I fear," he explained to Richelieu in one of his almost daily letters, "a great number of women who would spoil everything for me."

Inevitably there were women as "mistresses." The son of the Vert Galant perhaps had no alternative. There was the teen-age blonde, Marie de Hautefort, who terrified him. (He talked to her "only of dogs, birds and hunting," she complained to Madame de Motteville, *femme de chambre* of the queen.) And there was the teenage brunette, Marie-Louise de La Fayette, who may even have loved him; but when Louis said, "Come live with me at Versailles," she crossed herself and went to live in a convent in Paris. Louis's relief was almost audible, though he wrote a letter to Richelieu tell-

---

Louis, an ardent hunter since early boyhood, is shown in a contemporary engraving taking part in a stag hunt. In the fields of sport and war, to which he was devoted, Louis was fittingly brave. Only women frightened him.
BIBLIOTHEQUE NATIONALE

ing him of his melancholy (the writing wavers, a tear drops, one still sees the traces).

The pious, inhibited—and possibly tormented—Louis visited Louise, now Sister Angélique, a number of times at the convent of Sainte Marie (part of which still stands near the Place de la Bastille). His visit early in December, 1637, on the way to Saint Maur from Versailles was to effect an odd reconciliation with the queen. As Louis and Sister Angélique talked—and talked—in the parlor, a storm rose of such violence that he could neither return to Versailles nor go on to Saint Maur, where his bed, linen, and service had already preceded him. His apartment at the Louvre, a mile down the Seine, was not prepared for him. Guitaut, captain of the guard, now spoke up with his customary boldness. Since the queen was at the Louvre, he pointed out, the king would find supper and lodging. Louis rejected the idea and said they would wait out the storm. They waited. The storm became even more violent. Again Guitaut proposed the Louvre. Louis replied that the queen supped and went to bed too late for him. Guitaut said she would surely be glad to conform to his wishes. At last Louis agreed to the Louvre, and Guitaut galloped off to advise her of his coming and his desires.

"They supped together. The king spent the night with the queen, and nine months later Anne of Austria had a son, whose unexpected birth brought universal joy to the entire kingdom."

The account is that of Father Griffet, an eighteenth-century historian, and it is told with such a simple directness that it almost disarms one's suspicions. (The fatherhood of Louis XIV is still disputed.) And one could close this account of the birth of Versailles with the birth of its Sun King. Or one could—and perhaps should—close it with his father's last wish and leave out the un-becoming affair with the "beautiful Cinq-Mars." But if the affair is beyond the framework of Versailles's first château, it is still revelatory of the character of its begetter.

Always preferring that anyone close to the king be as close, politically, to himself, Richelieu had pushed forward the comely son of an old friend, and the young man had predictably caught the eye of the king. "Never," wrote Chavigny to Mazarin, "did the king have a more violent passion for anyone." Arriving at seventeen, Cinq-Mars's rise at court in the next two years was meteoric—from captain of a regiment of guards to "Monsieur le Grand," the Marquis de Cinq-Mars.

As Luynes had been thirty-nine to Louis's sixteen, so Louis was now thirty-nine to Cinq-Mars's nineteen. For Tallemant, who retails tawdry stories of the intimacy between Cinq-Mars and Louis, the relationship was clearly homosexual. On the other hand, this has never been "proved," and Cinq-Mars's own preference for Marion Delorme, a famous courtesan, has been well established, if only by Louis's spies and Louis's jealousy of her. That it was a turbulent and passionate relationship, however, is part of the archives: Richelieu himself drew up peace treaties for their joint signature.

Restlessly Cinq-Mars overreached himself. Turned enemy of Richelieu, he joined the "Spanish plot" against him,

Louis's château at Versailles, which he built as a hunting lodge in 1624, was made of brick and stone and was contemptuously described by observers as "a gentleman's small country house." Louis paid for it out of state funds.
ARCHIVES PHOTOGRAPHIQUES

The Marquis de Cinq-Mars

alienated Louis—and lost his head. At the hour of his scheduled decapitation the king, according to an apocryphal story, paused during a chess game, looked at his watch, and cynically remarked, "I would like to see the expression on Monsieur le Grand's face now." Poor Louis. "His loves," as Tallemant notes, "were strange loves, and he had nothing of the lover but jealousy." "He took no pleasure, as other men, in *la belle passion*." says Madame de Motteville. "Accustomed to bitterness, his *tendresse* was only that he might feel pain and suffering the more."

To no one's surprise Richelieu's death on December 4, 1642, was swiftly followed by the king's. Long ailing, Louis was not long in dying, being aided enormously by his doctors. In a single year Dr. Bouvard bled him forty-seven times, gave him two hundred and fifteen enemas and two hundred and twelve different drugs. Before dying the king bitterly accused Bouvard of his death.

And before dying Louis also confided his last wish in life to his confessor. If God should give him back his health, he said (he was, after all, only forty-one), he would, "as soon as I see my son able to ride and of majority age [thirteen] . . . put him in my place and . . . retire to Versailles with four of your priests, there to discuss holy matters, and to think no longer about anything but my soul and my salvation."

One month later, on May 14, 1643, Louis XIII was dead.

A Short Primer of Style

The latest studies in pedagogy show that good writing can be taught better by example than by precept. We recently came across a report of a seminar on poverty issued by the American Academy of Arts and Sciences. In one short section—a summary of "nine characteristics of poor populations"—the academicians have given such a fine epitome of elegant and precise expression that we quote it here in the hope that many of our readers may find it instructive. The way to point it up, we think, is to give the social engineers' version first and then put down the bare, blunt *meaning*, so that the full subtlety of their diction can be appreciated.

HOW TO SAY IT: "A level of monetary or nonmonetary recompense generally commensurate with low levels of occupational skills."

MEANING: They don't earn much.

HOW TO SAY IT: "The allocation of a very limited portion of a person's resources, abilities, and energies to the ownership, maintenance, and adornment of residential structures."

MEANING: They live in slums.

HOW TO SAY IT: "A versatile rather than constricted pattern of income acquisition which finds sources of income in various places, at varying times, and in varying degrees."

MEANING: They do lots of odd jobs.

HOW TO SAY IT: "The expectation that the major responsibility for exercising superordinate authority will be assumed by those at higher levels of skill and training."

MEANING: They expect their betters to run things.

HOW TO SAY IT: "A pattern of work involvement entailing predominantly nonspecialized physical labor."

MEANING: Mostly, the poor work with their hands.

HOW TO SAY IT: "A set of arrangements for producing and rearing children, the viability of which is not predicated on the consistent presence in the household of an adult male acting in the role of a husband and father."

MEANING: Dad is not home much of the time.

HOW TO SAY IT: "A set of pursuits outside the occupational sphere which provides direct and immediate emotional or physical gratification, and a quest for stimulating inner experience, characteristically involving strong drink."

MEANING: In their spare time they go in for sex, television, and liquor.

HOW TO SAY IT: "A pattern of educational involvement characterized by little formal schooling or sporadic schooling in localities where attendance is mandatory until the age of 16."

MEANING: They don't spend much time in school.

HOW TO SAY IT: "A mode of rearing children organized so as to minimize the duration of necessary inhousehold specialization. Most of a child's life is lived on the street or in the community rather than within the confines of a specific house."

MEANING: The kids aren't home much either.

It must be admitted, as a postscript, that even the greatest stylists occasionally slip. Further on in the A.A.A.S. report there is this painfully bald observation: "After long hours of sociological discourse, one fact remains clear: The poor do not have enough money."

DRAWINGS BY CHARMATZ

By E. M. HALLIDAY